Machine Vision
Inspection Systems
Volume 1

Scrivener Publishing
100 Cummings Center, Suite 541J
Beverly, MA 01915-6106

Publishers at Scrivener
Martin Scrivener (martin@scrivenerpublishing.com)
Phillip Carmical (pcarmical@scrivenerpublishing.com)

Machine Vision
Inspection Systems
Volume 1

Image Processing, Concepts,
Methodologies and Applications

Edited by

**Muthukumaran Malarvel,
Soumya Ranjan Nayak,
Surya Narayan Panda,
Prasant Kumar Pattnaik
and Nittaya Muangnak**

Scrivener
Publishing

WILEY

Wiley Global Headquarters
111 River Street, Hoboken, NJ 07030, USA

For details of our global editorial offices, customer services, and more information about Wiley products visit us at www.wiley.com.

Limit of Liability/Disclaimer of Warranty
While the publisher and authors have used their best efforts in preparing this work, they make no representations or warranties with respect to the accuracy or completeness of the contents of this work and specifically disclaim all warranties, including without limitation any implied warranties of merchantability or fitness for a particular purpose. No warranty may be created or extended by sales representatives, written sales materials, or promotional statements for this work. The fact that an organization, website, or product is referred to in this work as a citation and/or potential source of further information does not mean that the publisher and authors endorse the information or services the organization, website, or product may provide or recommendations it may make. This work is sold with the understanding that the publisher is not engaged in rendering professional services. The advice and strategies contained herein may not be suitable for your situation. You should consult with a specialist where appropriate. Neither the publisher nor authors shall be liable for any loss of profit or any other commercial damages, including but not limited to special, incidental, consequential, or other damages. Further, readers should be aware that websites listed in this work may have changed or disappeared between when this work was written and when it is read.

Library of Congress Cataloging-in-Publication Data

Names: Malarvel, Muthukumaran, editor. | Nayak, Soumya Ranjan, 1984– editor. | Panda, Sury Narayan, editor. | Pattnaik, Prasant Kumar, 1969– editor. | Muangnak, Nittaya, editor.
Title: Machine vision inspection systems / edited by Muthukumaran Malarvel, Soumya Ranjan Nayak, Sury Narayan Panda, Prasant Kumar Pattnaik and Nittaya Muangnak.
Description: Hoboken, NJ : Wiley-Scrivener, 2020. | Includes bibliographical references and index. | Contents: Volume 1. Image processing, concepts, methodologies and applications –
Identifiers: LCCN 2020020076 (print) | LCCN 2020020077 (ebook) | ISBN 9781119681809 (hardback) | ISBN 9781119681960 (adobe pdf) | ISBN 9781119682097 (epub)
Subjects: LCSH: Computer vision. | Computer vision–Industrial applications. | Engineering inspection–Automation. | Image processing. | Image processing–Digital techniques.
Classification: LCC TA1634 .M3354 2020 (print) | LCC TA1634 (ebook) | DDC 006.3/7–dc23
LC record available at https://lccn.loc.gov/2020020076
LC ebook record available at https://lccn.loc.gov/2020020077

Cover image: Pixabay.Com
Cover design by Russell Richardson

Set in size of 11pt and Minion Pro by Manila Typesetting Company, Makati, Philippines

Contents

Preface   **xi**

1   Land-Use Classification with Integrated Data   1
  D. A. Meedeniya, J. A. A. M Jayanetti, M. D. N. Dilini,
  M. H. Wickramapala and J. H. Madushanka
  1.1   Introduction   2
  1.2   Background Study   3
        1.2.1   Overview of Land-Use and Land-Cover Information   3
        1.2.2   Geographical Information Systems   4
        1.2.3   GIS-Related Data Types   4
                1.2.3.1   Point Data Sets   4
                1.2.3.2   Aerial Data Sets   5
        1.2.4   Related Studies   6
  1.3   System Design   6
  1.4   Implementation Details   10
        1.4.1   Materials   10
        1.4.2   Preprocessing   11
        1.4.3   Built-Up Area Extraction   11
        1.4.4   Per-Pixel Classification   12
        1.4.5   Clustering   14
        1.4.6   Segmentation   14
        1.4.7   Object-Based Image Classification   16
        1.4.8   Foursquare Data Preprocessing and Quality Analysis   20
        1.4.9   Integration of Satellite Images with Foursquare Data   21
        1.4.10 Building Block Identification   21
        1.4.11 Overlay of Foursquare Points   22
        1.4.12 Visualization of Land Usage   23
        1.4.13 Common Platform Development   23
  1.5   System Evaluation   25
        1.5.1   Experimental Evaluation Process   25
        1.5.2   Evaluation of the Classification Using Base
                Error Matrix   28

1.6   Discussion   31
       1.6.1   Contribution of the Proposed Approach   31
       1.6.2   Limitations of the Data Sets   32
       1.6.3   Future Research Directions   33
1.7   Conclusion   34
       References   35

2   **Indian Sign Language Recognition Using Soft
    Computing Techniques**   37
    *Ashok Kumar Sahoo, Pradeepta Kumar Sarangi
    and Parul Goyal*
2.1   Introduction   37
2.2   Related Works   38
       2.2.1   The Domain of Sign Language   39
       2.2.2   The Data Acquisition Methods   41
       2.2.3   Preprocessing Steps   42
               2.2.3.1   Image Restructuring   43
               2.2.3.2   Skin Color Detection   43
       2.2.4   Methods of Feature Extraction Used in the Experiments   44
       2.2.5   Classification Techniques   45
               2.2.5.1   K-Nearest Neighbor   45
               2.2.5.2   Neural Network Classifier   45
               2.2.5.3   Naive Baÿes Classifier   46
2.3   Experiments   46
       2.3.1   Experiments on ISL Digits   46
               2.3.1.1   Results and Discussions on the First
                         Experiment   47
               2.3.1.2   Results and Discussions on Second
                         Experiment   49
       2.3.2   Experiments on ISL Alphabets   51
               2.3.2.1   Experiments with Single-Handed Alphabet
                         Signs   51
               2.3.2.2   Results of Single-Handed Alphabet Signs   52
               2.3.2.3   Experiments with Double-Handed Alphabet
                         Signs   53
               2.3.2.4   Results on Double-Handed Alphabets   54
       2.3.3   Experiments on ISL Words   58
               2.3.3.1   Results on ISL Word Signs   59
2.4   Summary   63
       References   63

3   **Stored Grain Pest Identification Using an Unmanned Aerial
    Vehicle (UAV)-Assisted Pest Detection Model**   67
    *Kalyan Kumar Jena, Sasmita Mishra, Sarojananda Mishra
    and Sourav Kumar Bhoi*
    3.1   Introduction   68
    3.2   Related Work   69
    3.3   Proposed Model   70
    3.4   Results and Discussion   72
    3.5   Conclusion   77
          References   78

4   **Object Descriptor for Machine Vision**   85
    Aparna S. Murthy and Salah Rabba
    4.1   Outline   85
    4.2   Chain Codes   87
    4.3   Polygonal Approximation   89
    4.4   Moments   92
    4.5   HU Invariant Moments   96
    4.6   Zernike Moments   97
    4.7   Fourier Descriptors   98
    4.8   Quadtree   99
    4.9   Conclusion   102
          References   114

5   **Flood Disaster Management: Risks, Technologies,
    and Future Directions**   115
    Hafiz Suliman Munawar
    5.1   Flood Management   115
          5.1.1   Introduction   115
          5.1.2   Global Flood Risks and Incidents   116
          5.1.3   Causes of Floods   118
          5.1.4   Floods in Pakistan   119
          5.1.5   Floods in Australia   121
          5.1.6   Why Floods are a Major Concern   123
    5.2   Existing Disaster Management Systems   124
          5.2.1   Introduction   124
          5.2.2   Disaster Management Systems Used
                  Around the World   124
                  5.2.2.1   Disaster Management Model   125
                  5.2.2.2   Disaster Risk Analysis System   126
                  5.2.2.3   Geographic Information System   126

            5.2.2.4 Web GIS   126
            5.2.2.5 Remote Sensing   127
            5.2.2.6 Satellite Imaging   127
            5.2.2.7 Global Positioning System for Imaging   128
      5.2.3 Gaps in Current Disaster Management Technology   128
  5.3 Advancements in Disaster Management Technologies   129
      5.3.1 Introduction   129
      5.3.2 AI and Machine Learning for Disaster Management   130
            5.3.2.1 AIDR   130
            5.3.2.2 Warning Systems   130
            5.3.2.3 QCRI   131
            5.3.2.4 The Concern   131
            5.3.2.5 BlueLine Grid   131
            5.3.2.6 Google Maps   132
            5.3.2.7 RADARSAT-1   132
      5.3.3 Recent Research in Disaster Management   132
      5.3.4 Conclusion   137
  5.4 Proposed System   137
      5.4.1 Image Acquisition Through UAV   138
      5.4.2 Preprocessing   138
      5.4.3 Landmarks Detection   138
            5.4.3.1 Buildings   139
            5.4.3.2 Roads   139
      5.4.4 Flood Detection   140
            5.4.4.1 Feature Matching   140
            5.4.4.2 Flood Detection Using Machine Learning   141
      5.4.5 Conclusion   143
      References   143

6 Temporal Color Analysis of Avocado Dip for Quality Control   147
Homero V. Rios-Figueroa, Micloth López del Castillo-Lozano,
Elvia K. Ramirez-Gomez and Ericka J. Rechy-Ramirez
  6.1 Introduction   147
  6.2 Materials and Methods   148
  6.3 Image Acquisition   149
  6.4 Image Processing   150
  6.5 Experimental Design   150
      6.5.1 First Experimental Design   150
      6.5.2 Second Experimental Design   151

6.6   Results and Discussion   151
        6.6.1   First Experimental Design (RGB Color Space)   151
        6.6.2   Second Experimental Design ($L^*a^*b^*$ Color Space)   152
6.7   Conclusion   156
        References   156

**7   Image and Video Processing for Defect Detection in Key
        Infrastructure   159**
        Hafiz Suliman Munawar
7.1   Introduction   160
7.2   Reasons for Defective Roads and Bridges   161
7.3   Image Processing for Defect Detection   162
        7.3.1   Feature Extraction   162
        7.3.2   Morphological Operators   163
        7.3.3   Cracks Detection   164
        7.3.4   Potholes Detection   165
        7.3.5   Water Puddles Detection   166
        7.3.6   Pavement Distress Detection   167
7.4   Image-Based Defect Detection Methods   169
        7.4.1   Thresholding Techniques   170
        7.4.2   Edge Detection Techniques   170
        7.4.3   Wavelet Transform Techniques   171
        7.4.4   Texture Analysis Techniques   171
        7.4.5   Machine Learning Techniques   172
7.5   Factors Affecting the Performance   172
        7.5.1   Lighting Variations   173
        7.5.2   Small Database   173
        7.5.3   Low-Quality Data   173
7.6   Achievements and Issues   173
        7.6.1   Achievements   174
        7.6.2   Issues   174
7.7   Conclusion   174
        References   175

**8   Methodology for the Detection of Asymptomatic Diabetic
        Retinopathy   179**
        Jaskirat Kaur and Deepti Mittal
8.1   Introduction   180
8.2   Key Steps of Computer-Aided Diagnostic Methods   181
8.3   DR Screening and Grading Methods   183
8.4   Key Observations from Literature Review   188

8.5 Design of Experimental Methodology 189
8.6 Conclusion 192
    References 193

**9 Offline Handwritten Numeral Recognition Using
Convolution Neural Network** 197
Abhisek Sethy, Prashanta Kumar Patra and Soumya Ranjan Nayak
9.1 Introduction 198
9.2 Related Work Done 199
9.3 Data Set Used for Simulation 201
9.4 Proposed Model 202
9.5 Result Analysis 204
9.6 Conclusion and Future Work 207
    References 209

**10 A Review on Phishing—Machine Vision
and Learning Approaches** 213
*Hemamalini Siranjeevi, Swaminathan Venkatraman
and Kannan Krithivasan*
10.1 Introduction 213
10.2 Literature Survey 214
    10.2.1 Content-Based Approaches 214
    10.2.2 Heuristics-Based Approaches 215
    10.2.3 Blacklist-Based Approaches 215
    10.2.4 Whitelist-Based Approaches 216
    10.2.5 CANTINA-Based Approaches 216
    10.2.6 Image-Based Approaches 216
10.3 Role of Data Mining in Antiphishing 217
    10.3.1 Phishing Detection 219
    10.3.2 Phishing Prevention 220
    10.3.3 Training and Education 222
    10.3.4 Phishing Recovery and Avoidance 222
    10.3.5 Visual Methods 223
10.4 Conclusion 224
    Acknowledgments 224
    References 224

Index 231

Preface

This edited book aims to bring together leading researchers, academic scientists and research scholars to put forward and share their experiences and research results on all aspects of an inspection system for detection analysis for various machine vision applications. It also provides a premier interdisciplinary platform for educators, practitioners and researchers to present and discuss the most recent innovations, trends, methodology, applications and concerns, as well as practical challenges encountered and solutions adopted in the inspection system in terms of image processing and analytics of machine vision for real and industrial application. The book is organized into ten chapters,

Chapter 1 presents an overview of an automated methodology-based learning model classification technique for identifying the usage and coverage of land use in Sri Lanka by using satellite imagery data. This chapter also discusses the issue related to manual surveys and its limitations about the land-use of different regions.

Chapter 2 focuses on the Indian sign language recognition using machine learning algorithm in machine vision and pattern recognition research areas. The work is to translate acquired images or videos either offline or online to corresponding words, numbers or sentences representing the meaning of the input sign. The Direct Pixel Value, Hierarchical Centroid, Local Histogram features of Image Processing techniques are used as a feature in the experimental analysis. The classifiers used here are k-Nearest Neighbour and Neural Network.

Chapter 3 presents an unmanned aerial vehicle (UAV) assist the pest detection model to track pests in the stored grain (SG). This proposed model consists of four phases such as data acquisition, edge detection, feature extraction, and pest identification. In this model, the edge detection (ED) phase is focused on analyzing the data (pest in the SG images). Many standard edge detection (SED) methods such as Sobel, Prewitt, Roberts, Morphological, Laplacian of Gaussian (LoG), Canny etc. are used to track the shape, location, and quantity of pests in SG. The implementation of the methods are performed using MATLAB R2015b and evaluated using signal to noise ratio (SNR), peak signal to noise ratio (PSNR), and processing time (PT).

Chapter 4 describes object selection as a trade-off between performance and accuracy. Particularly, in machine vision time versus precision for object selection plays a crucial role in image analysis is addressed. These regions are a group of segmented pixels that are used for processing. Such regions are often represented by numbers called "object descriptors". Using such data, the authors compare and distinguish objects by matching the descriptors. Without loss of generality, these descriptors have certain properties like (a) invariance against geometrical transformations like translation, rotation and scaling, (b) Stability to noise and non-rigid local deformation, (c) Completeness.

Chapter 5 explores flood control and disaster management technologies based on image processing and machine learning. The main objective of this chapter is to develop an understanding of the flood risks, explore the existing systems for managing the risks and devise a flood management model through machine vision. Furthermore, this chapter discusses the limitations of the current technologies and suggests a reliable model to overcome the problems. Finally, this chapter elaborates on the system of how to detect flood-affected areas and determine rescue routes.

Chapter 6 discusses the color changes on the avocado dip under microwave conditions through the machine vision approach. This chapter analyzes the change of color in a* - b* space in terms of different treatments. Also, this chapter discusses real-time experimental analysis by various parameters.

Chapter 7 deliberates the defect detection on defective roads and bridges through computer vision-based techniques. This chapter discusses the basic steps involved in defect detection using image processing along with existing systems and presents the pros and cons of the different existing methods in terms of performance. Also, this chapter applies multiple image processing techniques to solve the various types of defects.

Chapter 8 presents the study and conducts experiments through machine vision techniques on diabetic retinopathy disease present in retinal fundus images. This chapter also discusses various factors of the disease that appears in the image and discusses the possible solutions in terms of image processing techniques. An effective analysis is shown for computer-aided solutions.

Chapter 9 provides a robust method to solve the ambiguities in handwritten the OCR system. This has been resolved using the Convolutional Neural Network (CNN) based approach. This state-of-the-art of

CNN-based approach for recognition of multiple handwritten numerals of various scripts is clearly shown here. It is also quite helpful to report the discriminate features of each individual and later lead to reporting a high recognition rate. At the simulation level we have listed the variance nature of the individual's images and through CNN we have reported a high recognition rate, which is quite helpful in building the automatic recognition system for handwritten numerals to have the solution for real-time problems.

Chapter 10 presents a detailed review of some of the attempts towards avoiding, detecting and preventing phishing in terms of visual methods. This chapter explains the frauds and criminal activities on phishing and, moreover, discusses the various solutions approached in recent years. Additionally, this chapter reviews the role of training and education on the reduction of phishing victims.

We have to start by thanking God Almighty for giving us the ability and opportunity to undertake to edit this book and to complete it satisfactorily. Completion of this book could not have been accomplished without the support of all editors starting from the "Call for Chapters" till their finalization. All the contributors have given their contributions amicably and is a positive sign of significant teamwork. The editors are sincerely thankful to all the members of Scrivener Publishing especially Martin Scrivener for providing constructive inputs and allowing an opportunity to edit this important book. We are equally thankful to all reviewers who hail from different places in and around the globe shared their support and stand firm towards quality chapter submissions. Finally, we are eternally grateful to the authors for contributing quality chapters.

Muthukumaran Malarvel
Soumya Ranjan Nayak
Surya Narayan Panda
Prasant Kumar Pattnaik
Nittaya Muangnak
April 2020

1

Land-Use Classification with Integrated Data

D. A. Meedeniya*, J. A. A. M Jayanetti, M. D. N. Dilini,
M. H. Wickramapala and J. H. Madushanka

*Department of Computer Science and Engineering,
University of Moratuwa, Sri Lanka*

Abstract

The identification of the usage and coverage of the land is a major part of regional development. Crowdsourced geographic information systems provide valuable information about the land use of different regions. Although these data sources lack reliability and possess some limitations, they are useful in deriving building blocks for the usage of the land, where the manual surveys are not up-to-date, costly, and time consuming. At present, in the context of Sri Lanka, there is a lack of reliable and updated land-use data. Moreover, there is a rapid growth in the construction industry, resulting in frequent changes in land-use and land-cover data. This paper presents a novel and an automated methodology based on learning models for identifying the usage and coverage of the land. The satellite imagery is used to identify the information related to land cover. They are integrated with Foursquare venue data, which is a popular crowdsourced geographic information, thus, enhancing the information level and the quality of land-use visualization. The proposed methodology has shown a kappa coefficient of 74.03%, showing an average land-use classification accuracy within a constrained environment.

Keywords: Geographic information system, land-cover identification, land-use classification, social computing, decision support system, satellite images, Foursquare data

Corresponding author: dulanim@cse.mrt.ac.lk

Muthukumaran Malarvel, Soumya Ranjan Nayak, Surya Narayan Panda, Prasant Kumar Pattnaik and Nittaya Muangnak (eds.) Machine Vision Inspection Systems (Vol. 1): Image Processing, Concepts, Methodologies and Applications, (1–36) © 2020 Scrivener Publishing LLC

1.1 Introduction

Regional planning and management are major concerns in the development strategy of a country. The information related to the coverage and usage of lands can be used to extract the features in an area and facilitate development activities. The land-use data are related to human activities, whereas the land-cover information represent the natural features and artificial constructions on the earth surface. Crowdsourced geographic information systems provide valuable information about the land use of different regions. At present, up-to-date data on land usage and coverage are not available for all the cities in Sri Lanka. This is due to the cost of labor, lack of the required technologies, and resources associated with the data surveys. Unavailability of a cost-effective way of obtaining such latest and reliable data is a bottleneck to the long-term planning and development of a region. This results in unplanned *ad hoc* developments, construction of unhealthy residential areas, deterioration of service and infrastructure, environmental pollution, increased traffic congestion, and so on [1], which can be widely seen in many urban areas in Sri Lanka. Therefore, up-to-date data on the usage and coverage of land are important to make strategic decisions on sustainable region planning.

The objective of this research is to design and develop a support system to classify the land-cover and land-use data using Google Satellite imagery [2] and Foursquare data, which is a type of volunteer geographic information (VGI), respectively [3]. The system produces a visualization of different types of land-use in each area (eg. residential, industrial, commercial, agriculture etc.) on a land-use map based on heterogeneous data sources including crowdsourced Foursquare data. Acquiring data on land cover and land use from different data types, which can be integrated into the classification system, will enhance the quality of the processed information [4].

Therefore, this research provides a novel way of identifying and classifying different forms of land-use data, specifically satellite imagery and Foursquare data, with the extensible features for other types of related data. The system refines the land-use mapping with the use of additional parameters, such as context-specific different data sources. Ultimately, the retrieved data can be used to monitor land-use changes in near real time [2]. Moreover, this study focuses on developing a common platform that enables the collaboration of heterogeneous data sources to produce enhanced land-use data. Further, this will increase the utility value of the retrieved information on land-cover and land-use, hence, widening the range of applicable applications from the results. Colombo district is selected as the study area considering the availability and sampling rates of different data sets and issues associated with data validation [4]. The proposed land-use visualization approach identifies and classifies different forms of land cover and land use in a selected area considering the satellite imagery and Foursquare data, respectively, and displays the classification on a land-use map.

The land-use data retrieved from the proposed methodology can be used to monitor land-use changes near real time. Analysis of these detailed snapshots of land-use enables authorities to detect a change and foresee its social and environmental consequences. This, in turn, will enable them to identify long-lasting sustainable solutions to urbanization issues in Sri Lanka.

The paper is structured as follows: Section II explores the related literature and Section III presents the design architectures of the system and Section IV describes the development process with the used techniques. Section V evaluates the validity of the proposed method, and finally, Section VI summarizes the research including future work.

1.2 Background Study

1.2.1 Overview of Land-Use and Land-Cover Information

The identification of the usage and coverage of the land is a major part of regional development. Land cover and land use are often interchangeably used in many information systems, despite the distinct difference between those two terms [1, 4]. Land cover refers to observable physical properties of land, such as the areas with trees, grounds, building, roads, water, and so on. On the other hand, land use refers to purposes for which lands are being used, such as residential, commercial, entertainment, and so on. It may be difficult to determine the actual purpose for which land is being used by solely using the information produced by a source of observation. For example, in the absence of additional information sources, it may be difficult to decide whether grasslands are used for agricultural activities or not. Moreover, there is a rapid growth in the construction industry, resulting in frequent changes in land-use and land-cover data.

As a summary, the land coverage and usage data are important to identify correctly and process timely manner in order to make decisions on regional development. However, it is challenging to obtain large-scale, latest data from reliable sources. The unplanned constructions may impact the region with unprogressive infrastructure, unhealthy residentials, and environment issues, such as traffic congestion and pollution.

1.2.2 Geographical Information Systems

A Geographical Information Systems (GIS) facilitates collection, store, process, analyze, and visualize data on the surface of the earth. Prior to the discovery of advanced technologies and concepts, a GIS primarily consisted of a database management system (DBMS) and a set of tools that allowed data to be retrieved from the DBMS. With the advent of the Internet and Web-based applications, as well as the increased utilization of mobile devices, the traditional notion of a GIS has been altered significantly. Particularly, the user base of GISs has expanded from traditional users, such as relevant public and private sector to just about anyone who uses an application built on top of a GIS in their mobile or other electronic devices.

Even though the primary functions, such as data storage, retrieval, visualization, and so on, are common to all GISs, the nature of these functions depends largely on the underlying application. Based on the area of application, GIS can be classified into different information system types, such as cadastral, land and property, image-based, natural resource management, spatial information systems, and so on.

The GIS can be used to find solutions to a wide variety of problems, such as determining and predicting the features of a particular location, identifying locations with particular characteristics, monitoring change over periods, determining the best route between different locations, modeling environmental and societal evolution over time, crime location mapping, disaster management, transportation planning, management, and so on.

1.2.3 GIS-Related Data Types

1.2.3.1 Point Data Sets

Point data are used to represent discrete data points that have no adjacent features. For example, in a GIS, the location of a place can be represented by a point location. The GIS data are of two categories, the spatially referenced data and the attribute data table associated with it. The spatially referenced data are represented in vector and raster forms. Foursquare data [3, 5] and OpenStreetMap data [6] are two popular GIS point data sources that can be utilized for the identification of land-use utilization at a detailed level.

Foursquare [3, 5] is a mobile-based social networking service that facilitates to acquire user-location information using check-in and search history; and recommend places near the user's current location. These data contain the names, locations, and types of places. When providing recommendations, the application makes use of its citizen-contributed database, the places a user goes, and the advice and comments given by other users on a place. This is a volunteered/crowdsourced VGI, that uses geographic data provided by the users. Thus, Foursquare data are used to identify land-use information with proper quality validation and consumes a low-cost mechanism.

OpenStreetMap [6] is a popular GIS data source that provides geographic data. This presents the physical features within a given area, such as commercial buildings, roads, waterways, railways, highways, and amenities using tags, and each of those tags describes a geographical attribute. Moreover, OpenStreetMap releases map data under a free and open license, which makes them available for researchers and as a data validation source.

1.2.3.2 Aerial Data Sets

An aerial data set is prepared by means of airborne methods and aerial photographs and Google satellite imagery some examples [2]. Satellite images of the Earth's surface captured by remote-sensing techniques have proven to be a useful data source for many research studies and applications in diverse fields [2, 7]. Satellite images enable wider geographical areas to be covered quickly with relative convenience. They provide a way of monitoring the Earth's surface, hence, eliminating the need to rely solely on labor-intensive processes, such as area frame surveys for maintaining up-to-date information on the Earth's surface, which tends to be a slow and a tedious process. Moreover, the digital format of satellite images enables to be directly processed digitally and integrated with other data sources with relative ease. Data retrieved from satellite images are used to successfully extract the required information on the land usage for decision making and predicting systems.

High elevation aerial photographs of the Earth's surface are a remote-sensing data source. They can be used to identify the coverage of lands. These visual interpretations are also used in conjunction with satellite images, particularly to fill areas which are not clear on satellite images due to prevalent atmospheric conditions, such as cloud cover at the time of capturing those. Aerial photographs are of high spatial resolution. Therefore, these images comprise a high level of information which is useful for various analytical and reference purposes associated with land-cover classifications. The spectral range of aerial photography is narrow, and therefore, a considerable number of photographs will have to be patched together to cover wider geographical areas. Further, the cost per surface unit is higher with aerial photographs compared with satellite images.

1.2.4   Related Studies

Among the variety of research studies, the study by Quercia and Saez [5], has described the feasibility of acquiring data from the locations of social-media users, considering the mining urban deprivation information in London city. This study has addressed the reliable, latest and inferring free data retrieval, and shown the use of Foursquare data in monitoring fine-grain resolutions, which cannot be obtained from other land-use data used in practice. However, this gives an insight into the limitations of Foursquare data such as demographic and geographic biases and the Foursquare categories not being fully structured. For instance, these can be biased by the penetration rate of the Foursquare data and a given location can be named with different category types based on the thinking patterns of the users who entered the Foursquare data.

A multidata approach (MDA) is presented by Bareth [4] to generate data related to land use. They have combined the traditional types of data for land usage with the information obtained from the different remote-sensing analysis. As a first step, remote sensing data were classified using supervised classification techniques and then the quality of the classified data was assessed. The second step of the research was to import the classified data into a GIS environment and overlay them with relevant 3rd-party data sources, such as official topographic or land-use data. The importance of this approach is that it enables useful and high-quality land-use information in various spatial databases, such as spatial biotope or biodiversity databases, spatial databases of national parks, and so on to be integrated with the results of remote-sensing analysis. Further, land-use data retrieved from official data sources can be integrated to MDA for cross-checking the results of remote-sensing analysis. Also, by incorporating the results of land-cover change models to MDA, they have simulated the change scenarios for the usage and coverage of the land.

According to the literature, satellite images are mainly used to identify urban land usage that covers a large area without frequent changes. However, it is challenging to obtain high-resolution images. Thus, there is a research direction toward the integration of these remote-sensing data with the social knowledge data for better analysis of the usage and coverage patterns of the land.

1.3   System Design

The primary focus of this study is to classify land usage into several categories, such as residential, hotels, restaurants, industrial, and so on. Two data sources google satellite images for the coverage and four-square point data for usage of the land are used for this study. First, the google satellite imagery is used to classify land-cover data that represent primitive categories, such as water, built-up, vegetation, and bare soil. Next, this output would be further differentiated using foursquare point data into the abovementioned land usage classes. Figure 1.1 shows the overall view of the proposed system.

System design mainly consists of four components. The data pre-processing component removes and purifies noises in the input data. The data classification component applies classification and clustering techniques on the preprocessed data. These results of heterogeneous data will be integrated into the data integration component. Then, data analysis component will evaluate the accuracy of the classified data. The main output of the system is a Shape file that adds a layer to Quantum Geographic Information System (QGIS). The QGIS is a free desktop application that supports different platforms. It has features to view, edit, and analyze geospatial data together with quality measures. The final system is expected to be used for urban planning and government officials who want to collect data, and so on.

Figure 1.2 shows the sequence diagram of the proposed Web application. It shows how such a user can easily retrieve the results produced by the system so that he can use this information in his respective work, such as sustainable urban development planning. First, the user will access a Web interface where he is provided with a google map. He can zoom in the map and select a rectangular area using the mouse pointer. The analyst can highlight the area from the map, which he wants the land-use classification. The common interface will send the boundaries (latitudes and

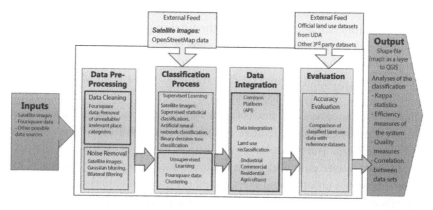

Figure 1.1 High-level design diagram.

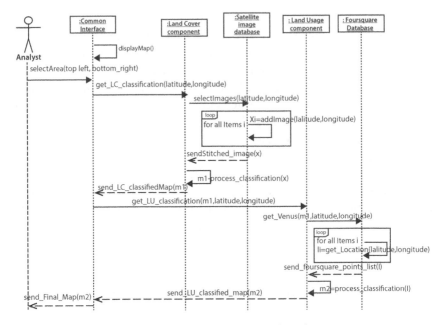

Figure 1.2 Process view of the land-use visualization Web application.

longitudes) of the area to the land-cover classification module, which will return the stitched image. Next, the common interface will send the land-cover classified map along with the boundaries to the land usage classification module. This module will get the Foursquare locations and their respective classes from the Foursquare database, perform the land-use classification, and return the final land usage classified map to the analyst. In addition, a legend is also provided with the different categories of land usage classes, such as residential, restaurants, hotels, and so on, and their assigned colors will also appear with the final map.

Figure 1.3 shows the architectural view of the proposed system, which complies with the overall view, and the components are described with the workflow given in Figure 1.4. The module "Input Data Manager" handles the input data types to the system. The current system uses satellite images, Foursquare data, and official land-use data. The architecture is designed in an extensible feature to incorporate other data types, such as OpenStreetMap. The module "Visualization Manager" visualizes the processed Foursquare data and point location data in terms of land-use classification with a color-coded layer based on the predefined categories and described in detail in the chapter. The logical layer comprises three main

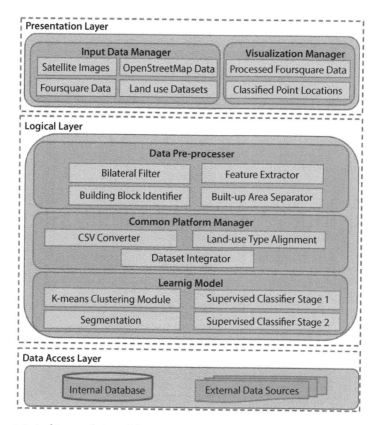

Figure 1.3 Architectural view of the system.

modules responsible to preprocess data, integrate data sources, and the learning process.

Figure 1.4 describes the workflow of the system, which is an extension of our previous work [7]. Initially, Google satellite imagery and Foursquare data of Colombo District, which contains instances of varieties of land uses were collected and preprocessed separately. The satellite imagery was subjected to bilateral filtering [8] to remove the Gaussian noise [9]. Next, edge enhancement techniques were applied to enhance the important features of satellite images, such as sharp edges, which helps to identify built-up areas. Foursquare data also need to be cleaned because they contain irrelevant and unreliable data, such as location names inserted with English and Tamil. Next, the preprocessed satellite images are classified using supervised learning techniques, such as random forest, and unsupervised classification techniques, such as k-means clustering. The foursquare point

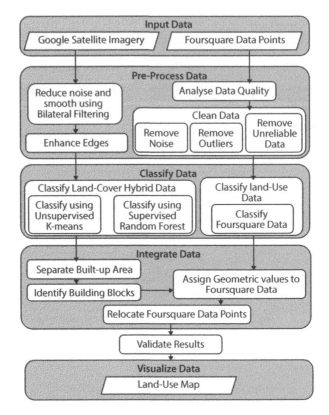

Figure 1.4 Workflow diagram of the system.

locations would be further differentiated into nine basic classes. Next, these two outputs will be integrated in order to produce the final land usage classified map. The common platform enables heterogeneous data sources to collaborate to produce enhanced land-use data. The implementation details are further discussed in the Implementation section.

1.4   Implementation Details

1.4.1   Materials

The data set considered for this study includes over 20,000 satellite images containing diverse features for each land-cover category. The differences in built-up areas were caused by differences in actual building structures and shapes, as well as due to lighting conditions and quality of the sensors used for capturing the images. Further, Google satellite images only include red, green, blue (RGB) bands, and certain land features are not well represented in these bands. Thus, developing a universal approach to automatically extract built-up areas to a satisfactory degree of accuracy is challenging.

This study has used 3863 foursquare points for the study area of around 700 square kms in Colombo District, All data records were consistent and complete and followed a common format and there were no discrepancies and duplications. Each record consisted of the location data such as name, geographical coordinates, category types the place belonged to, and the number of user and the check-ins. There were 10 main categories for Foursquare data, and 354 subcategories. However, some of the subcategories were not properly categorized under the main categories. In order to overcome this issue, this study has realigned foursquare categories and subcategories into nine land-use types.

1.4.2   Preprocessing

Initially, the images are smoothened using the bilateral filter, which effectively removes Gaussian noise while preserving the edge information of the images. The bilateral filter calculates the average of pixels surrounding a pixel and replaces it with the weighted average of intensities in neighboring pixels [10]. Foursquare being a VGI data set, the reliability of data is one of the key issues. In order to remove the unreliable data, the points with a user count below a given threshold value were removed, because the degree of the unreliability of the existence of a point tends to decrease with the number of unique users checked in for a given location [2]. Irrelevant data points and the records with unreadable names due to human or application errors at data entry were removed from the data set. The associated limitations, such as the unequal distribution of point data and the insufficient Foursquare data in unpopular regions, cannot be treated with preprocessing.

1.4.3   Built-Up Area Extraction

Computer vision techniques have been used to identify rooftops from satellite imagery. However, such approaches could only be used successfully when the built-up areas adhere to images with a fixed set of features or with a given hypothesis for rooftop areas developed by the researchers. The built-up areas in the set of satellite images that were available for this study had major variations from one image to another. These variations

Figure 1.5 Variations in features of built-up areas.

are partly caused by the differences in the resolution and quality of sensors that have been used to capture the images. The rest of the variations were caused by inherent differences in rooftop areas in terms of color and shape as indicated in Figure 1.5. Hence, it is challenging to find a universally applicable hypothesis to identify the built-up areas as suggested in related studies.

Several methods and techniques are available for the classification of land cover using remotely sensed data. Satellite image classification involves grouping individual pixels into a set of categories considering the spectral characteristics of pixels in various bands. These spectral classes are then matched to a set of predefined land-cover categories [11]. A single land-cover class may be represented with one or more spectral classes.

Land-cover classification approaches can be primarily classified into three categories. These include automated approaches, manual approaches, and hybrid approaches [12]. For the built-up area extraction process of this research, we followed a hybrid classification approach which involves supervised, as well as unsupervised, classification techniques. The tasks associated with the built-up area extraction is shown in Figure 1.6.

1.4.4   Per-Pixel Classification

Initially, a single round of supervised classification was used to obtain a land-cover classification. This approach failed to classify roads and building pixels to a satisfactory degree of accuracy due to high spectral similarities in pixels belonging to different land-cover classes. However, there was a distinct difference between the spectral characteristics of pixels belonging to vegetation and water classes from those of building and road classes. Based on the observations, a hybrid classification approach consisting two rounds of supervised classification was devised for the built-up area extraction process as indicated in Figure 1.5.

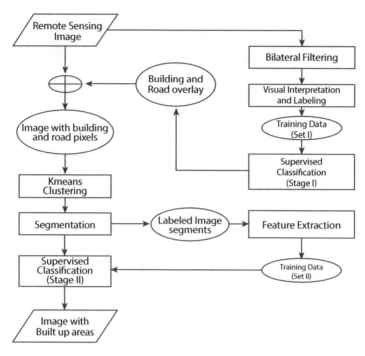

Figure 1.6 Workflow of the built-up area extraction process.

In order to extract building and road pixels from the rest of the image, the supervised per-pixel classification was used. Here, two classes of training samples were prepared. Class I included building and road pixels, and Class II included vegetation and water pixels. A random forest classifier [13] was trained using the prepared training samples, which were prepared by manually drawing polygons on a set of images corresponding to the two abovementioned classes and digitizing those to a obtain a set of polygon shapefiles. The trained classifier was then used for the classification of pixels in satellite imagery. A mask was prepared for the pixels that contain water and vegetation (Class II pixels), which were extracted using the trained random forest classifier. Initially, road and building pixels were extracted from the rest of the image using a supervised per-pixel classification. Then, object-based image classification was used to separate building pixels from the road pixels. This was used to mask out the satellite images, thereby extracting the building and road pixels (Class I pixels). Figure 1.7 (left) shows the original satellite image, (middle) the image with building and road pixels after the removal of vegetation and water pixels, and (right) the built-up areas identified by the supervised random forest classifier.

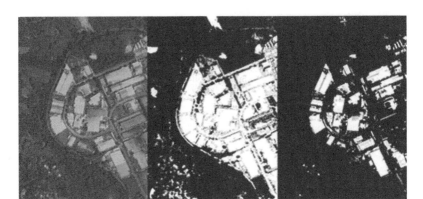

Figure 1.7 Original image (left). Image with building and roads (middle). Built-up areas (right).

1.4.5   Clustering

Prior to segmentation, the image intensity values are calculated using K-means clustering to group the homogeneous clusters. This was used to increase the homogeneity of the segments produced by the super pixel-based segmentation technique. The number of clusters (k) was determined by investigating the impact of a different number of clusters on the final output of the built-up area extraction process. It was observed that k=4 resulted in a high level of accuracy. Clustering was used prior to segmentation because the segmentation of clustered images resulted in more homogeneous segments in terms of textural and spectral properties of pixels rather than location.

1.4.6   Segmentation

The clustered image containing only the pixels of Class I (building and road pixels) was then segmented using a super pixel-based segmentation methodology called Simple Linear Iterative Clustering (SLIC) [14]. The SLIC was used because they are superior to traditional segmentation methodologies in terms of their high effectiveness at recognizing homogeneous segments with pixels, which are similar in terms of color and texture, regardless of how far apart they are in the image. The SLIC was partially used because of its simplicity which only requires the desired number of segments to be provided as an additional parameter. The number of segments was determined by the impact of a different number of segments on the final output of the built-up area extraction process.

It was observed that four segments per image resulted in the highest level of accuracy.

Segments produced with and without the application of clustering are indicated in Figure 1.8 and Figure 1.9, respectively. It can be clearly observed that clustering prior to segmentation has increased the homogeneity of segments in terms of color and texture rather than on location. The impact of the different number of clusters on the outcome of segmentation was visually analyzed, and four clusters seemed to produce the highest degree of homogeneity. The original satellite image is shown in Figure 1.9

Figure 1.8 A satellite image (left) and directly generated segments (middle and right).

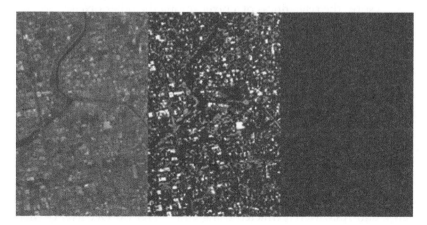

Figure 1.9 A satellite image (left) and segmented images (middle and right).

(left), also shown are the segments produced when it was clustered prior to segmentation (middle and right).

1.4.7   Object-Based Image Classification

After segmenting, each image segment was labeled into two classes. The built-up areas are represented by Class I, and Class II indicates the non–built-up areas. Then, the following texture features were extracted from the candidate regions:

- Contrast—a distinguishable feature of an image with respect to the difference of intensities between pixel over the image. The rooftop area has low contrast because that area of the images is similar to each other.
- Homogeneity—the closeness of pixel distribution ranging from 0 to 1. The rooftop regions have high homogeneity, because the images are similar.
- Dissimilarity—returns the degrees of disparity in the pixel distribution.
- Energy— a value which needs to be minimized, maximized, or optimized. It identifies the disorders in textures by considering certain quality distance among pixels. High textual uniformity values represent similar images.
- Correlation—an image registration and tracking technique that identifies changes in images. This is a simple and useful technique to extract information from an image and measures the relatedness of a pixel among the other pixels.
- Angular Second Moment (ASM)—returns a measure of textural uniformity that is pixel pair repetitions in an image.

A super pixel-based segmentation technique was used to segment the images because it efficiently reduces the image complexity. Further, as opposed to traditional segmentation techniques, super pixel-based segmentation can model many longer-range interactions between pixels. Thus, there are similar pixels in a super pixel, when considering the properties, such as color and texture.

The segments produced by the super pixel-based segmentation technique were then manually labeled into two classes: buildings and roads. From these segments, the texture information contrast, homogeneity, dissimilarity, energy, and ASM were extracted using Gray Level Co-Occurrence Matrix (GLCM) matrix. Then, the random forest classifier is trained using the created feature vectors. Figure 1.10 shows the input to the object-based image

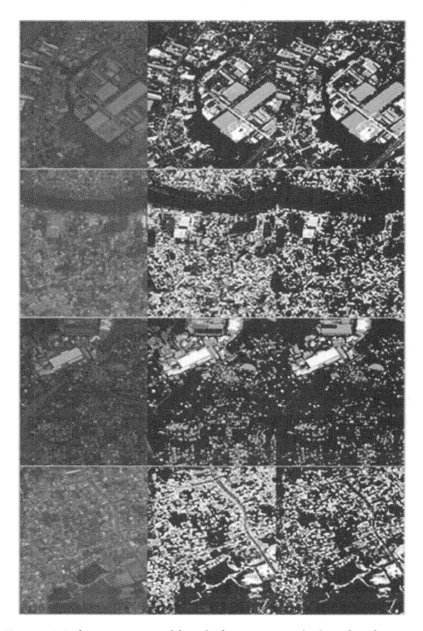

Figure 1.10 Built-up areas extracted from the first image using the devised pipeline.

classification step and the corresponding built-up areas that were identified from it by the classifier. After the extraction of features, each feature was normalized to get zero mean and unit standard deviation. As previously mentioned, the random forest learning model was trained using feature vectors. Accordingly, it was possible to extract the built-up areas to a reasonable degree of accuracy from images which were significantly different from one another in terms of different properties of land-cover categories as shown in Figure 1.10.

Algorithm 1 states the main processing steps of the system, highlighting the following:

> Process 1: supervised per-pixel classification is used to extract building and road pixels from the rest of the image as shown in Figure 1.7. This process used two classes of training samples, Class I includes building and road pixels, whereas class II contains vegetation and water pixels. The two functions, labeled as Class I and Class II, are used for this. A random forest classifier is trained using the prepared training samples. The input satellite image is then classified using the trained random forest classifier and was assigned to a classified image.

Algorithm 1: System Process
Data: satelliteImages
Result: classifySegmentedImage

```
Function main()

for image in trainingSamplesOfImages
      for pixel in image
            if typeOf(pixel).equals(building or
            road) then
                  labelAsClassI(pixel)
            else
                  labelAsClassII(pixel)
randomForestClassifier =
trainRandomForestClassifier(labelledPixels)
inputImage = Unclassified image
classifiedImage = classifyInputImage(inputImage,
randomForestClassifier)
clusteredImage = clusterInputImage(inputImage,
KmeansClustering)

mask = isolateWaterAndVegetationPixels(classified
Image)
imageWithRoadAndBuildingPixels = isolateRoad
AndBuildingPixels(clusteredImage, mask)
```

```
segmentedImage = imageSegmentation( imageWithRoad
AndBuildingPixels, SLIC)
for image in trainingSamplesOfSegmentedImages
    for segment in image
        if typeOf(segment).equals(building) then
            extractFeaturesAndLabelAsBuilding
            (segment)
        else
            extractFeaturesAndLabelAsRoad
            (segment)
objectBasedRandomForestClassifier =
trainRandomForestClassifier(extractedFeatures)
return classifySegmentedImage(segmentedImage,
objectBasedRandomForestClassifier)
```

Process 2: The input image is categorized into sets of homogeneous clusters using K-means clustering and assigned to clusteredImage. Clustering is performed prior to segmentation because it was observed to increase the homogeneity of the segments produced by the super pixel-based segmentation technique.

Process 3: Using the classified image produced in process 1, a mask, which contains only the water and vegetation pixels (Class II pixels), is prepared. Afterward, this was used to mask out the clustered image produced in process 2, thereby isolating the building and road pixels (Class I pixels) in it. The image, containing road and building pixels, was segmented (segmentedImage) using SLIC.

Process 4: The segments contained in a set of segmented images produced in Process 4 are labeled, and the training samples are prepared by extracting the features dissimilarity, homogeneity, energy, correlation, and ASM from all the images in trainingSamplesOfSegmentedImages.

Process 5: A random forest classifier is trained for object-based classification using the prepared training samples (using the function trainRandomForestClassifier).

Process 6: The segmented image produced in Process 5 is classified using the random forest classifier trained to obtain the final built-up area classification, using the function classifySegmentedImage.

1.4.8   Foursquare Data Preprocessing and Quality Analysis

The Foursquare data set for the Colombo District was analyzed to get a clear understanding of its properties, unique features, and possible issues. The Foursquare locations belonged to 10 different main categories, which fall into areas, such as travel, professional, outdoors, food, nightlife, residence, shopping, colleges, entertainment and event, and 354 subcategories.

The classification process becomes complex when there are a large group of subcategories. For instance, a given subcategory can belong to several categories. The data points tend to be found more in urban areas, whereas the density of the records tends to decrease when moving away from the urban areas; hence, not being equally distributed. Since Foursquare is a crowdsourced data set, the reliability of data was another key issue. The degree of the unreliability of the existence of a point tends to decrease with the number of unique users checked in for a given location. However, the data set for Colombo district showed a very low user count for most of the data points, having over 1500 records with less than 10 user counts.

Both a manual and an automated approach were carried out to analyze the quality of the Foursquare data. All data records were consistent and complete and followed a common format. There were no duplicate records to be found because all the data items were from a single source, and no integration of several data sources has been performed on the Foursquare data. There were no discrepancies in the given item set. None of the functional dependencies between the attributes has been violated. There were no missing values in any of the data records. Each record consisted of a unique name and a unique pair of latitude and longitude values.

The main use of Foursquare data for this research is to predict the usage of the land use in constructed areas. However, the original records contained points categorized as city, town, river, bridge, village, lake, road, and neighborhood, which were quite irrelevant for our research purpose. There were records where the user entered names that were not readable or partially readable. This was due to human or mobile or application error at data entry.

Related studies [3, 5] have shown the possible issues in the quality analysis process, suggesting the need for preprocessing of Foursquare data prior to integration. The irrelevant data points were removed from the original POI data set.

Unreliable data were removed by defining a threshold value, so the data points with a user count below the threshold were deleted. In order to remove the Foursquare category complexity, the Foursquare categories and subcategories were realigned to 9 land-use types, professional, administration, hospitals, education, transportation, residential, commercial, hotels, and recreation [7].

1.4.9   Integration of Satellite Images with Foursquare Data

The classification of satellite images resulted with the extracted built-up areas, as shown in Figure 1.5, was used as the input to the integration of the two data sources, extracted built-up area and the Foursquare point data set which are preprocessed and realigned. The land coverage was identified by the classified satellite images, and the usage was determined by the Foursquare data of the corresponding built-up areas. First, the built-up area was segmented to derive the building blocks and identify the associated Foursquare points, which overlaid on top of the segmented building blocks layer, to demonstrate land use.

1.4.10   Building Block Identification

Prior to segmentation, the built-up area image was converted to grayscale and then to binary, and the noise was reduced by applying filters. Then, a mask was applied to separate the foreground from the background, and the identified foreground was flood filled to fill the holes within the identified building block areas as shown in Figure 1.11.

Initially, the built-up area was further preprocessed to enhance the segmentation results. The images were converted to grayscale and binary; then the noise was reduced by applying filters. The foreground was separated from the background by applying a mask, and the holes within the building blocks were flood filled. Then, the building blocks were segmented and

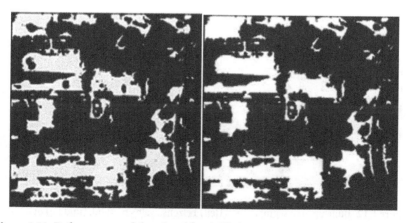

Figure 1.11 Built-up area and the related flood-filled area.

identified individually from the built-up areas. The segmentation process was done using three different methods, (1) Felzenszwalb's method [15], (2) quick shift method [16, 17], and (3) SLIC [14, 18] as depicted in Figure 1.12. The SLIC is a super pixel-based method, which uses K-means clustering and produces the best segmentation for the context. Finally, the Foursquare points were overlaid on the building blocks. The accuracy of the identified segments could be further enhanced by tuning the minimum number of segments parameter. However, certain segments identified did not include building blocks. To remove such segments, the percentage of black pixels within the identified segments were calculated and were removed if these did not reach the given threshold value.

1.4.11   Overlay of Foursquare Points

The next step in integration was to overlay the Foursquare points layer on the segmented built-up area image. Foursquare points that fall within the longitude and latitude region of each image were detected and rescaled by considering the width, height, and geographic coordinates of the image and was plotted on the top of the segmented built-up area image, as shown in Figure 1.13.

However, because the crowdsourced Foursquare data can be less accurate and unreliable, some of the Foursquare points do not overlay on the building blocks, instead falls close to the relevant built-up areas. Thus, based on a predefined threshold value, the data point that does not fall on the top of the building blocks was realigned to the closest build-up area [6].

As a next step, the geographical coordinates of Foursquare data points on each building block segment are derived by considering the midpoints

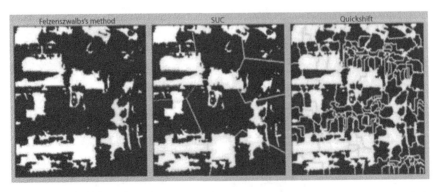

Figure 1.12 Built-up area segmentation (left) Felzenszwalb's method, (middle) quick shift method, and (right) SLIC.

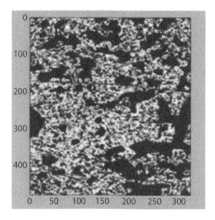

Figure 1.13 Foursquare integration.

and the difference between the longitude and latitude of its edge. Moreover, the process calculated the Euclidean distance from each data point to the midpoint of the associated building block. As mentioned above, the foursquare points that are outside the built-up area are assigned to the nearest building block based on the defined threshold radius. During the visualization process, the colored building blocks are merged into the final land-use visualization image.

1.4.12   Visualization of Land Usage

The identified usage and coverage information about the land are visualized into nine categories. Those types are administration, education, commercial, hospitals, recreation, transportation, professional, residential, and hotels. The building blocks where their land-use category could not be found was colored in white. The final land-use visualization image was created by the combination of all the colored, as well as white-colored, building blocks. Figure 1.14 shows the original satellite image with its land-use visualized image (right).

1.4.13   Common Platform Development

In order to devise a common platform to integrate heterogeneous data sources, research was conducted on the heterogeneous data sources available for land-use identification. Several free and commercial organizations provided point-of-interest (POI) data sets useful for land-use visualization [19]. The Gowalla POI data set, Facebook Places, the SimpleGeo Places,

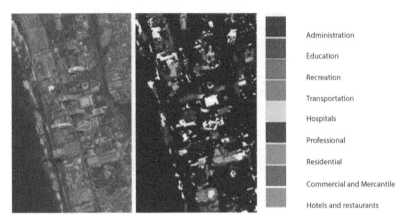

Figure 1.14 Original satellite image with the land-use visualization.

Google Places [20], locationary data set, factual data set, and OSM data set [21, 22] are some of the popular POI data sets available for land-use visualization. Most of these data sets contained millions of records useful for land-use type identification, where some were free to use, and some required a subscription charge. However, when analyzing the usefulness of those data sets, most of those covered different parts of the world and only a few data sets like OSM, Google places, and Facebook places were found to be useful with sufficient records, when it applies to the domain of Sri Lanka.

Most of the data sets were available as files that could be downloaded, whereas some data sets could be accessed through the APIs provided. Those data sets were to be found in several formats like json, csv, shp, xml, and so on. Different data sets had been classified according to their own set of land-use categories. Therefore, when integrating those heterogeneous data sets, the main challenges were to come up with a design that accommodates different formats and different land-use categories.

Figure 1.15 depicts the basic design for the common platform for heterogeneous data sources to collaborate. It accepts POI data sets of the formats json, xml, shp, and csv. If the formats are json, xml, or shp, they are converted to csv format using the csv conversion method. Afterward, the data set's land-use types are realigned into the nine land-use types we use for visualization. Afterward, the data points are integrated with the classified Google satellite images built-up area. When multiple land-use types are allocated to the same building block by different data sets, a decision supporting system is used where priority is given to the type with the highest user count.

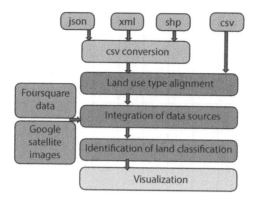

Figure 1.15 Common API design.

1.5   System Evaluation

1.5.1   Experimental Evaluation Process

The accuracy of the land-use visualization developed in this study was assessed using the official land-use data of Colombo district as the reference data set. Initially, there were 38 land-use categories in the official data set. In this study, we have realigned these categories into nine land-use types prior to the accuracy assessment. These types are commercial, administration, transportation, education, hotels and restaurants, hospitals, recreational, professional, and residential. The map areas with significantly low densities of Foursquare points were not considered for the accuracy evaluation to avoid the negative impact on the overall land-use identification accuracies caused by insufficient data. In this study, we have assumed that the approximate accuracy of the official data obtained via land-use surveys is 100%. We have selected 100 satellite images with a higher foursquare density as the test sample. The corresponding official images of the selected satellite images were downloaded in JPEG format, giving longitude and latitude ranges.

Different classification learning models were applied on the satellite images for the land-cover classification. Table 1.1 shows the obtained statistical metrics for different land types.

Naïve Bayesian method scored the lowest accuracy of 0.67. The SVM and k-NN classifiers have shown an accuracy of 0.76 and 0.82, respectively. Although the decision tree approach had an accuracy of 0.81, the random forest method showed a slight improvement with a score of 0.82. Of all the six approaches, the logistic regression method showed the highest accuracy

Table 1.1 Satellite image classification accuracy vs. learning models.

Learning model	Description	Category	Land-cover classification accuracy		
			Precision	Recall	F1-Score
Naïve Bayesian	Classification is based on the probabilistic knowledge with Bayes Theorem	Roads	0.72	0.54	0.61
		Buildings	0.46	0.73	0.56
		Vegetation	0.88	0.74	0.81
		Average	0.72	0.67	0.68
Support Vector Machine (SVM)	Nonparametric classification technique derived from statistical learning	Roads	0.98	0.56	0.71
		Buildings	0.75	0.80	0.77
		Vegetation	0.70	0.90	0.79
		Average	0.80	0.76	0.76
Decision Tree	Set of binary rules that apply sequentially to associate pixels into categories	Roads	0.90	0.79	0.84
		Buildings	0.62	0.88	0.73
		Vegetation	0.92	0.79	0.85
		Average	0.84	0.81	0.82

(Continued)

Table 1.1 Satellite image classification accuracy vs. learning models. (*Continued*)

Learning model	Description	Category	Land-cover classification accuracy		
			Precision	Recall	F1-Score
Random Forest	Ensemble classification and regression learning model that gives the mean prediction of the individual trees	Roads	0.91	0.80	0.85
		Buildings	0.64	0.88	0.75
		Vegetation	0.92	0.79	0.85
		Average	0.84	0.82	0.82
k-nearest neighbor (k-NN)	Consider the nearest training data set in the feature space to classify items	Roads	0.93	0.81	0.86
		Buildings	0.65	0.89	0.75
		Vegetation	0.91	0.80	0.85
		Average	0.85	0.82	0.83
Logistic regression	Models the link among a dependent and independent variable, to select the best fit.	Roads	0.91	0.85	0.88
		Buildings	0.77	0.81	0.79
		Vegetation	0.87	0.89	0.88
		Average	0.86	0.85	0.86

of 0.85. The precision of building land-cover category was remarkably low in comparison to two other land-cover categories, regardless of the machine learning technique used. The reason behind this can be interpreted by the visual interpretation of clusters that were obtained with k-NN clustering technique. The output of k-NN clustering indicates that the spectral characteristics of some pixels belonging to the building and roads land-cover classes are similar. This caused misclassifications to occur between buildings and roads and limited the accuracy of resulting land-cover classification.

The official land-use data were imported as a shapefile to a new QGIS project and assigned the allocated color code to the LU categories of the shapefile using the LU code. The classified satellite images were compared with the corresponding image from the official land-use classification shapefile. In this step, the longitudes and latitudes of the classified buildings in the satellite images were calculated, as shown in Figure 1.8. Then, the official land-use classification of that point was taken from the official LUC data and created the base error matrix as shown in Table 1.2. Accordingly, the satellite images were classified and compared with the corresponding official image.

1.5.2   Evaluation of the Classification Using Base Error Matrix

We have evaluated the accuracy of classifications using statistical metrics. We have used the base error matrix to calculate Total Accuracy/agreement [23], Kappa Coefficient [23–25], Commission Error, and Omission Error [23].

Total accuracy is the probability that the classifier has labeled an image pixel into the ground truth class. This measure on the correctness of the classified images, i.e., the ratio of the correctly classified pixels to the total pixels, is considered to create the error matrix as given in Equation 1. Thus, the accuracy is a measurement of the agreement among a standard, which is assumed to be correct and image classification of unknown quality. It is defined as accurate if the image classification is closely related to the standard.

Accordingly, the total accuracy of 78.894% is obtained for the proposed solution, where the number of correct plots is given by (87+56+42+79+4+9+9+23+5) and the total number of plots is 398.

$$\text{Total accuracy} = \frac{\text{Number\_of\_correct\_plots}}{\text{Total\_number\_of\_plots}} \times 100 \tag{1}$$

The commission error represents the pixels that belong to another category but are labeled as fitting to the considered category. Further, the

Table 1.2 Base error matrix.

		Official Reference Data Set									
		Professional	Hotels and Restaurants	Transportation	Commercial	Administration	Education	Residential	Outdoors and Recreational	Hospitals	Row Total
Classified Satellite Images	Professional	87	0	0	10	3	4	8	2	1	115
	Hotels and Restaurants	2	56	1	2	0	0	3	0	0	64
	Transportation	3	0	42	0	0	0	3	1	0	49
	Commercial	7	3	0	79	1	1	3	1	0	95
	Administration	3	0	2	1	4	0	0	0	0	10
	Education	2	0	0	0	0	9	0	0	0	11
	Residential	3	0	2	2	0	0	9	0	1	17
	Outdoors and Recreational	3	1	1	2	0	0	1	23	0	31
	Hospitals	1	0	0	0	0	0	0	0	5	6
	Column Total	111	60	48	96	8	14	27	27	7	398

omission error represents the pixels that belong to the truth category, but which is failed to be classified to the actual category. According to the base error matrix, the accuracy percentages are given in Table 1.3. The accuracy assessment measurements are calculated using the error or confusion matrix.

Kappa coefficient (K) [25] is a discrete multivariate technique that considers the ratio of the agreement between the output category and the reference data. This is used to identify whether a given data on land coverage by remote sensors are better than the data obtained by randomly assigned labels.

Equation 2 defines the Kappa coefficient, such that N is the total number of points, $\sum_{i=1}^{r}(x_{i+} \times x_{+i})$ is the sum of the products of row total and column total of the matrix, and $\sum_{i=1}^{r}x_{ii}$ is the sum of the diagonal values of the matrix. When K > 0.8, it represents strong agreement and high accuracy. The middle-agreement accuracy is defined when 0.4 < K< 0.8, otherwise, low-agreement accuracy is defined when K< 0.4.

Table 1.3 Accuracy percentages w.r.t. the Base error matrix.

Class	Agreement (%)	Commission error (%)	Omission error (%)
Professional	78.38	24.35	21.62
Hotel and restaurants	93.33	12.50	6.67
Transportation	87.50	14.29	12.50
Commercial	82.29	16.84	17.71
Administration	50.00	60.00	50.00
Education	64.29	18.18	35.71
Residential	33.33	47.06	66.67
Outdoors and recreational	85.19	25.81	14.81
Hospitals	71.42	16.67	28.57

$$K = \frac{N \sum_{i=1}^{r} x_{ii} - \sum_{i=1}^{r} (x_{i+} \times x_{+i})}{N^2 - \sum_{i=1}^{r} (x_{i+} \times x_{+i})} \qquad (2)$$

According to the base error matrix, we have obtained K = 0.7403, where N=398, $\sum_{i=1}^{r} (x_{i+} \times x_{+i}) = 29649$ and $\sum_{i=1}^{r} x_{ii} = 314$ for the land-use visualization.

Thus, the results we obtained by this methodology are at the middle level of agreement and accuracy [23, 26]. The analytical view of the agreement, commission error, and omission error of each land-use class are shown in Figure 1.16. The land-use classifications for the groups, such as administration, education and residential, are not classified well, because of the low density of Foursquare data. However, the categories with high-density Foursquare data, such as hotels, transportation, and outdoor, have shown high classification accuracies.

1.6 Discussion

1.6.1 Contribution of the Proposed Approach

This chapter has shown the possibility of using Foursquare data as a voluntary geographical information. Different data preprocessing and

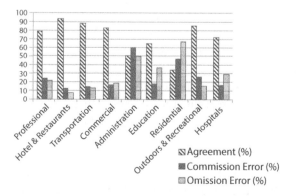

Figure 1.16 Agreement, commission error, and omission error analysis.

classification techniques were applied to analyze the accuracies of each learning model. We have proven that the land-use classification using both satellite imagery and Foursquare data is cost-effective and can be used effectively with complete data sets. The main objective of this research was to explore a novel approach to create an up-to-date land-use classification using Foursquare data and satellite imagery. Analysis of land-use data enables the authorities to carry new development plans. This, in turn, will enable to detect changes and foresee social and environmental consequences. Thus, the classification system could be used to retrieve valuable information required to enhance the decision-making process of organizations and processes, such as planning and management of cities, formulation of land-use policies, department of transportation, real estate agencies, development of commercial establishments, and so on. Retrieved information could also be used in the development of land-use models that can predict the evolution of land-use over periods.

1.6.2   Limitations of the Data Sets

Foursquare is a source of VGI and such sources tend to have inherent drawbacks, including location dependency, lack of reliability, incompleteness, and so on. The density of Foursquare data was particularly low in certain rural areas, as well as suburban areas [27]. Thus, one of the key issues found in the Foursquare data is that the uneven distribution of data over the region. Because of this, most of the buildings in the classified images of some areas did not have any Foursquare points overlapping with them. Moreover, the Foursquare points that do not overlap with a building block are realigned to the closest building block based on a defined threshold value.

In another point of view, considering the nature of the considered data with a possible human error occurs during the entering of Foursquare data, the land-use classification accuracy can be decreased, that is, the user-entered names may not readable or partially readable, due to human or mobile or application error at data entry. Thus, as a crowdsourced data, accuracy and reliability can be low in the associated Foursquare data. Another issue was the reliability of latitude and longitude value of a given location, because the previous study on Foursquare data for land-use mapping has shown deviation of the Foursquare point location with the real location. However, the degree of the unreliability of the existence of a point tends to decrease with the number of unique users checked in for a given location. Additionally, Foursquare data can contain irrelevant data, for the prediction of land use. This has limited the use of Foursquare data in identifying the land-cover classification of satellite imagery.

However, there are some tradeoffs that cause major limitations to be imposed on satellite images. Changing environment conditions, such as covered by clouds and fog, can reduce the quality of the satellite images. This tends to image coverage gaps which need to be filled using other data sources. Moreover, the quality of images largely depends on the technical specifications of the satellite sensors. In another direction, with the concept of smart cities and urban development in a given building, there can be different types of land-use categories. On the other hand, satellite images can be outdated. In a technical point of view, high spectral resolution reduces the signal-to-noise ratio, and therefore, when increasing spectral resolution, the background noise of the image also increases. Additionally, high radiometric resolution reduces the signal-to-noise ratio and have a negative impact on data storage and transmission rates. The high spatial resolution requires a decrease in data volume, because there are restrictions on data storage, transmission rates, and processing capabilities. Further, increasing the spectral resolution decreases spatial resolution and vice versa. This can result in inaccurate land-use and land-cover classification.

1.6.3   Future Research Directions

The proposed methodology can be fine-tuned by considering more complete data set with sufficient geotags of points that enhances land-use classification. The quality and information retrieval of data can be improved by considering a combination of land usage and coverage data from different sources. The issues caused by the unavailability of an adequate amount of Foursquare points can be mitigated by integrating different VGI sources, including OpenStreetMap and Flicker photos, which is a possible future direction. Moreover, the uncertainty analysis of Foursquare data is another possible future direction. This work can be extended for a generic platform to support multiple data resources and factors to improve the usage and coverage classification of land data.

Further, this research approach can be extended with surface roughness analysis using fractal dimension-based approaches. This idea was supported by the related study [28] that has described the related factors, such as spatial resolution and region of interests for complex object analysis. They have shown the methods of fractal dimension measurements considering the texture, color range, and distance of an image. Moreover, controlled images acquisition methods for the images with similar properties were described in the study of Nayak *et al.* [29]. They have shown the usefulness of the fractal dimension metric for similar color images. Further, the differential box-counting algorithm has extended to the color domain to estimate the fractal dimension of color images in the study of Nayak *et al.* [30]. They have shown the efficiency of using fractal dimensions to distinguish the surface roughness of the color images. Thus, applying these techniques is another future research direction of land-cover data classification.

1.7   Conclusion

Reliable data on the usage and coverage of land are significant for sustainable development; as opposed to traditional land-use information generation techniques that tend to be expensive in terms of resource consumption. Land-use information generated with a single source of volunteer geographic information often tends to have limitations due to coverage and accuracy issues associated with crowdsourced location data. Although these data sources lack reliability and possess some limitations, they are useful in deriving building blocks for the usage of the land, where the manual surveys are not up-to-date, costly, and time-consuming.

This paper presents a novel and an automated methodology based on learning models for identifying the usage and coverage of the land. The satellite imagery is used to identify the information related to land-cover. They are integrated with Foursquare venue data, which is a popular crowdsourced geographic information, thus enhancing the information level and the quality of land-use visualization. This paper assessed the possibility of integrating both satellite imagery that gives land-cover data and Foursquare data that indicate land-use data to identify the usage and coverage of land in a given region cost-effectively.

The main steps followed in this research includes the identification and segmentation of building blocks in satellite imagery, realignment and overlay of a transparent layer of Foursquare data with the satellite image layer, and finally, the identification and visualization of the usage and coverage of land data. These steps can be conveniently performed efficiently to generate timely and valid land-use information with minimal capital, labor, and other resource requirements. The obtained kappa coefficient of 74.03% proves that by combining satellite imagery with Foursquare data, up-to-date land-use information can be derived effectively to a reasonable degree of accuracy. The obtained land-use information could be used to retrieve valuable information required to enhance the decision-making process related to planning and management of cities, formulation of land-use policies, and so on. Retrieved information could also be used in the development of land-use models that can predict the evolution of land-use over periods.

This work can be extended for a common platform to facilitate new and up-to-date data sources to improve the land-use classification. Analysis of land-use data enables the authorities to carry new development plans. This, in turn, will enable to detect changes and foresee social and environmental effects.

References

1. López, E., Boccoa, G., Mendozaa, M., Duhaub, E., Predicting land-cover and land-use change in the urban fringe: A case in Morelia city, Mexico. *Landscape Urban Plann.*, 55, 4, 271–285, 2001.
2. Vanjare, A., Omkar, S.N., Senthilnath, J., Satellite image processing for land-use and land-cover mapping. *Int. J. Image Graphics Signal Process.*, 6, 10, 18–28, 2014.
3. Spyratos, S., Stathakis, D., Lutz, M., Tsinaraki, C., Using Foursquare place data for estimating building block use. *Environ. Plann. B Plann. Des.*, 43, 2, 1–25, 2016.
4. Bareth, G., Multi-data approach (MDA) for enhanced land-use/land-cover mapping. *The International Archives of the Photogrammetry, Remote Sensing and Spatial Information Sciences, XXXVII.* Part B8, pp. 1059–1066, 2008.
5. Quercia, D. and Saez, D., Mining urban deprivation from Foursquare: Implicit crowdsourcing of city land-use. *IEEE Pervasive Comput.*, 13, 2, 30–36, 2014.
6. Hu, T., Yang, J., Li, X., Gong, P., Mapping urban land-use by using Landsat Images and open social data. *Remote Sens.*, 8, 2, 151, 2016.
7. Jayanetti, J.A.A.M., Meedeniya, D.A., Dilini, M.D.N., Wickramapala, M.H., Madushanka, J.H., Enhanced land-cover and land-use information generation from satellite imagery and Foursquare data. *6th International Conference on Software and Computer Applications (ICSCA 2017)*, ACM, New York, pp. 149–153, 2017.
8. Kumar, B.S., Image fusion based on pixel significance using cross bilateral filter. *Signal Image Video P.*, 9, 5, 1193–1204, 2015.
9. Bhandari, A.K., Kumar, D., Kumar, A., Singh, G.K., Opti-mal sub-band adaptive thresholding based edge preserved satellite image denoising using adaptive differential evolution algorithm. *Neurocomputing*, 174, 698–721, 2016.
10. Gonzalez, R., Woods, R., Eddins, S., *Digital Image processing using MATLAB*, 2nd edition, Gatesmark Publishing, USA, 2009.
11. Abburu, S. and Golla, S.B., Satellite image classification methods and techniques: A review. *Int. J. Comput. Appl.*, 119, 8, 20–25, 2015.
12. Ghose, M., Pradhan, R., Ghose, S., Decision tree classification of remotely sensed satellite data using spectral separability matrix. *Int. J. Adv. Comput. Sci. Appl.*, 1, 5, 93–101, 2010.

13. Kulkarni, A.D. and Lowe, B., Random forest algorithm for land-cover classification. *Recent Innovation Trends Comput. Commun.*, 4, 3, 58–63, 2016.

14. Kim, K.S., Zhang, D., Kang, M.C., Ko, S.J., Improved simple linear iterative clustering superpixels, in: *IEEE International Symposium on Consumer Electronics (ISCE)*, pp. 259–260, 2013.

15. Felzenszwalb, P. and Huttenlocher, D., Efficient graph-based image segmentation. *Int. J. Comput. Vision*, 59, 2, 167–181, 2004.

16. Vedaldi, A. and Soatto, S., Quick shift and kernel methods for mode seeking, in: *European Conference Computer Vision*, pp. 705–718, 2008.

17. Achanta, R., Shaji, A., Smith, K., Lucchi, A., Fua, P., Süsstrunk, S., Slic superpixels. *EPFL Technical Report 149300*, 1–15, 2010.

18. Ranjitham, S., Superpixel based colour image segmentation techniques: A review. *Int. J. Adv. Res. Comput. Sci. Softw. Eng.*, 4, 9, 465–471, 2014.

19. Rae, A., Murdock, V., Popescu, A., Bouchard, H., Mining the web for points of interest, in: *35th International Conference on Research and Development in Information Retrieval (SIGIR)*, pp. 711–720, 2012.

20. Sappelli, M., Verberne, S., Kraaij, W., Recommending Personalized Touristic Sights Using Google Places, in: *36th International Conference on Research and Development in Information Retrieval (SIGIR)*, pp. 781–784, 2013.

21. Ming, W., Quingquan, L., Qui Qwu, H., Meng, Z., Quality analysis of Open Street Map Data, in: *8th International Symposium on Spatial Data Quality*, pp. 155–158, 2013.

22. Haklay, M., How good is Volunteered Geographical Information? A comparative study of OpenStreetMap and Ordnance Survey datasets Abstract. *Environ. Plann. B: Plann. Des.*, 37, 4, 682–703, 2010.

23. Tilahun, A. and Teferie, B., Accuracy assessment of land-use land-cover classification using Google Earth. *Am. J. Environ. Prot.*, 4, 4, 193–198, 2015.

24. How to calculate kappa, http://epiville.ccnmtl.columbia.edu/popup/how_to_calculate_kappa.html, 2019.

25. Viera, A.J. and Joanne, M.G., Understanding inter observer agreement: the kappa statistic. *Fam. Med.*, 37, 5, 360–363, 2005.

26. Kappa Inter-Rater Agreement, https://analyse-it.com/docs/220/standard/kappa_inter-rater_agreement.htm, 2019.

27. Noulas, A., Mascolo, C., Frias-Martinez, E., Exploiting Foursquare and Cellular Data to Infer User Activity in Urban Environments, in: *14th International Conference on Mobile Data Management*, pp. 167–176, 2013.

28. Nayak, S.R., Mishra, J., Palai, G., Analysing roughness of surface through fractal dimension: A review. *Image Vision Comput.*, 89, 21–34, 2019.

29. Nayak, S., Khandual, A., Mishra, J., Ground truth study on fractal dimension of colour images of similar texture. *J. Text. Inst.*, 109, 9, 1159–1167, 2018.

30. Nayak, S.R., Mishra, J., Khandual, A., Palai, G., Fractal dimension of RGB colour images. *Optik*, 162, 196–205, 2018.

Indian Sign Language Recognition Using Soft Computing Techniques

Ashok Kumar Sahoo[1]*, Pradeepta Kumar Sarangi[2] and Parul Goyal[3]

[1]Department of Computer Science and Engineering, Graphic Era Hill University, Dehradun, India
[2]Chitkara University Institute of Engineering and Technology, Chitkara University, Punjab, India
[3]School of Computing, Graphic Era Hill University, Dehradun, India

Abstract

Sign language recognition comes under the research dimension of pattern recognition. The work is to translate acquired images or videos either offline or online to corresponding words, numbers, or sentences representing meaning of the input sign. Here the work presented is recognition of Indian Sign Language. The application of this work is limited to Indian subcontinent where around 5% of the population is using Indian Sign Language to communicate with their external world. The direct pixel value, hierarchical centroid, local histogram features of image processing techniques are used in the experiments. The classifiers used here are k-Nearest Neighbor and Neural Network. The detailed work in this chapter is presented below.

Keywords: Indian sign language, feature extraction, histogram, hierarchical centroid, direct pixel value, naive Baÿes, k-nearest neighbor classifier, neural network classifier

2.1   Introduction

Sign language [1] is the communication medium for hearing-impaired people and hard hearing community. This is also helpful in communication

*Corresponding author: ashoksahoo2000@yahoo.com

Muthukumaran Malarvel, Soumya Ranjan Nayak, Surya Narayan Panda, Prasant Kumar Pattnaik and Nittaya Muangnak (eds.) Machine Vision Inspection Systems (Vol. 1): Image Processing, Concepts, Methodologies and Applications, (37–66) © 2020 Scrivener Publishing LLC

between speaking and nonspeaking community. A system, which can interpret sign language gestures to corresponding text or speech, is known as sign language recognition system. This will be helpful in exchange of information in various practical situations. The sign language used by people of Indian subcontinent is known as Indian Sign Language (ISL) [2].

The focus on this chapter is on computer recognition and translation of ISL in the English language domain to text. The work presented here is on vision-based computer recognition of ISL [3, 4]. This will be beneficial for better interaction to the unblessed community at common platforms. Data sets on ISL digits, alphabet, and a limited number of words are created, because no standard data sets are available. The data set available is proved to be sufficient, in terms of the number of training, as well as testing samples, which is compatible with experiments having feature vectors and classifiers available. Further, the data sets are tested on various combinations of feature extraction methods and classification techniques in order to obtain standardization in terms of data set, recognition accuracy, and consistency.

Some preprocessing steps and feature extraction techniques [5] (histogram, structural features, and feature vector inherited directly from an image matrix) in the pattern recognition process for performance improvement are conceived. A new pattern recognition process for video data set is experimented and is proved useful in recognition of dynamic gestures of ISL. For some clarity, the readers please note that the experiments are based on ISL digits, alphabets, and some designated words.

2.2   Related Works

The research works conducted by various authors till date at international and national levels are discussed in this section. As a big question arises, whether the signs in ISL are the same as the signs of international sign languages? To cater this question, the variations in sign languages, between international sign languages and with ISL are figured out. This indicates a new scope of research is available in ISL recognition. A limited number of researches have been conducted in India till date.

The Indian Sign Language (ISL) is a recognized sign language in India. It is mostly influenced by British Sign Language in the form of finger spelling system. However, it is not influenced by European sing languages. Rarely 5% [6–8] of deaf people attended deaf schools as reported. No formal ISL education available prior to 1926 as stated by Banerji [9] and concluded that different sign systems are followed in different schools. This implies that no standard sign languages are followed in schools. A number of schools were established to educate deaf people, and a few of them use ISL as a medium of instructions. In these schools, effective and proper audio visual supports are not available. The use of ISL is limited to short-term and vocational programs. A research was conducted [6] with more than a hundred deaf schools in 1975 and concluded that no standard ISL was used in those schools, only some kind of gestures are used in these schools. After 20 years, it is reported that the sign languages used in these schools are based on spoken English, regional spoken languages, or express their inability to provide a sign for every word. The teaching in these schools is based on a manual kind of communication. However, later on, it is agreed that ISL is a language of its own semantics and syntax.

Sign language gestures are different for each country and also dependent on the verbal language used in that country. The automatic recognition of sign language is dependent on the gestures performed by signers. The research in the automation of sign languages of different countries is at various levels and is mentioned in the study of Ashok *et al.* [10]. The developed countries in the world are having automatic recognition systems to aid deaf and hard hearing people. The systems developed and installed at various public places. However, the status of research in developing countries is in its early stage. The research facilities and data set availability in developed countries are also available in public domains. Same facilities in developing and underdeveloped countries are in the development stage. In order to develop a sign language recognition system, it is necessary to learn the current status of research at international and national levels. The detailed study on automatic recognition of ISL is not at par with the international sign languages because, at present, only a limited research has been conducted.

The organization of this chapter is as follows:

(i)   The Domain of the Sign Languages Used;
(ii) Data Acquisition Methods;
(iii) Preprocessing Steps;
(iv) Feature Extraction Methods Utilized;
(v)   Selection of Classification techniques;
(vi) Results and Discussions.

2.2.1   The Domain of Sign Language

In the ISL recognition system, one-handed and two-handed alphabet set (Figures 2.1 and 2.2), A to Z, digit set, 0 to 9 (Figure 2.3), and a limited number of ISL computer terminology (Figure 2.4) words are chosen for the experiments.

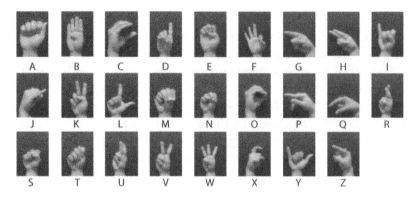

Figure 2.1 The ISL single-handed alphabet signs data set.

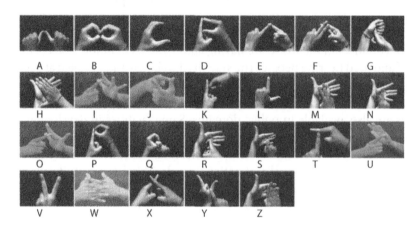

Figure 2.2 The ISL double-handed alphabet signs data set.

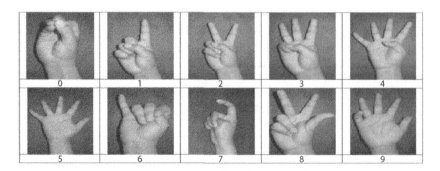

Figure 2.3 The ISL digit signs data set.

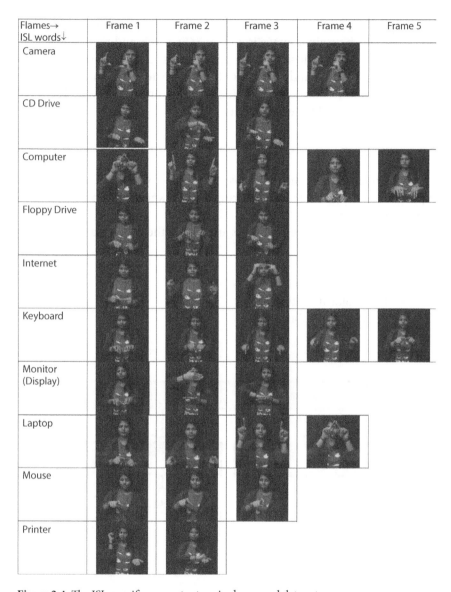

Flames→ ISL words↓	Frame 1	Frame 2	Frame 3	Frame 4	Frame 5
Camera					
CD Drive					
Computer					
Floppy Drive					
Internet					
Keyboard					
Monitor (Display)					
Laptop					
Mouse					
Printer					

Figure 2.4 The ISL-specific computer terminology word data set.

2.2.2   The Data Acquisition Methods

For data set acquisition, a dark background for uniformity and easy manipulation of images for feature extraction and classification is used. A Sony digital camera, Cybershot H70, is used for capturing the images. All images are captured with flashlight in an intelligent auto mode. The input images are stored in JPEG format because it is the most standard form of images nowadays. Each original image is 4608 × 3456 pixels and requires approximately five and half Mega Byte storage space. The images are cropped to 200 × 300 RGB pixels and requires only 25 kilobytes of memory space per image. The data sets on isolated digits, alphabet, and a set of word signs of ISL are also captured for experiments.

2.2.3   Preprocessing Steps

The implementation of the first phase of Figure 2.5 is the preprocessing of input image using image restructuring and background subtraction with skin color detection.

The following preprocessing steps are used in the experiments at various levels.

- Image restructuring,
- Skin color detection,
- Background subtraction.

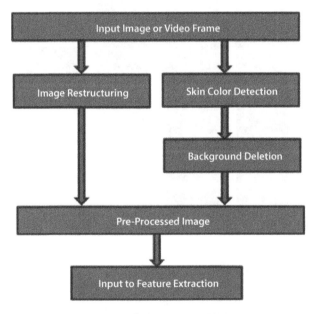

Figure 2.5 Image preprocessing steps of ISL signs.

2.2.3.1 Image Restructuring

The input images (static sign or frames extracted from input video) are furthered reduced to 20 × 30 pixel followed by a conversion to a binary image in the Matlab Software. The converted binary images are now treated as a pure numerical matrix order of 20 × 30. The zeros represent only the background data in the inputted image. The undesired information from ISL images is removed by deleting all border rows and columns having only zero values.

Several columns from the left and right sides, some rows from the top and from the bottom of the converted binary image were deleted because those rows/columns contain only "0." The preprocessed image matrix is now in the order of 17 × 16. This matrix is used as the input to the feature extraction process. The converted matrix is now reduced to a lower dimension; this is helpful in further reduction of dimension. The reduced image contains almost all information and differentiates it from other input signs.

2.2.3.2 Skin Color Detection

The skin colors from the sign images are spotted by an algorithm (Figure 2.6), and the backgrounds, including the body parts, are removed from each frame in the preprocessing stage. Image background and body parts are subtracted from each frame to extract the hand region and face by using the skin color detection algorithm described below. This is helpful in extracting valuable features from sign, and unwanted information is discarded.

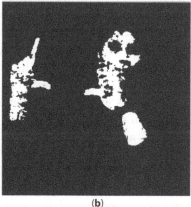

(a) (b)

Figure 2.6 (a) Original image and (b) thresholded skin color detected image.

By using the skin color detection algorithm, recognition rates of ISL signs have been enhanced.

2.2.4   Methods of Feature Extraction Used in the Experiments

Through the help of feature extraction [11], the higher dimensional data are reduced to lower the dimension. Because the original image contains a large amount of data to be processed, through the help of feature extraction process, we are able to reduce substantial size of data from the input images. Feature extraction is the process of extracting important numerical features from images. We have to reduce the image in such a manner that the image information must be contained in the extracted features. It is divided into two parts, namely, feature construction and feature selection.

It involves the processing of a large data set accurately. It is quite impossible to process a large amount of data in any computer system because it requires high computational power. Analyzing a huge number of variables involved requires also a large amount of memory and CPU power. Direct pixel value (DPV), local histogram, and hierarchical centroid (HC) feature extraction techniques used in this chapter.

In the DPV feature extraction method, the original image with higher dimension is reduced to a one-dimensional matrix with some preprocessing steps. Generally, a color image is converted to a grayscale image, which is a two-dimensional matrix and then the two-dimensional matrix is scaled to a one-dimensional matrix. This one-dimensional matrix is the DPV which represents the image.

In HC feature extraction method, the original image is divided into two subimages recursively and the center coordinates of each subimage is taken as valuable features for further processing. The center coordinates of each subimage are collected in a sequential manner and is used as a feature vector which indirectly represent the original image.

Histograms [13, 14] derived from an image describe global intensity distribution and is useful in representation of the image. These descriptions are helpful in solving pattern recognition problems as they are invariant to translations and rotations. The local histograms from images are also easy to compute. In this feature extraction technique, image bins are separated based on histogram frequency divisions and the evaluation of values. The image is first converted to grayscale image, because it is very hard in terms of computing power and space to process color images. The converted grayscale image contains only pixel values in the range 0 to 255. After extraction of histogram from images, the histograms are subdivided into eight equal bins of same range, and their frequencies are computed. For calculation of histogram bins in a given range, the other range grayscale values are turned off. Only the histogram bins of the given range are available, therefore, its frequencies can be summed up easily. This process is repeated for other range grayscale values also. In this way, local histogram bins are extracted and used as feature vector to the classification process.

2.2.5   Classification Techniques

In the previous discussion, the features extracted from images are inputted to any one of the classifier. In the experiments, classification techniques [15] are used to recognize the ISL signs.

With the help of a classification technique, an input image is identified to a class on the basis of training data set provided to classifier. Here, in the experiments, the task is to extract the text meaning of the input ISL signs. Classification techniques provide answers to possible inputs which are most likely matching to its possible output classes based on the training data provided. In this chapter, K-Nearest Neighbor (kNN) [16], Naive Bayes [18], and Neural Network classifier [18] are used for the recognition of the ISL symbols.

2.2.5.1   K-Nearest Neighbor

This classifier uses supervised leaning algorithm to classify objects on the concept of feature space. It was developed by Fix and Hodges. It uses the concept of nearest neighbor method to classify objects of each row data into one of the output classes. Each sample provided to the classifier should be equal to the training data in the form of number of columns. Each training data sample belongs to a particular output class. The group which represents an element might contain string array, numeric vector, or an array of strings. The group and training must have the same number of rows. Each group whether training or testing has a class number. The default assignment of class of this classifier uses majority rule. That means a sample point is assigned to a particular class based on the "k" nearest neighbor concept. When a sample is at the same distance as the two different classes, then a random number is used to break the tie.

2.2.5.2   Neural Network Classifier

This uses a two-layer feed-forward patternet network to solve a pattern classification problem using sigmoid output neurons [19]. The number of neurons may vary in the experiments on the hidden layer of artificial neural network. This is because of the varying results obtained from the experiments. The neural network has the same number output neurons as target values assigned to each input vector. It is a feed-forward network which can be trained for classification according to target classes.

The target vector for pattern recognition neural networks must consist of vectors of zeroes except for a 1 in element "i." The "i" is the class which represent the feature vector.

2.2.5.3 Naive Baÿes Classifier

It uses the applied supervised Bayesian learning technique in classifying objects. Its performance is comparable with decision tree and neural network classifiers. The performance of this classifier not degraded even on high-dimensional input feature vectors. The classification mechanisms of naïve Bayes classifier [20–22] depends on the Bayes theorem which is based on probability theory.

2.3 Experiments

2.3.1 Experiments on ISL Digits

A total of 5000 images representing 10 ISL digit signs are available in the data set for experiments.

The data set is divided into training and testing set prior to the experiments shown in Table 2.1. The details of the experiments on automatic recognition of digits (0-9) of ISL have been explained below. In experiment I, 70% of aggregate data set is used as a training set and the remaining 30% are used as a testing set. The training and testing data sets are reversed in experiment II.

The RGB images are converted into binary images and resized to 20×30 pixels, so that the important features can be extracted directly from the

Table 2.1 Division of data set into training and testing sets on ISL digits.

Experiments	Data set size	Training set	Testing set
I	100×10×5=5000 Images	70% from the first 70 signers	30% of the remaining 30 signers
II	-do-	30% of the last 30 signers	70% from the first 70 signers

image matrices with lower dimension. Unwanted information is removed from the images by deleting the rows/columns that contain all 0's from all four border sides.

The feature extraction method used for input to the recognition system for numeral ISL recognition is based on the structural features, known as HC, which was described earlier. The structural features are extracted directly from the sign images and were proven to provide a good representation of the numeral signs at higher levels of segmentation.

The kNN, naïve Baÿes, and neural network classifiers are used to classify ISL static numeral gestures to target classes (0-9).

2.3.1.1   Results and Discussions on the First Experiment

The summary of the experiments is listed in Table 2.2. When the training data are larger than the testing data, both classifiers produce good recognition accuracy. Experiments were also performed on data sets in which training and testing set are the same. It is also verified from the theory of classifiers, both classifiers produce their highest recognition results on same (training $\equiv$ testing) data set. It is interesting note that kNN classifier produces a 100% result when training and testing data are the same. When the training and testing data are the same and the classifier is naive Baÿes, the recognition rate is higher in case of a larger data set. When training and testing data are reversed, the results do not satisfy the expectations.

On average, the naive Baÿes classifier performance is 74.52%. This indicates that 24.48% of the testing data are misclassified. Similarly, 13.96% testing data set are misclassified in case of kNN classifier. The kNN classifier gives more accurate results in conducting these experiments.

Performances of both classifiers digitwise are shown in Figure 2.7. The digits "4" and "7" are more misclassified compared with the other digits. This is due to the orientation of hand positions in these signs. The digit

Table 2.2 The comparative recognition rates of naive Baÿes and kNN classifier on ISL digits.

	Classifier recognition rate (%)	
Experiment	Naive Baÿes	kNN
I	76.52	80.53
II	75.37	80.10
Average	74.52	80.32

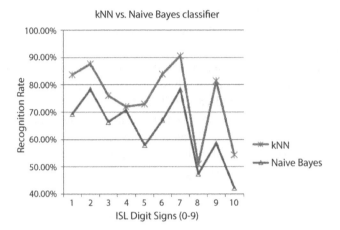

Figure 2.7 Comparison of results obtained from Naive Baÿes classifier versus kNN on ISL digits.

"4" misclassified with "3," "5," and with "9." Similarly, due to the similarity of the shape of signs in "0," "1," "6" with "7," misclassification occurs at digit "7." One more cause of this misclassification is the images are resized to 20×30, so feature vectors obtained from these signs are having similar values. In Figure 2.7, the class levels are shown from 1 to 10. Class level 1 indicates ISL digit "0," class level 2 indicates ISL digit "1," and finally, class level 10 indicates ISL digit "9." However, the maximum recognition rate is

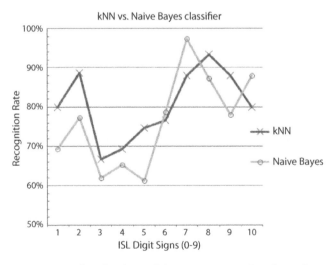

Figure 2.8 Comparison of results obtained from Naive Baÿes classifier vs. kNN on ISL digits.

more than 90% in the kNN classifier, but the minimum classification rate is around 40%. Because of this, the combination of feature vector and classifier cannot be used in the proposed system.

The results on data sets as mentioned in Table 2.1 for experiment II are also shown in Figure 2.8. The performance of kNN and naive Bayes classifiers is almost the same as experiment I. However, individual recognition rates of ISL digits are different as compared with experiment I.

2.3.1.2   *Results and Discussions on Second Experiment*

The same data sets used in the first experiment are also used here and are divided as training and testing samples. As per norms used by research community, the training set consists of 70% of the data and 30% are used as testing. The RGB images are converted into grayscale and resized to 20×30 pixels to extract important features from the image matrices. Structural features called the HC and DPV methods are used in conducting this experiment. The kNN and neural network classifiers are used to verify the recognition rates of the experiment.

Experiments are performed on different data sets and also on the same (30% or 70%) data set which is used as training, as well as testing for kNN and neural network classifiers. The results of the experiments on the same data set (training ≡ testing) have 100% accuracy. This means, if the user contributed to the data set earlier, the system definitely identifies the meaning of the actual gesture performed by the signer. The results from the different data sets (70% training and 30% testing) are shown in Table 2.3.

The performance of HC is less than that of experiment I as shown in Figure 2.9. This is because the level of segmentation level of HC feature extraction was reduced from 7 to 6. Instead of 256 features extracted, only 124 feature vectors are extracted from each image gesture to speed up the execution process. The pixel values of binary images are used as a feature vector in DPV

Table 2.3 The comparative recognition rates of naive Bayes and neural network classifier on ISL digits.

Feature extractor	Classifier classification, %	
	kNN	Neural network
DPV	78.60	97.17
HC	70.96	94.30
Average result	74.80	95.74

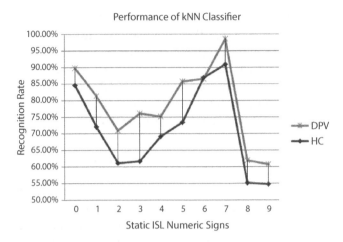

Figure 2.9 Performance of classifier kNN through DPV and HC feature vector on ISL digits.

method, so the result of this feature vector is better than that in the HC method. Because of this, misclassification rates are less as compared with experiment I.

The results of neural network classifier are better than kNN classifier, as the training process of this classifier is better than kNN is shown in Figure 2.10. The average results obtained from both feature extraction methods through neural network classifier is 95.74%. There is a similarity between "5" and "9." This is due to the shape similarity between these ISL signs. On the other hand, "8" and "9" are having same shape similarity. This is also the case seen in the ISL signs "4" and "5." We can infer here that the pair of techniques, namely, the neural network classifier with DPV feature extraction, will be helpful in the implementation of an automatic recognition system for ISL.

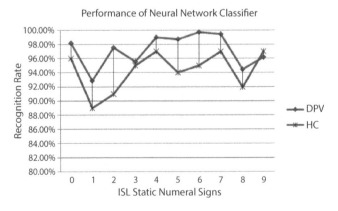

Figure 2.10 Performance of neural network classifier with DPV and HC feature extraction techniques.

2.3.2   Experiments on ISL Alphabets

The ISL alphabet [9] can be signed with either one hand or both hands. The character signs performed by using a single hand are known as single-handed character signs, and signs performed by both hands are known as double-handed character signs as described in the previous chapter. The experiments conducted at both levels are explained in the following sections.

2.3.2.1   *Experiments with Single-Handed Alphabet Signs*

The proposed recognition system is depicted in Figure 2.11. No standard data sets are available prior to the experiments on automatic recognition of ISL gestures proposed in this research. The data set created to conduct the experiments contains 2600 gestures which belong to the single-handed ISL characters. The input images are preprocessed before feeding into feature extraction and classification phases of the proposed system.

All 26 characters from English alphabet are included in the experiments. One hundred images per English ISL characters are collected. Therefore, a grand total of 2600 images are experimented for ISL character recognition. The images are cropped to 200 by 300 rgb pixels. The image background is estimated and deleted from the foreground cropped images in the image preprocessing step. This is helpful in uniform image background to the ISL

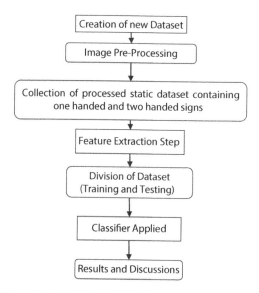

Figure 2.11 The ISL one-handed and two-handed character recognition system.

recognition system. Because the rgb images contain a large amount of data, these images are converted into grayscale images and are fed to the feature extraction phase. The images are further reduced to 40 by 50 pixels with help of the DPV feature extraction technique, and the image is converted into a one-dimensional array which contains 2000 element for each input ISL sign.

2.3.2.2 Results of Single-Handed Alphabet Signs

The kNN and neural network classifiers are used for prediction of target class to which the test data samples belong to. The performance of neural network classifier for testing data is plotted in the graph as shown in Figure 2.12 and Table 2.4. Local histogram features perform better as compared to HC and DPV feature extraction methods. Nevertheless, the results

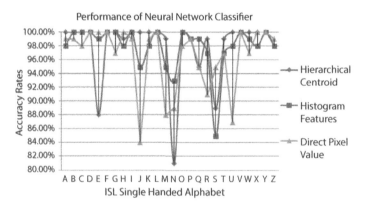

Figure 2.12 Neural network classifier's performance against three feature extraction techniques on ISL one-handed alphabet.

Table 2.4 Performance of kNN and neural network on one-handed ISL character.

Feature Vector → Classifier↓	Local histogram	DPV	HC	Sample size	Data set
kNN	56.79%	59.48%	51.02%	26×100 = 2600	Training = 70% Testing = 30%
Neural Network	95.3%	92.52%	93.37%	26×100 = 2600	Training = 70% Validation =10% Testing = 20%

produced by the three feature vectors through neural network classifier are similar.

Some of the ISL single-handed characters produce 100% recognition rates. The minimum recognition rate obtained from this experiment is around 80%. The highest results obtained are from local histogram features. Because 26 class levels are associated with this experiment, it is not easy to analyze the results as shown in Figure 2.12. Therefore, a detailed analysis is required for results of this experiment. As mentioned above, the average result of local histogram features is better than the DPV and HC feature vectors. This detailed result is analyzed in detail with the other results also. The detailed results, on ISL single characterwise, are derived from the confusion matrix of the neural network classifier.

The maximum misclassification rate reported is 15% for character "S." The overall misclassification rate is 4.7%. Among the three feature vectors with neural network classifier, this feature vector produces 92.52% recognition rates. From the classification confusion matrix, it is reported that about 31% of the single-handed characters were recognized with 100% accuracy. The maximum misclassification occurs at "F" with "J," and the misclassification rate is 7%.

As mentioned in the experiments, 26 input symbols are associated. Each input symbol is signed by using only one hand. Hence, there are possibilities in shape similarity in single-handed ISL alphabet. Therefore, the detailed analysis of the results on single-handed ISL alphabet is needed. Nine classes of 26 inputs are correctly classified. The difference between minimum and maximum classification accuracy is 15%. Due to this narrowness in classification accuracies, this combination of feature extraction technique and classification method can be useful in the proposed ISL recognition system. The input symbols "M" and "S" are misclassified with maximum probability of 9%. This is because the input symbols are very similar. The second maximum misclassification rate is only 4% and occurs at "J" with "C," and it appeared only once. The shape similarity between "M" and "S" is shown in Figure 2.13, and the shape similarity between "C" and "J" is shown in Figure 2.14.

2.3.2.3   Experiments with Double-Handed Alphabet Signs

The second data set on ISL alphabet contains gestures that belong to double-handed characters. A total of 2340 images, 90 signs per character, are available in the data set. The experimental conditions in the double-handed characters are the same as the single-handed characters. The proposed recognition system accepts any double-handed static ISL sign as input.

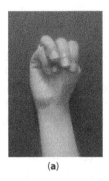 

(a)   (b)

Figure 2.13 Misclassification due to shape similarity between single-handed alphabets "M" and "S". (a) ISL Single Handed Aphabet "M". (b) ISL Single Handed Aphabet "S".

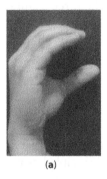 

(a)   (b)

Figure 2.14 Misclassification Due to Shape Similarity Between Single-Handed Alphabets "C" and "J". (a) ISL Single Handed Aphabet "C". (b) ISL Single Handed Aphabet "J".

Here, also, maximum accuracy occurs with neural network classifier. The selection of feature vectors and classifiers is user-dependent. The user can select any one of three feature vectors. Similarly, the user can select the classifier, but the performances of other classifiers are not better as compared with the neural network.

2.3.2.4   Results on Double-Handed Alphabets

It is clear from Figures 2.1 and 2.2 that the shapes of two-handed ISL characters are different from that of the one-handed ISL characters. The experiments which are carried out on one-handed ISL alphabet are also conducted on two-handed alphabet. The performance of kNN is not considerable versus all feature extraction techniques. Therefore, the results of kNN are excluded in the analysis of two-handed ISL characters.

The classification performance of local histogram feature technique is depicted in Table 2.4 and is better than HC and DPV feature vectors. Only 30 hidden neurons are required in the neural network. This helps to lessen the time requirements in the execution of the experiments. At this number of hidden neurons, the network performs good recognition results.

The performance of all three feature vectors against neural network classifier is shown in Figure 2.15. The minimum recognition accuracy of HC is 78.89%, 81.11% for DPV feature vector, and 93.33% for local histogram features. The maximum recognition rate for all feature vectors is 100%. Most of the ISL characters are having recognition accuracy of more than 95%. Only, on average, 3 of 26 characters are having a recognition accuracy below 90%. The local histogram feature vector gives higher recognition rates over other two feature vectors. This is only because the local histogram bins, which are extracted from sign images, are used as feature vectors. As already mentioned in the theory part of neural network classifier, the training data set is used to train the network, validation is used for stopping criteria, and the testing data set is used to test the performance of the system. From Figure 2.15, it is clear that the combination of local histogram features with neural network classifier can be used for an automatic ISL recognition system.

A detailed ISL characterwise classification accuracy is shown in Table 2.5. This gives a clear idea and a detailed comparison between the recognition rates of individual double-handed ISL characters and character wise comparison of recognition rates between the three feature extraction techniques. Only performances of double-handed characters "D," "H," and "W" are not 100%, but all other characters are recognized with 100% accuracy at any one of the feature vectors.

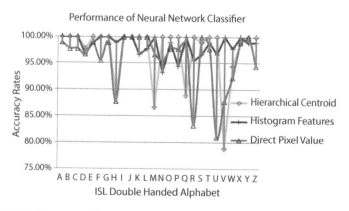

Figure 2.15 Performance of neural network classifier (double-handed ISL alphabets).

Table 2.5 Classification results of all three feature extraction methods against neural network classifier (double-handed ISL alphabets).

Characters (ISL)	Classification percentage		
	HC feature	DPV feature	Local histogram
A	100.00	98.89	100.00
B	100.00	97.78	100.00
C	100.00	97.78	100.00
D	97.78	96.67	96.67
E	100.00	98.89	98.89
F	100.00	95.56	100.00
G	100.00	98.89	100.00
H	88.89	87.78	98.89
I	100.00	100.00	100.00
J	100.00	100.00	100.00
K	100.00	100.00	96.67
L	100.00	100.00	97.78
M	86.67	96.67	100.00
N	100.00	95.56	93.33
O	100.00	97.78	98.89
P	100.00	97.78	94.44
Q	88.89	98.89	100.00
R	100.00	83.33	95.56
S	98.89	100.00	96.67
T	100.00	97.78	98.89
U	100.00	81.11	96.67
V	78.89	87.78	100.00
W	94.44	92.22	97.78

(Continued)

Table 2.5 Classification results of all three feature extraction methods against neural network classifier (double-handed ISL alphabets). (*Continued*)

Characters (ISL)	Classification percentage		
	HC feature	DPV feature	Local histogram
X	98.89	98.89	100.00
Y	100.00	100.00	98.89
Z	100.00	94.44	98.89
Aggregate	97.44	95.94	98.42

From Table 2.5, one interesting conclusion can be drawn. That is, if the majority voting method can be applied on feature vectors, 23 of the 26 characters guarantee 100% recognition results. The method to be followed is, if any one feature vector produces 100% recognition rate, this result should be retained for classification. For other three characters, the selection of feature vector should be the one which produced the highest recognition rates. If this selection criterion is followed, the system will guarantee at least 99% accurate results on double-handed ISL alphabet signs.

Six of 26 characters produce 100% recognition accuracy. Almost all characters produce reasonably good recognition results. The maximum misclassification occurs at "V" and "I" and also at "U" and "L." All other misclassifications are below 6%. The minimum misclassification of an ISL double-handed character is 16.67% and occurs at the letter "R." The misclassification of this letter is with letters "H," "M," "N," and "O."

The neural network classifier performance with local histogram feature vector classification confusion matrix is shown in Table 2.7. The aggregate misclassification rate of the confusion matrix is 4.70%. The difference between lowest classification character and highest classification character is 6.67%. This indicates that all classified characters are in the higher side, no significant difference is available. So, in the plotting of the recognition results of this experiment, the results obtained for all characters show a linear behavior. The maximum misclassification occurs at ISL double-handed character sign "N." This letter "N" is confused with letters "M" and "R" with a misclassification rate of 3.33% each with three instances out of 90. Twelve ISL double-handed letters performs 100% accurate recognition results. The percentage of 100% accurate recognition rate is 42.30%.

2.3.3 Experiments on ISL Words

The proposed method is described in Figure 2.16. Two to five frames are extracted from each input video of the ISL words [12] as described earlier.

The word set considered for the proposed ISL recognition system is shown in Table 2.6.

The frames extracted from video belong to a particular word are stored in a specific folder in the computer system for further processing. The frames are preprocessed with skin color detection algorithm. The preprocessed frames contain only binary information of hand and face. The features extracted from skin-filtered image frames are combined to represent the feature vector of a word. The feature vectors are divided into training set and testing set. Finally, the classification engine produces the results from the feature vectors.

A total of 1250 video files are collected from 25 signers. The number of frames extracted differs for each ISL word, because the hand positions and duration of each input video differ. The number of frames extracted from each ISL word is given in Table 2.7.

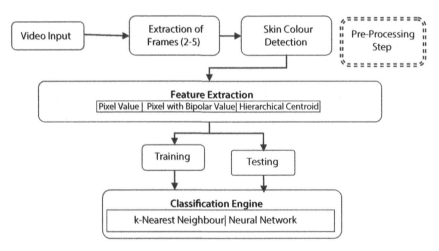

Figure 2.16 The proposed ISL gesture recognition system for specific ISL words.

Table 2.6 ISL-specific computer-related words.

ISL Sign	Camera	CD Drive	Computer	Floppy Drive	Internet
Class Reference	0	1	2	3	4
ISL Sign	Keyboard	Monitor (Display)	Laptop	Mouse	Printer
Class Reference	5	6	7	8	9

Table 2.7 Number of image frames per ISL word.

ISL word class	0	1	2	3	4	5	6	7	8	9
Number of frames/ word	4	3	5	3	3	5	3	4	3	2

In the DPV feature extraction method, original images (300×300) are resized to 40×40 pixels, and the image matrices were converted into one-dimensional arrays containing 1600 elements. As mentioned in Table 2.7, each ISL word can have two to five frames, so each instance of ISL word is having feature vector consisting of 3200 to 8000 elements, depending on the number of frames present in the input gesture. In order to normalize the feature space to 8000 elements each, the remaining elements of feature vectors of some gesture classes are padded with "0," A variation of this feature vector, called DPV with bipolar values (replacing "0" with "−1") is also used in conducting experiments. This is best suited for neural network classifiers.

Hierarchical centroid, which uses the center point division method of finding the centroid of the image as described in chapter III, is used as one of the proposed feature extraction techniques in conducting experiments. Iteratively, this method was performed six times to fetch 124 features out of each image frame. As discussed in the pixel value method, in this step also, each feature vector contains 620 elements with some of the elements assigned "0" values.

2.3.3.1 Results on ISL Word Signs

The performance of kNN classifier is summarized in Table 2.8 and can be visualized in Figure 2.17. The average recognition result of pixel value feature vector is 67.40%, whereas HC method accuracy rate is 84.60%. The conclusions from the results are that the combination of kNN with the HC method can be used as a gesture recognition system for ISL. The performance of class "2" and "9" are not encouraging because the number of frames associated with the feature vectors are less.

The results obtained from neural network classifier with all selected feature vectors are listed in Table 2.9. The DPV feature vector gives 100% recognition rates at four instances. Similarly, direct pixel with bipolar feature vector gives 100% recognition result at three instances, and HC gives 100% accuracy at only one instance.

The results obtained from DPV feature vector are better than any other method as shown in Table 2.10 and Figure 2.18. The results are very

Table 2.8 Performance of kNN classifier on ISL word set.

ISL Words→ Feature Extraction ↓	Performance of kNN (Recognition Rates in %)									
	Camera	CD Drive	Computer	Floppy Drive	Internet	Keyboard	Monitor (Display)	Laptop	Mouse	Printer
DPV	100.00	60.00	80.00	50.00	83.00	55.00	35.00	78.00	33.00	100.00
HC	100.00	47.00	75.00	79.00	100.00	92.00	100.00	100.00	53.00	100.00

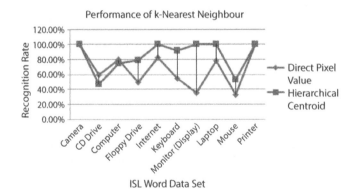

Figure 2.17 Comparison of results of all feature vectors against kNN classifier on ISL word data set.

encouraging for the research. It can also be observed from Figure 2.18 that the misclassification rate is about 3.00% on DPV feature vector. The misclassification rate of each individual class of ISL words is less than 10% in direct pixel feature extraction technique.

The performance of neural network with direct pixel bipolar values feature extractor is depicted in Figure 2.18. The number of hidden neurons

Table 2.9 Recognition rates of neural network classifier against all feature vectors (on ISL word data set).

ISL Words → Feature Extraction ↓	Performance of Neural Network Classifier (Against all three Feature Extraction Methods) (Recognition Rate in %)									
	Camera	CD Drive	Computer	Floppy Drive	Internet	Keyboard	Monitor (Display)	Laptop	Mouse	Printer
DPV	100.00	93.60	96.80	96.00	100.00	95.20	94.40	100.00	94.40	100.00
DPV (Bipolar)	100.00	98.40	100.00	74.40	90.40	88.80	90.40	93.60	92.00	100.00
HC	93.70	96.80	92.00	84.80	96.00	95.20	91.20	98.40	83.20	100.00

Table 2.10 Summary of results obtained from all classifiers and all feature vector (ISL word data set).

Feature Vector → Classifier ↓	Comparison of kNN vs. Neural Network Classifier (Against all 3 Feature extraction methods) (Recognition Rate in %)				
	DPV	DPV (Bipolar)	HC	Sample size	Data set
kNN	67.40	–	84.60	10×125 = 1250	Training = 1250 Testing = 850
Neural network	97.00	96.70	93.70	10×125 = 1250	Training = 60% Validation = 20% Testing = 20%

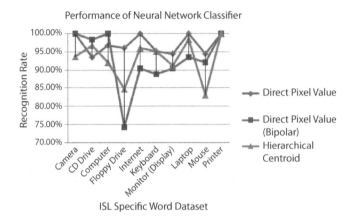

Figure 2.18 Comparison of results of all feature vectors against neural network classifier (ISL word data set).

required for best performance of the network is 55. The error rate of training, validation, and testing are similar with direct pixel feature extraction method. The number of hidden neurons required in this experiment restricts the performance of this experiment.

The comparative analysis of results of kNN classifier is shown in Figure 2.19. However, in this case, the performance of HC is better than the DPV feature vector. The aggregate performance of HC feature vector is 84.60% and 67.40% of the DPV feature extractor as shown in Figure 2.19. These

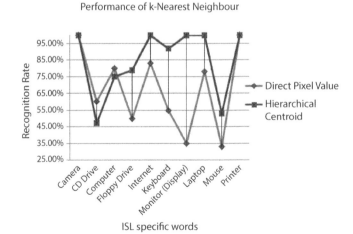

Figure 2.19 Comparison of results obtained from DPV and HC feature extraction methods on kNN Classifier (ISL word data set).

results are far below as compared with neural network classifier on the same feature vectors also. Therefore, the focus of analysis of results of this experiment is on neural network classifier. For comparison purpose, the kNN classifier is used.

2.4 Summary

The research question is to develop an ISL recognition system because its unavailability. The research proposed the design, development, and implementation of an automatic recognition system for ISL. A system has been designed and successfully tested with adequate accuracy on ISL digits, single-handed alphabet, double-handed alphabet, and specific words. The system is able to interpret meaning of ISL signs (Derivation of text from ISL signs).

No standard data sets are available prior to the proposed system. The data sets created is sufficient in terms of the number of sign samples, accuracy, stability, and consistency. Some preprocessing steps have been enhanced as per requirements of the proposed system. Three feature extraction techniques are proposed, and they have been very useful in the experiments. The performance of the system is tested by using various classification techniques. Finally, an automatic recognition system has been designed which is able to handle ISL inputs at digit, alphabet, and word levels.

The study can further be clubbed together to provide an integrated development environment that can append the existing data set better in terms of recognition accuracy and consistency. The research can be integrated in the future with hand-held devices, such as smart phones, palmtops, and so on. This study can also be useful for researchers in this field afterward. They can use the existing data sets, compare their systems with outcomes of this research.

References

1. Brill, R., *The Conference of Educational Administrators Serving the Deaf: A History*, Gallaudet University Press, Washington DC, 1986.
2. Zeshan, U., Vasishta, M.M., Sethna, M., Implementation of Indian Sign Language in Educational Settings. *Asia Pacific Disabil. Rehabilitation J.*, 10, 1, 16–40, 2005.
3. Ananth Rao, G. and Kishore, P.V.V., Selfie Video Based Continuous Indian sign Language Recognition System. *Ain Shams Eng. J.*, 9, 4, 1929–1939, 2018.

4. Sahoo, A.K. and Ravulakollu, K.K., Vision based Indian sign language character recognition. *J. Theor. Appl. Inf. Technol.*, 67, 2, 770–780, 2014.

5. Mingqiang, Y., Kidiyo, K., Joseph, R., A Survey of Shape Feature Extraction Techniques. *Pattern Recognit.*, 15, 7, 43–90, 2008.

6. Vasishta, M.M., Woodward, J., Wilson, K., Sign Language in India: Regional Variation within the Deaf Population. *Indian J. Appl. Linguist.*, 4, 2, 66–74, 1978.

7. Anuja, K., Suryapriya, S., Idicula, S.M., Design and Development of a Frame Based MT System for English-to-ISL. *World Congress on Nature & Biologically Inspired Computing (NaBIC), Coimbatore*, pp. 1382–1387, 2009.

8. Zeshan, U., *Sign Language of Indo-Pakistan: A Description of a Signed Language*, John Benjamin Publishing Co, Philadelphia, Amsterdam, 2000.

9. Banerji, J.N., *India International Reports of Schools for the Deaf*, pp. 18–19, Volta Bureau, Washington City, 1978.

10. Sahoo, A.K., Mishra, G.S., Ravulakollu, K.K., Sign language recognition: state of the art. *J. Eng. Appl. Sci.*, 9, 2, 116–134, 2014.

11. Antunes, D.R., Guimarães, C., Garcia, L.S., Oliveira, L., Fernande, S., A Framework to Support Development of Sign Language Human-Computer Interaction: Building Tools for Effective Information Access and Inclusion of the Deaf. *5th International Conference on Research Challenges in Information Science*, Gosier, pp. 1–12, 2011.

12. Vamvakas, G., Gatos, B., Perantonis, S.J., Handwritten Character Recognition through Two-Stage Foreground Subsampling. *Pattern Recognit.*, 43, 8, 2807–2816, 2010.

13. Ilunga-Mbuyamba, E., Avina-Cervantes, J.G., Lindner, D., Guerrero-Turrubiates, J., Chalopin, C., Automatic brain tumor tissue detection based on hierarchical centroid shape descriptor in Tl-weighted MR images. *International Conference on Electronics, Communications and Computers*, Cholula, pp. 62–67, 2016.

14. Tu, B., Zhang, X., Kang, X., Zhang, G., Wang, J., Wu, J., Hyperspectral image classification via fusing correlation coefficient and joint sparse representation. *Geosci. Remote Sens. Lett.*, 15, 3, 340–344, 2018.

15. Mohan, G. and Subashini, M.M., MRI Based Medical Image Analysis: Survey on Brain Tumor Grade Classification. *Biomed. Signal Process. Control*, 39, 139–161, 2018.

16. Mehmood, A., Mukherjee, M., Ahmed, S.H., Song, H., Malik, K.M., NBC-MAIDS: Naïve Bayesian Classification Technique in Multi-Agent System-Enriched IDS for Securing IoT Against DDoS Attacks. *J. Supercomput.*, 74, 10, 5156–5170, 2018.

17. Kong, Y., Gao, J., Xu, Y., Pan, Y., Wang, J., Liu, J., Classification of autism spectrum disorder by combining brain connectivity and deep neural network classifier. *Neurocomputing*, 324, 63–68, 2019.

18. Sharma, M., Pal, R., Sahoo, A.K., Indian Sign Language Recognition Using Neural Networks and kNN Classifiers. *J. Eng. Appl. Sci.*, 9, 8, 1255–1259, 2014.

19. Mourgias-Alexandris, G., Tsakyridis, A., Passalis, N., Tefas, A., Vyrsokinos, K., Pleros, N., An All-Optical Neuron with Sigmoid Activation Function. *Opt. Express*, 27, 7, 9620–9630, 2019.

20. Mitchell, T.M., *Machine Learning*, McGraw-Hill Science/Engineering/Math, USA, 1997.

21. Calders, T. and Verwer, S., Three Naive Bayes Approaches for Discrimination-Free Classification. *Data Min. Knowl. Discovery*, 21, 2, 277–292, 2010.

22. Guo, L., Rivero, D., Dorado, J., Munteanu, C.R., Pazos, A., Automatic feature extraction using genetic programming: an application to epileptic EEG classification. *Expert Syst. Appl.*, 38, 8, 10425–10436, 2011.

3

Stored Grain Pest Identification Using an Unmanned Aerial Vehicle (UAV)-Assisted Pest Detection Model

Kalyan Kumar Jena[1,2,3]*, Sasmita Mishra[2], Sarojananda Mishra[2] and Sourav Kumar Bhoi[3]

[1]Utkal University, Bhubaneswar, India
[2]Department of Computer Science Engineering and Applications, Indira Gandhi Institute of Technology, Sarang, India
[3]Department of Computer Science and Engineering, Parala Maharaja Engineering College, Berhampur, India

Abstract

Detecting pests in stored grain (SG) accurately is a major issue in the current scenario. It is very much essential to monitor the SG in order to take preventive measures to cease the further growth of pests in the SG. This can be done by capturing the images of SG with the help of UAVs, high-definition drones, cameras, sensors, and so on. Many methods have been introduced to detect the pests in the SG. However, no method is fully efficient in each and every situation. In this chapter, a UAV-assisted pest detection model is proposed in order to track the pests in the SG. This proposed model consists of four phases, such as data acquisition, edge detection (ED), feature extraction, and pest identification. In this model, we have only focused on the ED part by analyzing the data (pest in the SG images). Many standard ED (SED) methods, such as Sobel, Prewitt, Roberts, Morphological, Laplacian of Gaussian (LoG), Canny, are used to track the shape, location, and quantity of pests in SG. The implementation of the methods are performed using MATLAB R2015b and evaluated using signal to noise ratio (SNR), peak SNR (PSNR), and processing time (PT).

Keywords: SG, pests, UAV, SED, SNR, PSNR, PT

*Corresponding author: kalyankumarjena@gmail.com

Muthukumaran Malarvel, Soumya Ranjan Nayak, Surya Narayan Panda, Prasant Kumar Pattnaik and Nittaya Muangnak (eds.) Machine Vision Inspection Systems (Vol. 1): Image Processing, Concepts, Methodologies and Applications, (67–84) © 2020 Scrivener Publishing LLC

3.1   Introduction

Grain plays an important role for the survival of human society. It is considered as one of the important basic needs of human society. Human without grain is like bike without fuel. Stored grain (SG) is a major concern in the today's era. Several reasons are there for the loss of SG. The loss of SG due to pests is one of them. Loss of SG leads to food crisis in a global scale. Everyone has to be alert about this issue, otherwise it leads to a very serious problem to the human society globally. About 5% to 10% and 20% loss of SG by pests are caused in developed countries and developing counties, respectively [1]. So, it is essential to track the shape, location, and quantity of pests in the SG in order to take preventive measures for their growth. The SG pests can be broadly classified as primary SG pests and secondary SG pests [80, 81]. Several primary SG pests are lesser grain borer (LGB), rice weevil (RW), granary weevil (GW), angoumois grain moth (AGM), and so on, and several secondary SG pests are rust red flour beetle (RRFB), confused flour beetle (CFB), saw toothed grain beetle (STGB), flat grain beetle (FGB), warehouse moth (WM), Indian meal moth (IMM), and so on. Pest classification is shown in Figure 3.1.

In this work, a UAV [38, 39]-assisted pest detection model is proposed to monitor the SG pests by capturing the images of SG periodically. If any pest is found in the SG, these images will be sent to the information center (IC) and then these images will be collected from the IC for processing and analysis. The captured images will be processed by the help of standard edge detection (SED) methods, such as Sobel [40–43], Prewitt [44–46], Roberts [47–49], Morphological [54], LoG [50–53], Canny [55–58], and several other image processing approaches [59–79] to track the shape, location, and quantity of pests in the SG [1–37]. The outputs of SED methods are compared and evaluated using signal to noise ratio (SNR), peak SNR (PSNR), and processing time (PT).

The main contributions in this chapter are stated as follows:

1. A UAV-assisted pest detection model is proposed to track the shape, location, and quantity of pests in the SG to take preventive measures for the further growth of the pests in the SG.
2. The SG images will be captured by the UAVs and transferred to the IC. The captured images will be collected from the IC and then processed by using SED methods, such as Sobel, Prewitt, Roberts, Morphological, LoG, Canny, and other for pest detection.
3. MATLAB R2015b is used for the implementation of SED methods, and SNR, PSNR, and PT are taken as performance metrics.

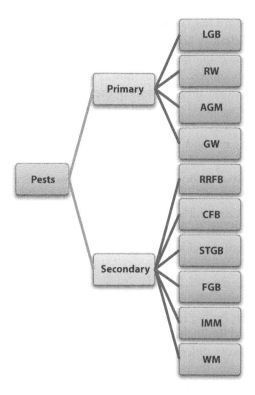

Figure 3.1 Pest classification over SG.

The rest of the chapter is organized as follows: Sections II, III, IV, and V describe the related works, proposed model, results and discussion, and conclusion of the work, respectively.

3.2   Related Work

Several works have proposed by several researchers to identify the pests in the SG [1–37]. In this section, some of the works were discussed. Qin *et al.* [1] focuses on spectral residual (SR) saliency ED mechanism to detect the pests in SG. It mainly focuses on the image logarithmic spectrum as part of the information of the image. The rest of the spectrum is changed to airspace for obtaining the results (ED). It is based on the processing in frequency domain. Shen *et al.* [2] proposed a deep neural network-based technique to identify and detect the insects in SG. In this work, faster R-CNN is used to focus the regions of insects in the images as well as to classify the insects in the regions. An advanced inception network can be developed for feature map extraction. Solà *et al.* [3] proposed a multiplex PCR method to identify and detect the pests, such as *Sitotroga cerealella, S. oryzae, Sitophilus granarius, Rhyzopertha dominica,* and *S. zeamais,* which are hidden in grain kernels. This method may be used for decision making (commercial) to satisfy the demands in the current market scenario.

Kaushik and Singhai [4] proposed an integrated and environment monitoring-sensing system for the detection of contamination and insect infestation in SG. This method may monitor the quality of grain. The sensor data may help in the prediction of essential information and provide alerts for taking preventive actions. Liu *et al.* [6] proposed a deep learning-based pestnet method to detect and classify multiclass pests. The pestnet method focuses on CSA, Convolutional Neural Network (CNN), Region Proposal Network (RPN), Position-Sensitive Score Map (PSSM), Fully Connected (FC), as well as contextual Region of Interest (RoI) mechanisms. The pestnet method can be evaluated by using MPD2018 data set as well as newly referred pest image data set. Priyadarsini *et al.* [7] focuses on a device (smart) to explore the negative effects on the pest bugs in case of land (harvesting), as well as in the water body PH level. It is mainly focused on the identification of the PH value and the control of pest for better agriculture. In order to repel several types of insects, different ultrasonic waves are produced.

3.3   Proposed Model

The proposed model is mentioned in Figure 3.2. This model is focused on UAV-assisted pest detection model for the detection of pests over the SG. It is very essential to track each and every pest in the SG in order to take preventive measures for further loss of SG. The UAVs or high-definition drones can be used to monitor the SG at regular intervals. The UAVs will capture the SG images at regular intervals and send these images to the IC. The captured images can be taken from the IC for analysis periodically. If any pest is detected, then the captured images will be processed immediately in order to track the position, shape, and quantity of pests. It can be done by using four phases discussed as follows.

1. Data Acquisition: According to the proposed model presented in Figure 3.2, the data (SG image) is collected periodically using the help of UAVs. The UAVs periodically take images of SG for pest detection. The data are transferred by the UAV to the IC using the Internet connection from the UAV to the IC.
2. Edge detection: After collecting the image the IC process the images for detecting the pests over the SG. It uses the SED

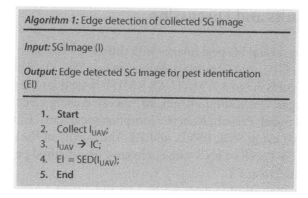

Algorithm 1: Edge detection of collected SG image

Input: SG Image (I)

Output: Edge detected SG Image for pest identification (EI)

1. **Start**
2. Collect I_{UAV};
3. $I_{UAV} \rightarrow IC$;
4. $EI = SED(I_{UAV})$;
5. **End**

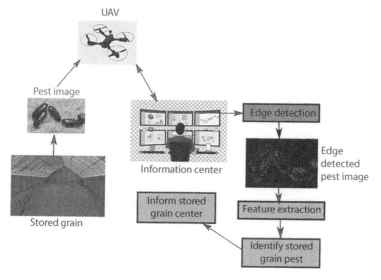

Figure 3.2 Proposed UAV-assisted pest detection model for SG.

method to find the edges in the SG image. This is performed to identify the object (pest) in the SG images. Algorithm 1 presents the ED of collected SG image.

3. Feature Extraction: Then the feature of the image is extracted by using a classifier which takes the input (many images transferred by the UAV) and uses a learning algorithm to detect the pest over the SG. The features are then compared to detect many types of pests over the SG.

4. Pest Identification: After comparing the features, the pests are identified. Then, the pest information is sent to the SG center using the Internet connection for taking preventive measures for the safety of SG.

3.4   Results and Discussion

In this work, several SG pest images with different sizes, such as RW, LGB, RRFB, CFB, GW, are taken from source images [80, 81] which are mentioned in Figures 3.3 to 3.7. MATLAB R2015b is used for the processing of SG pest images. The SG pest images are processed using several SED methods, such as Sobel, Prewitt, Roberts, Morphological, LoG, Canny methods and evaluated using SNR, PSNR, and PT. The quality of the output image increases if the PSNR or SNR value increases. The method performs faster if it deals with lesser PT.

From the analysis of Figures 3.3 to 3.10 and Tables 3.1 to 3.3, it is concluded that the morphological method detects the pests in a better way as compared with other methods, and it processes the images with less PT. However, the PSNR and SNR values of Canny method is higher as compared with others. From the analysis of RW image as mentioned in Figure 3.3, morphological method detects the RW from image in a better way, and its PT is 0.01 unit. However, Sobel, Prewitt, and Roberts method try to detect the RW. However, the results of these methods are not so

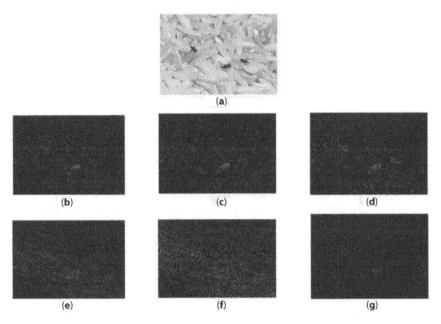

Figure 3.3 Processing of RW (1280 × 853). (a) Original image and results using (b) Sobel, (c) Prewitt, (d) Roberts, (e) LoG, (f) Canny, and (g) morphological methods.

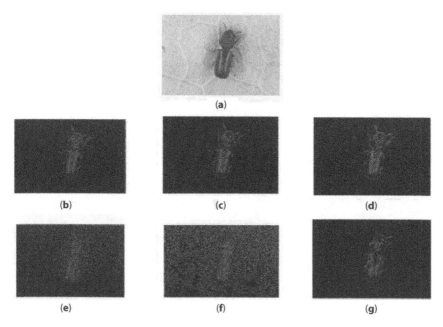

Figure 3.4 Processing of LGB(800 × 534). (a) Original image and results using (b) Sobel, (c) Prewitt, (d) Roberts, (e) LoG, (f) Canny, and (g) morphological methods.

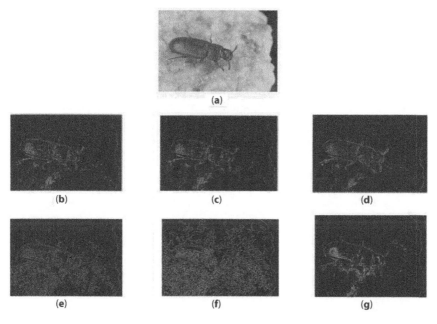

Figure 3.5 Processing of RRFB (640 × 426). (a) Original image and results using (b) Sobel, (c) Prewitt, (d) Roberts, (e) LoG, (f) Canny, and (g) morphological methods.

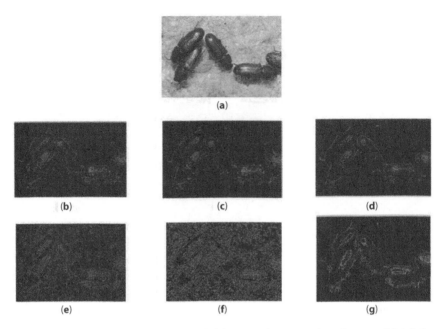

Figure 3.6 Processing of CFB (750 × 511). (a) Original image and results using (b) Sobel, (c) Prewitt, (d) Roberts, (e) LoG, (f) Canny, and (g) morphological methods.

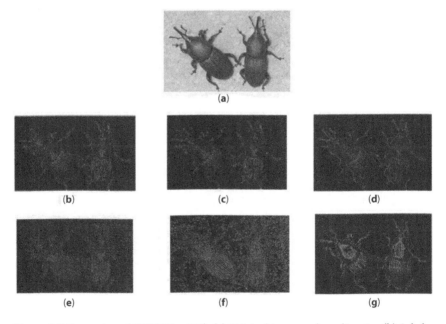

Figure 3.7 Processing of GW (800 × 502). (a) Original image and results using (b) Sobel, (c) Prewitt,(d) Roberts, (e) LoG, (f) Canny, and (g) morphological methods.

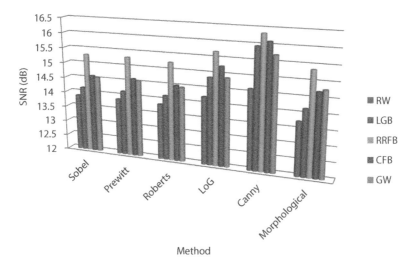

Figure 3.8 SNR (dB) representation of several methods.

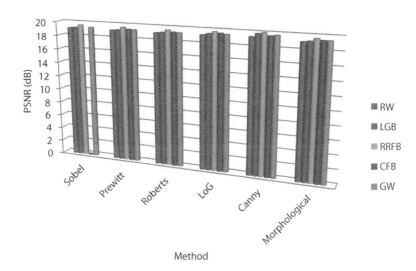

Figure 3.9 PSNR(dB) representation of several methods.

good as compared with the morphological method. The LoG and Canny methods are not able to identify the RW. From the analysis of LGB and RRFB images, as mentioned in Figures 3.4 and 3.5, respectively, morphological method detects the LGB and RRFB pests from images in a better way as compared with other methods, and its PT are 0.03 and 0.01 units, respectively. However, Sobel, Prewitt, and Roberts methods try to detect

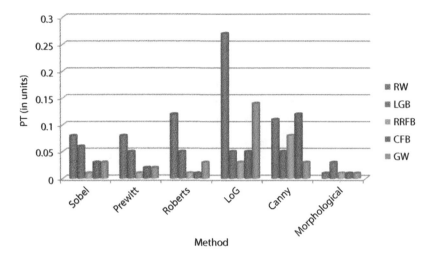

Figure 3.10 PT (in units) representation of several methods.

Table 3.1 Evaluation of methods using SNR(dB) value.

Method	RW	LGB	RRFB	CFB	GW
Sobel	13.87	14.15	15.29	14.59	14.55
Prewitt	13.87	14.15	15.30	14.60	14.55
Roberts	13.84	14.14	15.24	14.51	14.46
LoG	14.23	14.87	15.69	15.25	14.89
Canny	14.62	15.95	16.34	16.11	15.72
Morphological	13.75	14.16	15.36	14.71	14.78

Table 3.2 Evaluation of methods using PSNR(dB) value.

Method	RW	LGB	RRFB	CFB	GW
Sobel	19.09	19.18	19.55	19. 32	19.29
Prewitt	19.09	19.18	19.57	19.32	19.29
Roberts	19.09	19.17	19.54	19.29	19.27
LoG	19.20	19.39	19.69	19.52	19.41
Canny	19.32	19.78	19.95	19.58	19.70
Morphological	19.07	19.18	19.58	19.37	19.37

Table 3.3 PT (in units) calculation of several methods.

Method	RW	LGB	RRFB	CFB	GW
Sobel	0.08	0.06	0.01	0.03	0.03
Prewitt	0.08	0.05	0.01	0.02	0.02
Roberts	0.12	0.05	0.01	0.01	0.03
LoG	0.27	0.05	0.03	0.05	0.14
Canny	0.11	0.05	0.08	0.12	0.03
Morphological	0.01	0.03	0.01	0.01	0.01

the LGB and RRFB pests, and LoG and Canny methods also try to detect the LGB and RRFB from the images. However, the results of LoG and Canny methods are not so good as compared with Sobel, Prewitt, and Roberts methods.

Similarly, from the analysis of CFB and GW images, as mentioned in Figures 3.6 and 3.7, respectively, morphological method detects the CFB and GW pests from images in a better way as compared with others, and its PT is 0.01 unit in both cases. However, Sobel, Prewitt, and Roberts methods try to detect the CFB and GW, and LoG and Canny methods also try to detect the CFB and GW pests from the images. However, the results of LoG and Canny methods are not so good as compared with the Sobel, Prewitt, and Roberts methods.

3.5 Conclusion

In this chapter, a UAV-assisted pest detection model is proposed which mainly consists of four phases, such as data acquisition, ED, feature extraction, and pest identification. In this work, we have only focused on the ED part by analyzing the pests in the SG images. The implementation of the SED methods is performed using MATLAB R2015b and evaluated using SNR, PSNR, and PT. From the results, it is observed that morphological ED method detects the edges well with lower PT. In the future, this SED method will be taken in our pest detection model. Then, the edge detected images are given to a classifier for learning to identify the pests accurately. This proposed model will be a better solution for the prevention of SGs.

References

1. Qin, Y., Wu, Y., Wang, Q., Yu, S., Method for pests detecting in stored grain based on spectral residual saliency edge detection. *Grain Oil Sci. Technol.*, 2, 33–38, 2019.
2. Shen, Y., Zhou, H., Li, J., Jian, F., Jayas, D.S., Detection of stored-grain insects using deep learning. *Comput. Electron. Agric.*, 145, 319–325, 2018.
3. Solà, M., Riudavets, J., Agusti, N., Detection and identification of five common internal grain insect pests by multiplex PCR. *Food Control*, 84, 246–254, 2018.
4. Kaushik, R. and Singhai, J., An approach for the development of a sensing system to monitor contamination in stored grain, in: *2019 6th International Conference on Signal Processing and Integrated Networks (SPIN)*, IEEE, pp. 880–884, 2019.
5. Kumari, R., Jayachandran, L.E., Ghosh, A.K., Investigation of diversity and dominance of fungal biota in stored wheat grains from governmental warehouses in West Bengal, India. *J. Sci. Food Agric.*, 99, 7, 3490–3500, 2019.
6. Liu, L., Wang, R., Xie, C., Yang, P., Wang, F., Sudirman, S., Liu, W., PestNet: An end-to-end deep learning approach for large-scale multi-class pest detection and classification. *IEEE Access*, 7, 45301–45312, 2019.
7. Priyadarsini, J., Karthick, B.N., Karthick, K., Karthikeyan, B., Mohan, S., Detection of PH value and Pest control for eco-friendly agriculture, in: *2019 5th International Conference on Advanced Computing & Communication Systems (ICACCS)*, IEEE, pp. 801–804, 2019.
8. Glen, N., Korol, O., Andre, L., Robert, F., Tom, G., Extracting pest risk information from risk assessment documents, in: *2019 ACM/IEEE Joint Conference on Digital Libraries (JCDL)*, IEEE, pp. 368–369, 2019.
9. Losey, S.M., Daglish, G.J., Phillips, T.W., Orientation of rusty grain beetles, Cryptolestes ferrugineus (Coleoptera: Laemophloeidae), to semiochemicals in field and laboratory experiments. *J. Stored Prod. Res.*, 84, 101513, 2019.
10. Njoroge, A., Affognon, H., Richter, U., Hensel, O., Rohde, B., Chen, D., Mankin, R., Acoustic, Pitfall Trap, and Visual Surveys of Stored Product Insect Pests in Kenyan Warehouses. *Insects*, 10, 4, 105, 2019.
11. Jian, F., Influences of stored product insect movements on integrated pest management decisions. *Insects*, 10, 4, 100, 2019.
12. McCulloch, G.A., Mohankumar, S., Subramanian, S., Rajan, T.S., Rahul, C., Surendran, R., Walter, G.H., Contrasting patterns of phylogeographic structuring in two key beetle pests of stored grain in India and Australia. *J. Pest Sci.*, 92, 3, 1249–1259, 2019.
13. Banga, K.S., Kotwaliwale, N., Mohapatra, D., Giri, S.K., Techniques for insect detection in stored food grains: An overview. *Food Control*, 94, 167–176, 2018.
14. Daglish, G.J., Nayak, M.K., Arthur, F.H., Athanassiou, C.G., Insect pest management in stored grain, in: *Recent Advances in Stored Product Protection*, pp. 45–63, Springer, Berlin, Heidelberg, 2018.

15. Athanassiou, C.G. and Rumbos, C.I., Emerging pests in durable stored products, in: *Recent Advances in Stored Product Protection*, pp. 211–227, Springer, Berlin, Heidelberg, 2018.

16. Golden, G., Quinn, E., Shaaya, E., Kostyukovsky, M., Poverenov, E., Coarse and nano emulsions for effective delivery of the natural pest control agent pulegone for stored grain protection. *Pest Manage. Sci.*, 74, 4, 820–827, 2018.

17. Eliopoulos, P.A., Potamitis, I., Kontodimas, D.C., Estimation of population density of stored grain pests via bioacoustic detection. *Crop Prot.*, 85, 71–78, 2016.

18. Stejskal, V., Hubert, J., Aulicky, R., Kucerova, Z., Overview of present and past and pest-associated risks in stored food and feed products: European perspective. *J. Stored Prod. Res.*, 64, 122–132, 2015.

19. Hammond, N.E.B., Hardie, D., Hauser, C.E., Reid, S.A., Can general surveillance detect high priority pests in the Western Australian Grains Industry? *Crop Prot.*, 79, 8–14, 2016.

20. Li, Y.Y., Fields, P.G., Pang, B.P., Coghlin, P.C., Floate, K.D., Prevalence and diversity of Wolbachia bacteria infecting insect pests of stored products. *J. Stored Prod. Res.*, 62, 93–100, 2015.

21. Santiago, R.M.C., Rabano, S.L., Billones, R.K.D., Calilung, E.J., Sybingco, E., Dadios, E.P., Insect detection and monitoring in stored grains using MFCCs and artificial neural network, in: *TENCON 2017-2017 IEEE Region 10 Conference*, IEEE, pp. 2542–2547, 2017.

22. Zhu, C., Wang, J., Liu, H., Mi, H., Insect identification and counting in stored grain: Image processing approach and application embedded in smartphones. *Mobile Inf. Syst.*, 2018, 2–5, 2018.

23. Tigar, B.J. and Hursthouse, A.S., Using elemental profiling to determine intrinsic markers to track the dispersal of *P rostephanus truncatus*, a pest of stored grain with alternative natural hosts. *Entomol. Experiment. Appl.*, 160, 1, 83–90, 2016.

24. Engl, T., Eberl, N., Gorse, C., Krüger, T., Schmidt, T.H., Plarre, R., Kaltenpoth, M., Ancient symbiosis confers desiccation resistance to stored grain pest beetles. *Mol. Ecol.*, 27, 8, 2095–2108, 2018.

25. Neethirajan, S., Karunakaran, C., Jayas, D.S., White, N.D.G., Detection techniques for stored-product insects in grain. *Food Control*, 18, 2, 157–162, 2007.

26. Cox, P.D. and Collins, L.E., Factors affecting the behaviour of beetle pests in stored grain, with particular reference to the development of lures. *J. Stored Prod. Res.*, 38, 2, 95–115, 2002.

27. Armitage, D.M., Cogan, P.M., Wilkin, D.R., Integrated pest management in stored grain: Combining surface insecticide treatments with aeration. *J. Stored Prod. Res.*, 30, 4, 1994.

28. Yang, Y., Peng, B., Wang, J., A system for detection and recognition of pests in stored-grain based on video analysis, in: *International Conference on Computer and Computing Technologies in Agriculture*, pp. 119–124303–319, Springer, Berlin, Heidelberg, 2010.

29. Herron, G.A., Resistance to grain protectants and phosphine in coleopterous pests of grain stored on farms in New South Wales. *Aust. J. Entomol.*, 29, 3, 183–189, 1990.

30. Elmouttie, D., Kiermeier, A., Hamilton, G., Improving detection probabilities for pests in stored grain. *Pest Manage. Sci.*, 66, 12, 1280–1286, 2010.

31. Eliopoulos, P.A., Potamitis, I., Kontodimas, D.C., Estimation of population density of stored grain pests via bioacoustic detection. *Crop Prot.*, 85, 71–78, 2016.

32. Baker, J.E., Dowell, F.E., Throne, J.E., Detection of parasitized rice weevils in wheat kernels with near-infrared spectroscopy1. *Biol. Control*, 16, 1, 88–90, 1999.

33. Nayak, M.K., Daglish, G.J., Byrne, V.S., Effectiveness of spinosad as a grain protectant against resistant beetle and psocid pests of stored grain in Australia. *J. Stored Prod. Res.*, 41, 4, 455–467, 2005.

34. Stefanazzi, N., Stadler, T., Ferrero, A., Composition and toxic, repellent and feeding deterrent activity of essential oils against the stored-grain pests *Tribolium castaneum* (Coleoptera: Tenebrionidae) and *Sitophilus oryzae* (Coleoptera: Curculionidae). *Pest Manage. Sci.*, 67, 6, 639–646, 2011.

35. Stejskal, V., Aulický, R., Kučerová, Z., Lukáš, J., Method of sampling and laboratory extraction affects interpretation of grain infestation by storage pests. *J. Plant Dis. Prot.*, 115, 3, 129–133, 2008.

36. Flinn, P.W., Hagstrum, D.W., Reed, C., Phillips, T.W., United States Department of Agriculture–Agricultural Research Service stored-grain area-wide Integrated Pest Management program. *Pest Manage. Sci Formerly Pestic. Sci.*, 59, 6-7, 614–618, 2003.

37. Shah, M.A. and Khan, A.A., Imaging techniques for the detection of stored product pests. *Appl. Entomol. Zool.*, 49, 2, 201–212, 2014.

38. Mozaffari, M., Saad, W., Bennis, M., Nam, Y.H., Debbah, M., A tutorial on UAVs for wireless networks: Applications, challenges, and open problems. *IEEE Commun. Surv. Tutorials*, 21, 2334–2360, 2019.

39. Atencia, C.R., Del Ser, J., Camacho, D., Weighted strategies to guide a multi-objective evolutionary algorithm for multi-UAV mission planning. *Swarm Evol. Comput.*, 44, 480–495, 2019.

40. Gupta, S. and Mazumdar, S.G., Sobel edge detection algorithm. *Int. J. Comput. Sci. Manage.Res.*, 2, 1578–1583, 2013.

41. Chaple, G. and Daruwala, R.D., Design of Sobel operator based image edge detection algorithm on FPGA, in: *International Conference on Communication and Signal Processing, IEEE*, pp. 788–792, 2014.

42. Patel, J., Patwardhan, J., Sankhe, K., Kumbhare, R., Fuzzy inference based edge detection system using Sobel and Laplacian of Gaussian operators, in: *Proceedings of the International Conference and Workshop on Emerging Trends in Technology*, New York, USA, pp. 694–697, ACM, 2011.

43. Gao, W., Xiaoguang, Z., Lei, Y., Huizhong, L., An improved Sobel edge detection, in: *3rd International Conference on Computer Science and Information Technology*, vol. 5, IEEE, pp. 67–71, 2010.

44. Zhou, R.-G., Han, Y., Yu, C., Feng-Xin, L., Quantum image edge extraction based on improved Prewitt operator. *Quantum Inf. Process.*, 18, 9, 261, 2019.

45. Lofroth, M. and Ebubekir, A., Auto-focusing approach on multiple micro objects using the prewitt operator. *Int. J. Intell. Rob. Appl.*, 2, 4, 413–424, 2018.

46. Ye, H., Bin, S., Shili, Y., Prewitt edge detection based on BM3D image denoising, in: *2018 IEEE 3rd Advanced Information Technology, Electronic and Automation Control Conference(IAEAC)*, IEEE, pp.1593–1597, 2018.

47. Amer, G., Mahmoud, H., Ahmed, M.A., Edge detection methods, in: *2015 2nd World Symposium on Web Applications and Networking (WSWAN)*, IEEE, pp.1–7, 2015.

48. Srivastava, D., Rashi, K., Shubhi, G., Implementation and statistical comparison of different edge detection techniques, in: *Advances in Computer and Computational Sciences*, pp. 211–228, Springer, Singapore, 2017.

49. Singh, S. and Rakesh, S., Comparison of various edge detection techniques, in: *2015 2nd International Conference on Computing for Sustainable Global Development (INDIACom)*, IEEE, pp. 393–396, 2015.

50. Wan, J., Xiaofu, H., Pengfei, S., An iris image quality assessment method based on Laplacian of Gaussian operation, in: *MVA*, pp. 248–251, 2007.

51. Mohamad, A.S., Nur, S.A.H., Muhammad, N.N., Roszymah, H., Jameela, S., Automated detection of human RBC in diagnosing sickle cell anemia with Laplacian of Gaussian filter, in: *2018 IEEE Conference on Systems, Process and Control (ICSPC)*, IEEE, pp. 214–217, 2018.

52. Saad, O.M., Ahmed, S., Lotfy, S., Mohammed, S.S., Automatic arrival time detection for earthquakes based on Modified Laplacian of Gaussian filter. *Comput. Geosci.*, 113, 43–53, 2018.

53. Ghosal, S.K., Jyotsna, K.M., Ram, S., High payload image steganography based on Laplacian of Gaussian (LoG) edge detector. *Multimedia Tools Appl.*, 77, 23, 30403–30418, 2018.

54. Yu-Qian, Z., Gui, W.H., Chen, Z.C., Tang, J.T., Li, L.Y., Medical images edge detection based on mathematical morphology, in: *Engineering in Medicine and Biology 27th Annual Conference, IEEE*, pp. 6492–6495, 2006.

55. Wang, M., Jesse, S.J., Yifei, J., Xianfeng, H., Lei, G., Liping, X., The improved canny edge detection algorithm based on an anisotropic and genetic algorithm, in: *Chinese Conference on Image and Graphics Technologies*, pp. 115–124, Springer, Singapore, 2016.

56. Xin, G., Chen, K., Hu, X., An improved Canny edge detection algorithm for color image, in: *10th International Conference on Industrial Informatics*, IEEE, pp. 113–117, 2012.

57. Othman, Z. and Azizi, A., An adaptive threshold based on multiple resolution levels for canny edge detection, in: *International Conference of Reliable Information and Communication Technology*, Springer, Cham, pp. 316–323, 2017.

58. Shanmugavadivu, P. and Kumar, A., Modified eight-directional canny for robust edge detection, in: *International Conference on Contemporary Computing and Informatics*, IEEE, pp. 751–756, 2014.

59. Nayak, S.R., Mishra, J., Khandual, A., Palai, G., Fractal dimension of RGB color images. *Optik*, 162, 196–205, 2018.

60. Nayak, S.R. and Mishra, J., Analysis of Medical Images Using Fractal Geometry, in: *Histopathological Image Analysis in Medical Decision Making*, pp. 181–201, IGI Global, 2019.

61. Nayak, S.R., Mishra, J., Palai, G., Analysing roughness of surface through fractal dimension: A review. *Image Vision Comput.*, 89, 21–34, 2019.

62. Jena, K.K., Mishra, S., Mishra, S.N., Bhoi, S.K., Nayak, S.R., MRI brain tumor image analysis using fuzzy rule based approach. *J. Res. Lepidoptera*, 50, 98–112, 2019.

63. Nayak, S.R. and Mishra, J., A modified triangle box-counting with precision in error fit. *J. Inf. Optim. Sci.*, 39, 113–128, 2018.

64. Jena, K.K., Mishra, S., Mishra, S.N., Bhoi, S.K., 2L-ESB: A two level security scheme for edge based image steganography. *Int. J. Emerging Technol.*, 10, 29–38, 2019.

65. Nayak, S.R., Mishra, J., Palai, G., An extended DBC approach by using maximum Euclidian distance for fractal dimension of color images. *Optik*, 166, 110–115, 2018.

66. Jena, K.K., Bhoi, S.K., Nayak, M.K., Baral, C.K., Patro, D.M.K., Mohanty, S.S., A smart watering system using IoT. *Pramana Res. J.*, 69, 3, 527–535, 2019.

67. Nayak, S.R., Ranganath, A., Mishra, J., Analysing fractal dimension of color images, in: *IEEE International Conference on Computational Intelligence and Networks*, CINE, pp. 156–159, 2015.

68. Jena, K.K., Mishra, S., Mishra, S.N., An edge detection approach for fractal image processing, in: *Examining Fractal Image Processing and Analysis*, Hershey, Pennsylvania, pp. 1–22, IGI Global, 2019.

69. Nayak, S.R., Mishra, J., Padhy, R., A new extended differential box-counting method by adopting unequal partitioning of grid for estimation of fractal dimension of grayscale images, in: *Computational Signal Processing and Analysis*, pp. 45–57, Springer, Singapore, 2018.

70. Das, S.K., Nayak, S.R., Mishra, J., Fractal geometry: The beauty of computer graphics. *J. Adv. Res. Dyn. Control Syst.*, 9, 10, 76–82, 2017.

71. Jena, K.K., Mishra, S., Mishra, S.N., An algorithmic approach based on CMS edge detection technique for the processing of digital images, in: *Examining Fractal Image Processing and Analysis*, Hershey, Pennsylvania, pp. 252–272, IGI Global, 2019.

72. Nayak, S.R., Khandual, A., Mishra, J., Ground truth study on fractal dimension of color images of similar texture. *J. Text. Inst.*, 109, 1159–1167, 2018.

73. Jena, K.K., Mishra, S., Mishra, S.N., Bhoi, S.K., An entropy based thresholding approach for image edge detection. *J. Appl. Sci. Comput.*, 2, 309–322, 2019.

74. Nayak, S.R., Mishra, J., Jena, P.M., Fractal analysis of image sets using differential box counting techniques. *Int. J. Inf. Technol.*, 10, 39–47, 2018.

75. Jena, K.K., Bhoi, S.K., Maharana, P.K., Das, P.R., Senapati, P.K., A smart and secure home automation system using IoT. *Universal Rev.*, 8, 3, 125–132, 2019.

76. Nayak, S.R., Mishra, J., Palai, G., A modified approach to estimate fractal dimension of gray scale images. *Optik*, 161, 136-145, 2018.

77. Jena, K.K., Nayak, S.R., Mishra, S., Mishra, S.N., Vehicle number plate detection: An edge image based approach, in: *4th Springer International Conference on Advanced Computing and Intelligent Engineering*, Advances in Intelligent Systems and Computing, 2019.

78. Nayak, S.R., Mishra, J., Padhy, R., An improved algorithm to estimate the fractal dimension of gray scale images, in: *International Conference on Signal Processing, Communication, Power and Embedded System, IEEE*, pp. 1109–1114, 2016.

79. Nayak, S.R., Mishra, J., Jena, P.M., Fractal dimension of grayscale images, in: *Progress in Computing, Analytics and Networking*, pp. 225–234, Springer, Singapore, 2018.

80. https://www.agric.wa.gov.au/pest-insects/insect-pests-stored-grain

81. https://www.google.com/search?q=primary+and+secondary+stored+grain+pests&sxsrf=ACYBGNQvb6AbxvSe5qzHXD9Lo7-TqYwSSw:1575972076386&source=lnms&tbm=isch&sa=X&ved=2ahUKEwihy6e-6armAhUqxjgGHRjuD9AQ_AUoAXoECBIQAw&biw=1600&bih=789

4

Object Descriptor for Machine Vision

Aparna S. Murthy[1*] and Salah Rabba[2]

[1]EIT, PEO, Canada
[2]Ryerson University, Toronto, Canada

Abstract

In this chapter, we discuss various object identifying techniques in a two-dimensional plane. Object descriptors of different kinds and data structures used to store them are discussed. The comparison of object is based on the constructed data structure. The properties of the object, such as invariance and completeness, are also encoded as a set of descriptors. We discuss the chain code and polygonal approximation, the boundary descriptors for matching the objects. The boundary descriptors are also called contours, whereas moments, Fourier descriptor, and Quadtree are property descriptors used in template matching. The broad classification is that boundary describes the shape of the object, whereas the region descriptors describe the content of the object. Depending on the application, we have to use either boundary or region descriptors for template matching or feature extraction.

Keywords: Polygonal approximation, moments, Zernike polynomial, quadtree

4.1 Outline

Object selection is a tradeoff between performance and accuracy. Particularly, in machine vision, time versus precision for object selection plays a crucial role. With digital images, there are regions of image which are of interest. These regions are a group of segmented pixels that are used for processing. Such regions are often represented by numbers called "object descriptors."

Corresponding author: aparnasm11@gmail.com

Muthukumaran Malarvel, Soumya Ranjan Nayak, Surya Narayan Panda, Prasant Kumar Pattnaik and Nittaya Muangnak (eds.) Machine Vision Inspection Systems (Vol. 1): Image Processing, Concepts, Methodologies and Applications, (85–114) © 2020 Scrivener Publishing LLC

Using such data, we compare and distinguish objects by matching the descriptors. Without loss of generality, these descriptors have certain properties:

a. Invariance against geometrical transformations, like translation, rotation, and scaling;
b. Stability to noise and nonrigid local deformation;
c. Completeness.

Invariant properties say rotation-invariance makes the recognition independent of orientation. Position invariance also means immune to perspective and affine transformations. Two objects are said to have a complete set when they are of same shape. We say that the objects are similar when they have the same descriptors. It is very important to recognize objects from different viewpoints. In essence, a descriptor should enable identifying objects in an efficient and unique way. Because universal identifiers are hard to be designed, the best performance is obtained by choosing the properties listed.

To represent a region, there are two characteristics, namely,

External: Pixels around or boundary of the object. This is used to choose the shape of the object that is defined by its boundary.
Internal: Pixels within the region, they are reflective of properties, such as color, texture, or area, which is commonly the region of interest.

Shape and region descriptors are arrangement of pixels around a boundary or within the area. Boundary descriptors are around the object, and edges can be used to detect them while region descriptors are heuristic or property-based. Examples of some simple descriptors include length of a boundary. This delineates the number of pixels all along the boundary. The diameter of the boundary is the distance measure between two points. Major and minor axes that are perpendicular to one another as in case of an ellipse that defines the four points within a boundary or forms a box. The ratio of the axes called eccentricity is an important metric. Curvature is difficult to be defined, so depending on the traversal in the clockwise direction, a vertex is said to be "convex segment" if slope is positive else "concave segment."

Bounding box is a common technique used in object selection. It has some difficulty when encountered patches or parts those are not available. Figure 4.1 shows the workflow of the part identifier using bounding box.

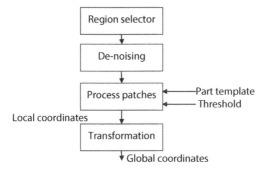

Figure 4.1 Workflow of part selection using bounding box part template.

A boundary or perimeter called "contour" is a set of points in a region that represents a set of pixels within and outside the region of choice. The contour generally refers to the shape of the object. The points are found traversing either clockwise or counter-clockwise direction. This path of traversal is described in terms of connectivity, four-way or eight-way are the common representations.

$$\begin{bmatrix} 0 & 0 & 0 & 0 & 0 \\ 0 & 0 & 1 & 0 & 0 \\ 0 & 1 & x & 1 & 0 \\ 0 & 0 & 1 & 0 & 0 \end{bmatrix} \qquad \begin{bmatrix} 0 & 1 & 1 & 1 & 0 \\ 0 & 1 & x & 1 & 0 \\ 0 & 1 & 1 & 1 & 0 \\ 0 & 0 & 0 & 0 & 0 \end{bmatrix}$$

"x" represents the center pixel and the neighboring ones represent the connectivity information. The four-way connectivity considers neighboring nine pixels, of which four pixels represent the connectivity as ones. With eight-way connectivity, all the neighboring eight pixels are included. A boundary or region can have both types of connectivity, and they are complementary. If the boundary pixels are eight-way connected, the region will be four-way connected and vice-versa.

4.2 Chain Codes

Chain codes came into the field of computer vision in the 1960s by Freeman. Chain codes as the name suggests is used to check the boundaries of an object by storing position relative to adjacent pixels. The direction of connectivity can be four-way or eight-way as shown below:

		North,0		
	West,3	Origin	East,1	
		South,2		

(a) Four-way connectivity

	North West,7	North,0	North East,1	
	West,6	Origin	East,2	
	South West,5	South,4	South East,3	

(b) Eight-way connectivity

The four-way connectivity has an origin, north with a code of 0, east code of 1, south code of 2, and west has a code 4. Similarly, the eight different directions have eight codes, 0 through 7. The integers represent boundary by straight lines of specific direction and length. The direction of each line is coded by a number arrangement called "chain code." The first difference is calculated by counting the number of positions required to get to the second number in counter-clockwise direction.

Chain code: (Start) 0 1 1 0 0 1 2 2 2 3 3 3
First difference: 3 0 1 0 3 3 0 0 2 0 0

Chain code provides the close contour of the object boundary along with direction and angle of finding the pixels, that is the advantage of the eight-way connectivity.

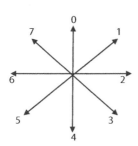

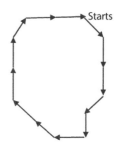

Chain code: (Starts) 3 4 4 5 4 6 7 7 0 0 1 2 2

First difference: 7 0 7 1 6 7 0 7 0 6 6 0

If the start point changes the code is different, we need "starting point invariance." This is obtained by considering a code to represent the digits, such as integers. We can shift the digits cyclically. The least integer is returned as the initial point or start point invariant code descriptor. In addition to this, we can have a rotation-independent code. This is accomplished by expressing code as difference of the code, because relative descriptor will totally remove rotation dependency. Scale invariance is a bit tricky since the points change, and hence, boundary needs to be resampled.

Shape numbers are the first difference of a boundary code that is used to identify an object. The number of digits in the shape number is described as "order n." The first difference is treated in a circular fashion independent of rotation; the coded value that defines the boundary depends on its orientation.

Noise can drastically change the edges as seen after edge detector for boundary identification. Say if salt and pepper noise is added, then some extra points would change the code. Noise filtering can be done using Fourier transformation with an advantage of returning a global descriptor. Even region descriptors are an alternate solution. Modern-day corner detectors have an advantage. They decompose the intensity using principal component analysis (PCA) to detect the corners uniquely.

4.3   Polygonal Approximation

Chain codes are time-consuming with multistep processing. In certain cases, having boundary descriptor is sufficient. Linear piecewise approximations are frequently used, which resemble the perimeter of a polygon. A closed curve, with the number of segments of the polygon if is equal to the number of points along the boundary such that they are continuous, accounts to polygonal approximation. As seen in Figure 4.2, parsing is done considering the cells around the boundary is enclosed within a wall. This technique is called the "minimum perimeter polygons."

Let $a(x_1,y_1)$, $b(x_2,y_2)$, $c(x_3,y_3)$ be three points,

$$X = \begin{bmatrix} x_1 & y_1 & 1 \\ x_2 & y_2 & 1 \\ x_3 & y_3 & 1 \end{bmatrix}$$

$$\text{sgn}(a,b,c) = \det(X)$$

$$= \begin{cases} >0 & \text{if } (a,b,c) \text{ are in counterclockwise direction} \\ =0 & \text{if } (a,b,c) \text{ are collinear} \\ <0 & \text{if } (a,b,c) \text{ are in clockwise direction} \end{cases}$$

Definition: Form a list with vertex being W(White) or B(Black). The concave vertices must be in sequential order, and the leftmost, upper vertex V_0 is a W. There are two crawlers, W_c and B_c. W_c crawls along the convex vertices and B_c crawls along the mirrored concave B vertices.

Algorithm: V_0 is the initial vertex, V_K is the current and V_L is the last vertex

1. Set $W_c = B_c = V_0$
2. $\text{sgn}(V_L, W_c, V_K) > 0$, lies to the positive side of line through V_L, W_c

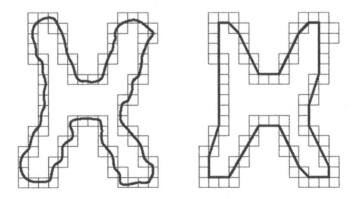

Figure 4.2 Minimum perimeter polygon approximation.

3. $sgn(V_L,W_c,V_K) \le 0$ and $sgn(V_L,B_c,V_K) \ge 0$
   V_K is next vertex to be examined, if V_K is convex then
   $Wc = V_K$
   Else $Bc = V_K$
4. $sgn(V_L,W_c,V_K) \le 0$ and $sgn(V_L,B_c,V_K) < 0$
   B_c is the next vertex to be examined, $V_L = B_c$
5. $W_c = B_c = V_L$
6. Continue until the first vertex is reached.

Merging Algorithm:

This approach is to merge points along the boundary unless it fits the least-square error line and until an error threshold is greater than other lines. At the "Start," we consider the lines, namely, Line-1 and Line-2. Each line has segments (e_1, e_2) and (e_3, e_4, e_5), respectively. Let, $e_1 + e_2 < T$ and $e_3 + e_4 + e_5 > T$, choose Line-1 since it is lesser than the second-line threshold value. This line connects, such that adjacent nodes are formed as vertices.

The merging condition is the preset threshold value that is compared for each line on the basis of the segment length.

Splitting algorithm: Here, the line is divided into segments again until the criterion is fulfilled. Say the line shown has four segments that are orthogonal, e_1, e_2, e_3 and e_4, respectively, from the start node.

$e_1 < T$ $e_2 > T$ $e_3 < T$ and $e_4 < T$, if maximum distance is greater than threshold choose it as the next vertex. Continue with similar segmentation until the final vertex is met.

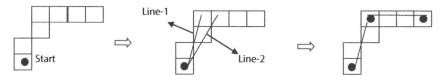

Figure 4.3 Adjacent pixel for selection of the vertex forming the boundary.

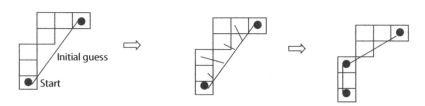

Figure 4.4 Selection of adjacent vertex based on segmentation.

4.4   Moments

Digital images contain vast amount of data. Analysis and interpretation of an image acquired by imaging system, such as robotic vision, medicine, and so on, have issues that worsen the quality of image. Generally, $f(x, y)$ is the ideal image, and $g(x, y)$ is the observed image, then we have $g=D(f)$, where D is the degradation ratio. The real imaging system can be modeled by space invariance convolution and noise that are used to transform the spatial coordinates.

In recent years, recognition of objects that are deformed is gaining momentum. There are three main approaches, namely, brute-force, image normalization, and invariant features. In the first method, a search into the parametric space of all possible image degradation, that is, image is scaled, blurred, and deformed version. In the second, it is an ill-posed problem because it is a difficult inverse problem. Third approach is extensively used to describe objects using a set of measurable quantities called invariants that are not sensitive to deformations. Normally, one invariant does not have enough discrimination power, and many invariants $I_1, I_2....I_n$ are used simultaneously. Each object is, thus, represented in an N-dimensional metric space called feature space.

Categorizes based on mathematical tool are:

1. Shape descriptors
2. Transform coefficient features
3. Differential invariants
4. Moment invariants

Moment: Moments describe area or region by regional shape descriptors. It is a scalar measure based on geometric properties. Area or region in an affine plane is defined as

$$A(S) = \int \int I(x,y)dxdy \tag{1}$$

Alternatively,

$$A(S) = \sum_x \sum_y I(x,y)\Delta A \tag{2}$$

With $I(x,y) = \begin{cases} 1, & \text{for pixel within the shape} \\ 0, & \text{otherwise} \end{cases}$

Perimeter of a curve closing in say S, is given in the parametric x(t), y(t) coordinates

$$P(S) = \int \sqrt{x^2(t) + y^2(t)} \tag{3}$$

Discrete region has a perimeter as

$$A(S) = \sum_i \sqrt{(x_i - x_{i-1})^2 + (y_i - y_{i-1})^2} \tag{4}$$

Compactness is the ratio of the area and perimeter, expressed as

$$C(S) = \frac{4\pi A(S)}{P^2(S)} \tag{5}$$

The enclosed area that is the boundary measures the efficiency within the region.

Moment properties:
Moments are used to statistically recognize patterns with model-based vision. Some complex applications are occlusion could assume features to be extracted by means of in-fill for missing parts. Moments are global descriptors that are used to describe shapes.

Two-dimensional Cartesian moments of order p, q m_{pq} for pixel $I(x, y)$ is given in the form

$$m_{pq} = \int_{-\infty}^{\infty}\int_{-\infty}^{\infty} x^p y^q I(x,y)\, dx\, dy \tag{6}$$

For digital images moments are,

$$m_{pq} = \sum_x \sum_y x^p y^q I(x,y)$$

The zero-order moments are shown below,

$$m_{00} = \sum_x \sum_y I(x,y)\,\Delta A$$

Where, ΔA is the area of a pixel. The first-order moments are given as seen in equation (7) and (8),

$$m_{10} = \sum_x \sum_y x I(x,y)\,\Delta A \tag{7}$$

$$m_{01} = \sum_x \sum_y y I(x,y)\,\Delta A \tag{8}$$

Generally, the center of mass $(\bar{x},\bar{y})$ is calculated from the ratio first and zero order moments,

$$\bar{x} = \frac{m_{10}}{m_{00}} \quad and \quad \bar{y} = \frac{m_{01}}{m_{00}}$$

If we look at the transformation of scales, such as brightness with m_{pq} moments, then m'_{pq} is the transformed moments, we have the relation

$$m'_{pq} = \alpha m_{pq}$$

α is the factor by which the transformation is accomplished. We are looking at some invariants, such as position, rotation, and size. With the center known, the centralized moments that is invariant is defined as:

$$\mu_{pq} = \sum_x \sum_y (x-\bar{x})^p (y-\bar{y})^q I(x,y)\Delta A \tag{9}$$

The first-order centralized moment is given as:

$$\mu_{01} = \sum_x \sum_y (y - \bar{y})^1 I(x, y) \Delta A$$
$$\mu_{01} = \sum_x \sum_y y I(x, y) \Delta A - \sum_x \sum_y \bar{y} I(x, y) \Delta A$$
$$\mu_{01} = m_{01} - \bar{y} \sum_x \sum_y I(x, y) \Delta A$$

(10)

From, $\bar{y} = \dfrac{m_{01}}{m_{00}}$, we get

$$\mu_{01} = m_{01} - \frac{m_{01}}{m_{00}} * m_{00} = 0$$

$$\mu_{01} = \mu_{10} = 0$$

(11)

Second-order moments,

$$\mu_{20} = \sum_x \sum_y (x - \bar{x})^2 I(x, y) \Delta A$$

(12)

$$\mu_{20} = \sum_x \sum_y \left(x^2 - 2x\bar{x} + \bar{x}^2\right) I(x, y) \Delta A$$

Splitting each term and substituting $\bar{x}$ is written as:

$$\mu_{02} = m_{20} - 2 \frac{m_{10}}{m_{00}} m_{10} + \left(\frac{m_{10}}{m_{00}}\right)^2 m_{00}$$

$$\mu_{02} = m_{20} - \frac{m_{10}^2}{m_{00}}$$

(13)

It can be seen from equation (11), which is a nondescriptive form, whereas equation (13) has a descriptive capability.

4.5 HU Invariant Moments

It is shown that centralized moments are translational invariant only. To augment invariance for rotation and scale, we need to normalize the central moments and that is defined as:

$$\eta_{pq} = \frac{\mu_{pq}}{\mu_{00}^{\gamma}} \qquad (14)$$

$$\gamma = \frac{p+q}{2} + 1 \quad \forall \ p+q \geq 2$$

Seven invariants moments or called as Hu's moments are listed below

$$M1 = \eta_{20} + \eta_{02}$$
$$M2 = \left(\eta_{20} - \eta_{02}\right)^2 + 4\eta_{11}^2$$
$$M3 = \left(\eta_{30} - 3\eta_{21}\right)^2 + \left(3\eta_{21} - \eta_{03}\right)^2$$
$$M4 = \left(\eta_{30} + \eta_{12}\right)^2 + \left(\eta_{21} + \eta_{03}\right)^2$$
$$M5 = \left(\eta_{30} - 3\eta_{21}\right)\left(\eta_{30} + \eta_{21}\right) + \left((\eta_{30} + \eta_{12})^2 - 3(\eta_{21} + \eta_{03})^2\right)$$
$$\qquad + (3\eta_{21} - \eta_{03})\,(\eta_{21} + \eta_{03})\,(3\left(\eta_{30} + \eta_{12}\right)^2 - \left(\eta_{21} + \eta_{03}\right)^2)$$
$$M6 = (\eta_{20} - \eta_{02})\left(\left(\eta_{30} + \eta_{12}\right)^2 - \left(\eta_{21} + \eta_{03}\right)^2\right)$$
$$\qquad + 4\eta_{11}\left(\eta_{30} + \eta_{12}\right)\left(\eta_{21} + \eta_{03}\right)$$
$$M7 = \left(3\eta_{21} - \eta_{03}\right)\left(\eta_{30} + \eta_{12}\right)\left(\left(\eta_{30} + \eta_{12}\right)^2 - 3\left(\eta_{21} + \eta_{03}\right)^2\right)$$
$$\qquad + \left(3\eta_{12} - \eta_{30}\right)\left(\eta_{21} + \eta_{03}\right)(3\left(\left(\eta_{12} + \eta_{30}\right)^2 - \left(\eta_{21} + \eta_{03}\right)^2\right))$$

$$(15)$$

4.6   Zernike Moments

Zernike moment gives rotation-invariant moment that is obtained by using polar representation for centralized moments.

$$
Z_{pq} = \frac{p+1}{\pi} \int_{0}^{2\pi} \int_{0}^{\infty} V_{pq}{}^* \left(r,\theta\right) f\left(r,\theta\right) r \, dr \, d\theta \tag{16}
$$

p is the magnitude, and q is the radial direction, and '*' denotes the complex conjugate of the Zernike polynomial V_{pq}
$V_{pq}(r, \theta) = R_{pq}(r)e^{iq\theta}$ where R_{pq} is real-valued polynomial and $0 \leq q \leq |p|$

$$
R_{pq} = \sum_{m=0}^{\frac{p-|q|}{2}} (-1)^m \frac{(p-m)!}{m!\left(\dfrac{p+|q|}{2}-m\right)!\left(\dfrac{p-|q|}{2}-m\right)!} r^{p-2m} \tag{17}
$$

The polynomials of lower degree are given as below:

$R_{00}(r) = 1$
$R_{11}(r) = r$
$R_{22}(r) = r^2$
$R_{20}(r) = r^2 - 1$
$R_{31}(r) = 3r^2 - 2r$

If we plot these polynomials, we find that they are orthogonal within the unit circle so the shapes within the area of interest have to be remapped.
Advantages of Zernike moments:

1. They are rotational invariant.
2. They are orthogonal and hence less redundancy.
3. Accurate with detailed shapes.
4. They are useful for image reconstruction, and the number of moments improves the accuracy during reconstruction.
5. Sharper shapes can be used in classification.

4.7   Fourier Descriptors

Fourier descriptors are frequency analysis carried out by choosing a small set of Fourier coefficients that describe the shape. Fourier description of a curve has two steps: first, definition of the curve and second is expanding using Fourier transform. A Fourier description of given image gets a set of spatial frequencies that fit the boundaries. The first dc component is average value of coordinates, second gives the radius of circle that fits the points and higher-order components describe the details associated with higher frequencies.

Let c (t) be a continuous curve given as: $c(t) = \sum_k c_k f_k(t)$

where c_k is coefficient of expansion and $f_k(t)$ defines the basis functions.

Fourier expansion can be written as: $c(t) = \sum_k c_k e^{i\omega k t}, \omega = \dfrac{T}{2\pi}$ where T is the period.

It defines the orthogonal basis of a function that is $\displaystyle\int_0^T f_k(t) f_j(t) dt = 0$

$$\therefore c_k = \int_0^T c(t) e^{-ik\omega t}$$

Rewriting in the trigonometric form,

$$c(t) = c_0 + \sum_{k=1}^{\infty} c_k e^{ik\omega t} + c_{-k} e^{-ik\omega t}$$

$e^{ik\omega t}$ and $e^{-ik\omega t}$ are complex conjugate vectors with c_k and c_{-k} complex numbers written as

$$c_k = c_{k,1} - ic_{k,2} \text{ and } c_{-k} = c_{k,1} + ic_{k,2}$$

Substituting in the c (t) equation and simplifying, we get

$$c(t) = c_0 + 2 \sum_{k=1}^{\infty} \left(c_{k,1} \cos(k\omega t) + c_{k,2} \sin(k\omega t) \right)$$

Defining: $ak = 2c_{k,1}$ and $bk = c_{k,2}$

$$\therefore c(t) = \frac{a_0}{2} + \sum_{k=1}^{\infty}\left(a_k \cos(k\omega t) + b_k \sin(k\omega t)\right) \qquad (18)$$

a_k and b_k are the Fourier descriptors that control the frequency and add up to the curve definition. Considering the orthogonal property, the descriptors can be rewritten as:

$$a_k = \frac{2}{T}\int_0^T c(t)\cos(k\omega t)dt$$

$$b_k = \frac{2}{T}\int_0^T c(t)\sin(k\omega t)dt$$

Fourier descriptors are not insensitive to geometrical changes. Changes in these constraints can be seen in the transformation. For example, rotation of a point in the complex plane by an angle θ is indicated as $e^{i\theta}$, repeating this transformation for every point along the curve results in Fourier descriptor that affects all the points equally by multiplying with a constant. Hence, rotation implies a multiplication by a constant term.

Invariant descriptors are complex form of coefficients. The advantage of these descriptors is that they do not have negative frequencies that are more prone to noise.

4.8   Quadtree

Quadtree is a region descriptor that is a data structure used to decompose in a regular fashion. Depending on the data that is decomposed, a variety of quadtree flavors are available. In our context, we use lines, curves, regions, and volumes. In this chapter, we discuss quadtree as a two-dimensional binary image region.

Consider a region as shown below that illustrates a region of interest. 0s indicate pixels outside the region, whereas 1s represent the pixel within.

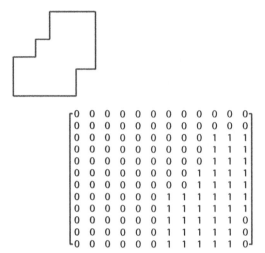

$$\begin{bmatrix}
0 & 0 & 0 & 0 & 0 & 0 & 0 & 0 & 0 & 0 & 0 & 0 \\
0 & 0 & 0 & 0 & 0 & 0 & 0 & 0 & 0 & 0 & 0 & 0 \\
0 & 0 & 0 & 0 & 0 & 0 & 0 & 0 & 0 & 1 & 1 & 1 \\
0 & 0 & 0 & 0 & 0 & 0 & 0 & 0 & 0 & 1 & 1 & 1 \\
0 & 0 & 0 & 0 & 0 & 0 & 0 & 0 & 0 & 1 & 1 & 1 \\
0 & 0 & 0 & 0 & 0 & 0 & 0 & 0 & 1 & 1 & 1 & 1 \\
0 & 0 & 0 & 0 & 0 & 0 & 0 & 0 & 1 & 1 & 1 & 1 \\
0 & 0 & 0 & 0 & 0 & 0 & 1 & 1 & 1 & 1 & 1 & 1 \\
0 & 0 & 0 & 0 & 0 & 0 & 1 & 1 & 1 & 1 & 1 & 1 \\
0 & 0 & 0 & 0 & 0 & 0 & 1 & 1 & 1 & 1 & 1 & 0 \\
0 & 0 & 0 & 0 & 0 & 0 & 1 & 1 & 1 & 1 & 1 & 0 \\
0 & 0 & 0 & 0 & 0 & 0 & 1 & 1 & 1 & 1 & 1 & 0
\end{bmatrix}$$

Quadtree is subdivided successively into four quadrants, namely, northwest, northeast, southwest, and southeast as shown in Figure 4.5(a). These are further divided into subquadrants and so on, until we obtain all 1s or 0s that is entirely disjoint from one another. The process is shown in Figure 4.5(b) as a tree with a root and four-leaf nodes. Leaf nodes are either WHITE or BLACK to indicate that the block is within or outside the region of interest. All other nodes can be collectively called as GRAY.

The common operation using quadtree is tree traversal, this involves examining the node adjacent to each other. The nodes represent the edges or pixels that are touching each other. To perform the operations as generic as possible, the location of nodes must be done independently that is irrespective of node size. It is simple to locate neighbors in the vertical or horizontal direction. In this case, the tree has to be either ascended or descended while searching for neighbors.

Quadtree is a very useful representation of binary images. It can be compared with binary trees, and hence, the complexity is similar. The simplest way of representation of the data structure is to use arrays. By using arrays, segregation and merging are simple to use and traverse. Region representation as collection of maximal blocks in a given area is a common way of decomposing an image. Each region is determined by using metrics, such as centers and radii of the blocks. Representation, such as triangles or hexagonal tessellation, can also be done.

Set of operations: Most important application of quadtree involves its support for operations, such as union and intersection. The union of two leaf nodes is identified and merged resulting in a union operation, one node is WHITE and other is GRAY then union results in GRAY. Such operations

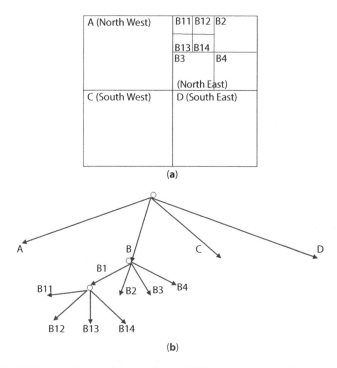

Figure 4.5 (a) Four quadrants of the quadtree. (b) The tree structure of the quadtree, based on quadrant as shown by their direction.

are used when merging of leaf nodes or splitting them for analysis. Other transformations, like scaling, are easy to process, whereas rotation and translation do not preserve the geometrical properties of the image.

Geometric properties: Computing of area and moments is easy with quadtree. To find the area we need to traverse the quadtree in postorder and sum up the peripheral BLACK blocks. For a level k, area is 2^{2k}. Another common property is "connected components" of a graph. This is a two-step process, first scan row by row assign label to BLACK pixels that are adjacent as you travel in one direction. As you traverse if you come across equivalence, merge the equivalent and relabel accordingly. The execution time and space consideration is $\Theta(B*\log B)$, where B is the number of BLACK nodes of the quadtree. This shows that the dependency on the number of BLACK blocks rather than the size of the blocks. Moments can be easily computed from the nodes that are BLACK. The centroid, area, and shape of the object can be easily identified using moments. Perimeter computation is done using quadtree like the label components we need to look for adjacent WHITE blocks. For each WHITE block found, the length of the side is added.

ALGORITHM:

1. Take M × N image and crop it to $2^k * 2^k$
2. Decompose the image using a fixed threshold
3. Divide the image into four quadrants
4. Iteratively divide into $2^m * 2^m$, where $m \leq k$
5. Store the nodes in the form of array
6. Inspect the blocks for connected components or any other operations

4.9   Conclusion

In this chapter, we discuss the object identifier technique using a few descriptors. We have seen that there are two characteristics that are used to identify objects mainly using pixels. The pixel boundary of the object is used to define shape and properties that are listed as area, color, and so on. Based on shape and region, we define the pixels that are important around and/or within a given region of interest. The commonly used Chain codes, polygonal approximation and its variants are used to define the boundary and shape of objects, whereas moments and QT are region descriptors. When compared with boundary descriptors, region descriptors provide more information, such as texture details and other statistical features. The order of moments describes the shape and certain characteristics of the region be it statistical or image properties. The Zernike moments are rotational invariant, whereas Fourier descriptors filters noise and provides certain features that are useful about the region of interest. All of the models are implementable in a given programming language, such as OpenCV or Python.

CODE: A. Moment Calculation
Input: Binary image

Output : First-order to third-order moments

```
function [Center,All]=IM_Moments(Blk)

I22=Blk;
[R1,C1]=size(I22);
I22(R1,:)=0;
```

```
I22(:,C1)=0;
I=find(I22);
[j,i]=ind2sub(size(I22),I);
momNT=@(p,q) sum((i.^p).*(j.^q).*double(I22(I)))  ;

m00=momNT(0,0);
m01=momNT(0,1);
m10=momNT(1,0);
m02=momNT(0,2);
m11=momNT(1,1);
m20=momNT(2,0);
m03=momNT(0,3);
m30=momNT(3,0);
xx=floor(m10/m00);
yy=floor(m01/m00);

Center=[xx,yy];
All=[m00,m01,m10,m11,m02,m20,m03,m30];
End
```

B. Hu's Invaraints
Input: 4x4 matrix

Output: Invariant moments

```
function INmoments = Hu_Moments(et)
INmoments(1) = et(3,1) + et(1,3);
INmoments(2) = (et(3,1) - et(1,3))^2 + (4*et(2,2)^2);
INmoments(3) = (et(4,1) - 3*et(2,3))^2 + (3*et(3,2)
- et(1,4))^2;
INmoments(4) = (et(4,1) + et(2,3))^2 + (et(3,1) +
et(1,4))^2;
INmoments(5) = (et(4,1) - 3*et(2,3))*(et(4,1) +
et(2,3))*((et(4,1) + et(2,3))^2 - 3*((et(3,2) +
et(1,4))^2)) + (3*(et(3,2) - et(1,4)))*(et(3,2) +
et(1,4))*(3*(et(4,1) + et(2,3))^2 - (et(3,2) +
et(1,4))^2);
INmoments(6) = (et(3,1) - et(1,3))*((et(4,1)+et(2,3))^2-
(et(3,2)+ et(1,4))^2) + 4*et(2,2)*((et(4,1) + et(2,3))*
(et(3,2) + et(1,4)));
```

```
INmoments(7) = (3*et(3,2) - et(1,4))*(et(4,1) + et(2,3))*
((et(4,1) + et(2,3))^2 - 3*(et(3,2)-
et(1,4))^2) - (et(4,1) - 3*et(2,3))*
(et(3,2) + et(1,4))*(3*(et(4,1) + et(2,3))^2 -
(et(3,2) + et(1,4))^2);
end
```

C. Quadtree decomposition
Input: Image of size 256 x256

Output: Decomposed blocks of the quadtree

FN= <name of the image file>

```
Img=imread(FN);
I2=rgb2gray(Img);
thres=0.09;

Node=InitSplit(I2);        %%level-1
[Ro,Co]=size(I2);
Ro_Lvl= log2(Ro);
Co_Lvl = log2(Co);

[Lvl2,Lvl3,Lvl4,Lvl5]=SubSplit2(Node,Ro_Lvl-2);
%%Higher level >=2
DC1=QTdecomp(Lvl3,thres);
[Blk]=Lvl3Disp(DC1);

figure(1), imshow(Blk,[]),hold on

function [Node]=InitSplit(Img)
 Node=struct('RtDir',{},'Level',{},'Dir',{},'Xoff',{},
 'Yoff',{},'Data',{}) ;
 [Ro,Co]=size(Img);
Mx=Ro/2 ;  My=Co/2;
Node(1).RtDir=0;
Node(1).Level=1;
Node(1).Data=Img(1:Mx,1:My);   % P1=AA(1:midx,1:midy);
Node(1).Xoff={[1,Mx]};
Node(1).Yoff={[1,My]};
```

```
Node(1).Dir=1;        %% 'NW'
Node(2).RtDir=0;
Node(2).Level=1;
Node(2).Data=Img(1:Mx,My+1:Co);  %
P2=AA(1:midx,midy+1:Co);
Node(2).Xoff={[1,Mx]};
Node(2).Yoff={[My+1,Co]};
Node(2).Dir=2;        %%'NE'
Node(3).RtDir=0;
Node(3).Level=1;
Node(3).Data=Img(Mx+1:Ro,1:My);  %
P3=AA(midx+1:Ro,1:midy);
Node(3).Xoff={[Mx+1,Ro]};
Node(3).Yoff={[1,My]};
Node(3).Dir=3;        %%%'SW'
Node(4).RtDir=0;
Node(4).Level=1;
Node(4).Data=Img(Mx+1:Ro,My+1:Co);
%P4=AA(midx+1:Ro,midy+1:Co);
Node(4).Xoff={[Mx+1,Ro]};
Node(4).Yoff={[My+1,Co]};
Node(4).Dir=4;          %%%'SE'
end

 function [Sub1,Sub2,Sub3,Sub4]=SubSplit(Nodes,TTl)
Init=2;
Cnt=1;
while(Cnt~=TTl)
    switch (Init)
        case 2
   S1=Split(Nodes(1),Nodes(1).Dir);
   S2=Split(Nodes(2),Nodes(2).Dir);
   S3=Split(Nodes(3),Nodes(3).Dir);
   S4=Split(Nodes(4),Nodes(4).Dir);
Sub1=vertcat(S1,S2,S3,S4);
case 3
    for i=1:4
         S11(i,:)=Split(S1(i),S1(i).Dir);
         S22(i,:)=Split(S2(i),S2(i).Dir);
         S33(i,:)=Split(S3(i),S3(i).Dir);
```

```
            S44(i,:)=Split(S4(i),S4(i).Dir);

        end
    Sub2=vertcat(S11,S22,S33,S44);
        case 4
            for i=1:4
                for j=1:4
                    SN1(i,j,:)=Split(S11(i,j),S11(i,j).
                    Dir);
                      SN2(i,j,:)=Split(S22(i,j),S22(i,j).
                      Dir);
                        SN3(i,j,:)=Split(S33(i,j),S33(i,j).
                        Dir);
                          SN4(i,j,:)=Split(S44(i,j),
                          S44(i,j).Dir);
                end
            end
Sub3=vertcat(SN1,SN2,SN3,SN4);
        %case 5
        otherwise
            for i=1:4
                for j=1:4
                    for k=1:4

                        SN11(i,j,k,:)=Split(SN1(i,j,k),
                        SN1(i,j,k).Dir);
                        SN22(i,j,k,:)=Split(SN2(i,j,k),
                        SN2(i,j,k).Dir);
                          SN33(i,j,k,:)=Split(SN3(i,j,k),
                          SN3(i,j,k).Dir);
                            SN44(i,j,k,:)=Split(SN4(i,j,k),
                            SN4(i,j,k).Dir);

                    end
                end
            end
            Sub4=vertcat(SN11,SN22,SN33,SN44);
    end

    Init=Init+1;
    Cnt=Cnt+1;
```

```
   end
  end

function [SubNd]=Split(TNode,flag)
Dt=TNode(1).Data;
[Ro,Co]=size(Dt);
Sx1=Ro/2 ;  Sy1=Co/2;

SubN(1).RtDir=flag;
SubN(1).Level=TNode(1).Level+1;
SubN(1).Dir=1;     %% 'NW'
SubN(1).Data=Dt(1:Sx1,1:Sy1);  % P1=AA(1:midx,1:midy);
SubN(1).Xoff={[1,Sx1]};
SubN(1).Yoff={[1,Sy1]};

SubN(2).RtDir=flag;
SubN(2).Level=TNode(1).Level+1;
SubN(2).Dir=2;     %% 'NE'
SubN(2).Data=Dt(1:Sx1,Sy1+1:Co);  %
P2=AA(1:midx,midy+1:Co);
SubN(2).Xoff={[1,Sx1]};
SubN(2).Yoff={[1,Sy1+1]};

SubN(3).RtDir=flag;
SubN(3).Level=TNode(1).Level+1;
SubN(3).Dir=3;     %% 'SW'
SubN(3).Data=Dt(Sx1+1:Ro,1:Sy1);  %
P3=AA(midx+1:Ro,1:midy);
SubN(3).Xoff={[1,Sx1+1]};
SubN(3).Yoff={[1,Sy1]};

SubN(4).RtDir=flag;
SubN(4).Level=TNode(1).Level+1;
SubN(4).Dir=4;     %% 'SE'
SubN(4).Data=Dt(Sx1+1:Ro,Sy1+1:Co);  %
P4=AA(midx+1:Ro,midy+1:Co);
SubN(4).Xoff={[1,Sx1+1]};
SubN(4).Yoff={[1,Sy1+1]};
SubNd=SubN;
end
```

```
function [XCord,YCord,Center,Combo]=Lvl3Disp(DC1)
%%%%%%%%%%%%%%%%%%%for 2D 16x4   %%%%%%%%%%%%%%%%%%%%%%%%%
%%%%%%%%%%%%%%%%%%%%%%%%%

Dt1=DC1;
[p,q]=size(Dt1);
for i=1:p
    %%%%%%%%%%%%%%%%%%%%%%Combining the quadrants
%%%%%%%%%%%%%%%%%%%%%%%%%%%%%%%
   XX1(i)=Comb1(Dt1(i,:));
 end

[p,q]=size(XX1);

i=1; j=1;
while(i <=16)
      ZZ1(j)=Comb2(XX1(i:i+3),j);

   i=i+4;
   j=j+1;
end

%%%%%%%%%%Function for combining %%%%%%%%%%%%%%%%%%%%%%%
%%%%%%%%%%%%%

function [FComb]=Comb1(P1)
 C1=horzcat(P1(1).Data,P1(2).Data);
  C2=horzcat(P1(3).Data,P1(4).Data);

FComb.RtDir=P1(1).RtDir;
FComb.Level=P1(1).Level-1;
FComb.Data=vertcat(C1,C2);
end

function [FComb]=Comb2(P1,Dir)
 C1=horzcat(P1(1).Data,P1(2).Data);
  C2=horzcat(P1(3).Data,P1(4).Data);

FComb.RtDir=Dir;
FComb.Level=P1(1).Level-1;
```

```
FComb.Data=vertcat(C1,C2);
end

function [FComb]=FinComb(P1)
 C1=horzcat(P1(1).Data,P1(2).Data);
  C2=horzcat(P1(3).Data,P1(4).Data);

FComb.Level=P1(1).Level-1;
FComb.Data=vertcat(C1,C2);
end

function [DeCo]=QTdecomp(N1,thres)
[xx,yy]=size(N1);
tmp=N1(xx,yy);
Lvl=tmp.Level;
switch(Lvl)
        case 2
          DeCo=LvlSplit2(N1,thres);
      otherwise
          DeCo=LvlSplit3(N1,thres);

end

end

function [DeC]=LvlSplit3(N1,thres)
[p,q]=size(N1);
for i= 1:p
    for j=1:q

    DeCo1(i,j)=Decompose(N1(i,j),thres);
end
end
DeC=DeCo1;

end

function [DeC]=LvlSplit2(N1,thres)
[p,q]=size(N1);
for i= 1:p
```

```
    for j=1:q

      DeCo1(i,j)=Decompose(N1(i,j),thres);
    end
end
DeC=DeCo1;

end

function [DeCNd]=Decompose(Node,thres)
Dt=Node.Data;
S = qtdecomp(Dt,thres);
blocks = repmat(uint8(0),size(S));

for dim =[16 8 4 2 1];
 numblocks = length(find(S==dim));
if (numblocks > 0)
  values = repmat(uint8(1),[dim dim numblocks]);
  values(2:dim,2:dim,:) = 0;
  blocks = qtsetblk(blocks,S,dim,values);
end
end
blocks(end,1:end) = 1;
blocks(1:end,end) = 1;

DeCNd(1).RtDir=Node.RtDir;
DeCNd(1).Level=Node.Level;
DeCNd(1).Dir=Node.Dir;
DeCNd(1).Data=blocks;
DeCNd(1).Xoff=Node.Xoff;
DeCNd(1).Yoff=Node.Yoff;
DeCNd(1).sparse=S;
end
```

Output :

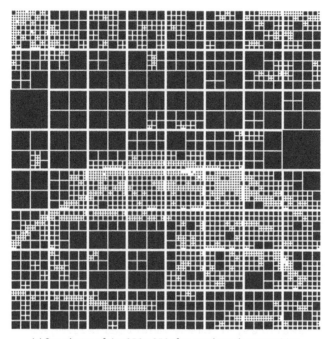

(a) Sample eye of size 256 × 256 after quadtree decomposition

D. Moment based region descriptor after decomposing using quadtree

Input: Image of size 512 x 512
Output : as shown in figure –
FN-<Input file name>

```
Img=imread(FN);
I2=rgb2gray(Img);
thres=0.2;
Node=InitSplit(I2);        %%level-1
[Ro,Co]=size(I2);
Ro_Lvl= log2(Ro);
Co_Lvl = log2(Co);

[Lvl2,Lvl3,Lvl4,Lvl5]=SubSplit2(Node,Ro_Lvl-2);
%%Higher level >=2
DC1=QTdecomp(Lvl3,thres);
Bound=550;
```

```
[MBlk,OCnt]=CntAndComb(DC1,Bound);
[C2Blk]=Lvl3Disp(MBlk);


[EyRt,EyLt,ERtAddr,ELtAddr,IBlk]=SelectBloc(OCnt,MBlk);
[CEyRt,AllEyRt]=IM_Moments(EyRt);
[CEyLt,AllEyLt]=IM_Moments(EyLt);
Rt=1;Lt=2;
[Center,EFeatRt,MiscRt]=GeometryCal
(AllEyRt,ERtAddr,Rt);
[Center2,EFeatLt,MiscLt]=GeometryCal
(AllEyLt,ELtAddr,Lt);
figure(2), imshow(I2) , hold on
plot(Center(1),Center(2),'r*');
plot(EFeatRt(:,1),EFeatRt(:,2),'m*');
plot(Center2(1),Center2(2),'c*');
plot(EFeatLt(:,1),EFeatLt(:,2),'g*');
plot(AvgPt(1),AvgPt(2),'b*');
plot(NuCent(:,:,1),NuCent(:,:,2),'k*');
hold off


function
[Center,EFeatures,Misc]=GeometryCal(AllMm,Addr,flag)
m00=AllMm(1);
m01=AllMm(2);
m10=AllMm(3);
m11=AllMm(4);
m02=AllMm(5);
m20=AllMm(6);
m03=AllMm(7);
m30=AllMm(8);


xx=floor(m10/m00);
yy=floor(m01/m00);


Mu20=(m20/m00) -xx^2;
Mu02=(m02/m00) -yy^2;
Mu11=(m11/m00)-xx*yy;


RoGx=(m20/m00)^0.5 ;
RoGy=(m02/m00)^0.5 ;
RoG=((Mu20+Mu02)/m00) ^0.5;
```

```
Mu30=(m30/m00) -xx^3;
Mu03=(m03/m00) -yy^3;
Skx= Mu30/(Mu20^1.5);
Sky= Mu03/(Mu02^1.5);

alpha=floor(abs((0.5*(Mu20+Mu02+((4*Mu11^2)-(Mu20
-Mu02)^2)^0.5))^0.5));
beta=floor(abs((0.5*(Mu20+Mu02-((4*Mu11^2)-
(Mu20-Mu02)^2)^0.5))^0.5)) ;

Foci=((alpha ^2 -beta ^2)^0.5) ;
c=Foci/2;
theta=0.5*atan(beta/(alpha-c)) +(alpha<c)*pi/2;

%%%%%%%%%%%%%%%%%%%%%%%%%%%%%%%%%%%%%%%%%%%%%%%%%%%%
%%%%
if(flag==1)
h=floor(m10/m00)+24;
k=floor(m01/m00)+24;
else
h=floor(m10/m00)-24;
k=floor(m01/m00)+24;
end
if(flag==0)
   Center(1)=Addr(1)+h;
Center(2)=Addr(2)+k;
else
Center(1)=Addr(1,1)+h;
Center(2)=Addr(2,1)+k;
end
step=16;
Tau=linspace(0,360,step)'.*(pi/180);
r1=(7/4)*alpha;
r2=beta;
xcc = Center(1)+r1*cos(Tau) ;
ycc = Center(2)+r2*sin(Tau) ;

RoG=[RoG RoGx RoGy]; Skew=[Skx Sky];
EFeatures=[xcc ycc];
Misc=[alpha beta theta RoG Skew];
end
```

Output:

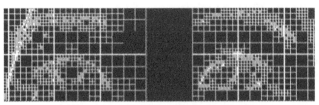

(a) Decomposed based on the threshold value

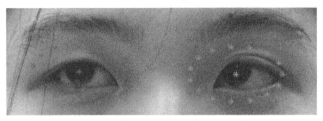

(b) Moment based boundary identification of the eyes

References

1. Nixon, M. and Aguado, A., *Feature extraction and Image processing*, Second edition, Academic Press is an imprint of Elsevier, Linacre House, Jordan Hill, Oxford OX2 8DP, UK, 2008.
2. Gonzalez, R.C. and Woods, R.E., *Digital Image Processing*, Second edition, Prentice Hall, Upper Saddle River, New Jersey 07458, 1992.
3. Seychell, D. and Debono, C.J., Efficient object selection using depth and texture information, in: *2016 Visual Communications and Image Processing (VCIP)*, IEEE Chengdu, China, pp. 1–4, 2016.
4. Smith, B.A., Yin, Q., Feiner, S.K., Nayar, S.K., Gaze locking: passive eye contact detection for human? Object Interaction, ACM Symposium on User Interface Software and Technology (UIST), pp. 271-280, 2013. http://www.cs.columbia.edu/CAVE/databases/columbia_gaze/
5. Vishnu Muralidharan (2020). Hu's Invariant Moments (https://www.mathworks.com/matlabcentral/fileexchange/52259-hu-s-invariant-moments), MATLAB Central File Exchange. Retrieved March 24, 2020.
6. https://www.mathworks.com/products/matlab.html
7. Samet, H., The quadtree and related Hierarchical data structures. *Comput. Surv.*, 16, 2, 187–260, 1984.

Flood Disaster Management: Risks, Technologies, and Future Directions

Hafiz Suliman Munawar

University of New South Wales (UNSW), Sydney, Australia

Abstract

Flood control and disaster management deal with reduction or prevention of devastating effects caused by floodwater. The overall aim of this research is to develop an understanding about the flood risks on a global scale, explore the existing systems for managing the risks and devise a flood management model to overcome the gaps existing in the current technology. Floods as a disaster will be viewed in detail along with an analysis of the threats to community and economy. The identification of a problem domain and working towards a true solution for managing the damage and destruction caused by flood, is crucial. The use of technology for effective disaster response is also investigated along with its limitations. Various advancements in the disaster management technologies are explored and the gaps are identified. Finally, a machine learning and image processing based solution is proposed for flood management. The system is formulated so as to overcome the limitations of the current technologies and present a robust and reliable model for early flood detection and management.

Keywords: Flood, flood risks, flood management, disaster management, machine learning, edge detection, Artificial Neural Network, artificial intelligence

5.1 Flood Management

5.1.1 Introduction

The main objective of this chapter is to highlight flood related risks that exists globally and investigate the use of current systems for managing

Email: h.munawar@unsw.edu.au

Muthukumaran Malarvel, Soumya Ranjan Nayak, Surya Narayan Panda, Prasant Kumar Pattnaik and Nittaya Muangnak (eds.) Machine Vision Inspection Systems (Vol. 1): Image Processing, Concepts, Methodologies and Applications, (115–146) © 2020 Scrivener Publishing LLC

these risks. A detailed analysis of flood related disasters is done along with the threats they pose to the economy and community. This research is focused towards analysing the past and present occurrences of global floods, in order to understand the existing risks. The steps taken by various nations to deal with these instances of floods are also explored.

This section aims to understand the existing risks by analysing the past and present instances of global floods and the manner in which they have been tackled by different nations. The use of technology and the gaps in the existing system will also be discussed in different chapters and sections of this thesis to cover all aspects under consideration. The division of this section will be in further four sections, as follows:

Section 1.2 focuses on the flood threats that exists globally. The past instances of floods in different countries will be explored while moving towards the current situation in this domain.

Section 1.3 is aimed towards analysing the flood risks existing in Pakistan specifically. As Pakistan is susceptible to natural calamities like monsoon floods and, being an under developed country, lacks the state-of-the-art technology to deal with such disasters, this section will look into the current threats posed to the country.

Section 1.4 This section investigates the flood risks in a developed country like Australia and reviews the flood instances in past to determine the countries current state in terms of flood management.

Section 1.5 This section will link the current information about floods and their losses. Existing literature will be explored to find the reasons behind regarding floods as disasters to present the rationale for this study.

5.1.2   Global Flood Risks and Incidents

Hazards and risks associated with climate change have been studied for a long time. The threats and losses caused by floods are found to be higher than any other natural disaster. Increased urbanization is considered to be the reason behind this increased risk of floods. More land usage and growth of commercial areas have led to the development of communities in the coastal areas and river basins, which are naturally prone to flood [1]. Globally, the risk of floods is mapped using technology but these maps have not been successfully implemented on a local level yet. To aid disaster preparedness among flood prone communities, flood related information on local level needs to be gathered. Proper systems should be developed and implemented to facilitate this cause.

There is a global risk of floods which makes it crucial for all nations to take the necessary measures, in order to prepare and respond to such disasters. Various studies have been conducted to analyze the risks of floods in a specific country. These studies add to the existing enormous amount of data that conforms the threats and risks related to floods. According to an estimate of flood related economic loss in the year 2012, there was a total of 19 billion US dollars that the world lost owing to floods in various regions of the world [2]. This is a huge loss in a single year and indicates an alarming situation that is threatening the economy of the world. The increasing meddling of mankind with nature is linked to exposure of more people to the risks of floods than ever before. According to predictive analysis into the future, these flood hazards are likely to increase and cause huge damage to economy, infrastructure and lives of the people In general. Another major factor contributing to such hazards is dramatic climate change which is the cause behind many other natural disasters like drought, storms, heat waves and bush fires [3].

Hirabayashi *et al.* [4] linked flood risks with various climate change factors, which are expected to happen until the end of this century. The predictive analysis done in this domain, confirms the possibility of a dramatic increase in occurrence of flood globally. Countries in Southeast Asia and eastern Africa are particularly at a higher risk. These risks are expected to get doubled or even exceed this limit till the twentieth century with a growing rate of huge and dramatic destruction by the end of twenty first century. Figure 5.1 illustrates the graph of past flood incidents and the

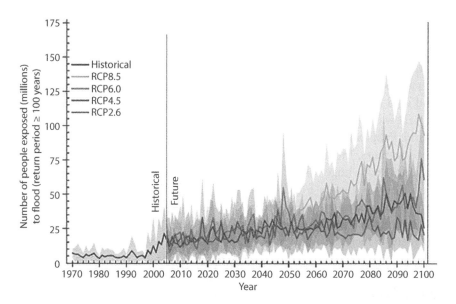

Figure 5.1 The number of people exposed to flood.

future predictions. According to these forecasts, drastic climate changes are expected in future, making the need for flood management and coping measures, even more crucial than ever.

Natural disasters like floods hold diverse risks causing widespread effects. These floods can cause either direct or indirect damage. The extent to which a disaster causes suffering for an individual or a company determines the nature of damage. Damage can be classified as either direct or indirect. Floods can cause losses to people, companies, economies, industries and governments. The classification is not concrete and damages can be referred to as direct and indirect and also measured in terms of their tangibility [5]. Direct damages include loss of lives, injuries, destruction of infrastructure, vehicles and damage to crops and animals. Indirect damage refers to the societal disruption, psychological trauma and disturbed pattern of production and consumption of goods.

5.1.3   Causes of Floods

A number of factors can be held responsible for the incidence of floods. Some of these factors are associated with climate like heavy rainfalls, storms or sudden melting of snow. The human driven factors contributing to flood risks include urbanization and lack of water storage reservoirs, dams or levees. Increased urbanization leads to addition of water-proof surfaces to the land which alters the natural drainage system making the area more prone to floods. It also leads to construction of more homes on floodplains. Poorly maintained infrastructure in urban areas also add to the risk of floods. However, most of the flood related risks are associated with dramatic climate change which is one of the major factors contributing to floods, along with other natural calamities like droughts, heat waves and wild bush fires. According to global weather data analysis, incidences of heat waves and floods have considerably increased in many parts of the world. Pakistan is ranked at top most among the countries with immensely hot summers. Incidents of wild bush fire in Russia and drought in China have caused a huge loss of lives and a significant damage to economy as well. The US Centre for Climate and Energy Solution regarded the year 2010 as a turning point in the conditions of global climate. An increase in heat waves is associated with increased precipitations, which indicates a substantial increase in the risk of floods due to global warming [3]. Climate change analysis have further revealed that for each unit increase in temperature, the rate of precipitation is doubled. A study in the Netherlands pointed out that for a rise in temperature with a margin of 12 degree centigrade, the precipitation rates have doubled to that of the rates recorded in the previous years, indicating a clear rise in the overall risk of floods due to changing weather [6].

5.1.4   Floods in Pakistan

Climate change has become the main factor causing increased incidences of floods in Pakistan, over the last few decades. Glacier melting and monsoon rains are two major weather related conditions which resulted in a rise of flood risks in the country. Most of the flood incidents happen in the late summers, when the monsoon rains are on their peak. These heavy rainfalls occur due to a storm that rise from the Bay of Bengal and enters Pakistan through Rajasthan (India).

Inland floods lower the GDP by 1% each year, according to the statistics by World Resources Institute. In addition to that, the disaster management, flood relief and rescue activities increase the burden on the economy of Pakistan.

In addition to the casualties and destruction of the country's infrastructure, floods have caused major setbacks to the agriculture sector of Pakistan. Pakistan depends on its agriculture to meet its food needs and to engage in foreign trade by exporting crops to other countries. Flood incidents have devastated the farm lands severely depleting rice and wheat crops of Pakistan [3].

There are two types of floods, which commonly happen in Pakistan. These are flash floods and riverine floods. Flash floods occur in hilly areas and consist of a rapid gush of water flow that builds up in a few hours after a causative phenomenon. These floods leave no time to evacuate the area and are quick and highly destructive. Most of the destruction caused by this type of flood is due to their high torrent and the fragments carried by them. Major causes include heavy rains, glacier melting and breakage of dams. These floods last for a short time period but are often sudden and unexpected and destroy buildings, houses and infrastructure, in addition to a large number of fatalities. Riverine floods are caused by an overflow of water from natural or artificial water bodies like dams and rivers. These floods are slow in their manifestation and typically last for several weeks. They turn into flash floods in hilly areas, due to a higher velocity of water.

At some point, floods have affected all the provinces of Pakistan. Specifically, Punjab and Sindh have been affected by flood incidents most frequently. The northern areas of the country along with Khyber Pakhtunkhwa and Gilgit are affected by the torrents originating from hilly areas. Monsoon storms and torrents were considered to be the major causes of floods in Pakistan in the past. But due to rapid rise in global warming and melting of glaciers, the flood incidents now happen in peak summer season as well, due to extremely hot temperatures [3]. Flood statistics from the year 1991 to date shows that Pakistan has faced severe devastation and setbacks owing to floods. A huge portion of population was displaced during the floods that occurred between 2008 and 2009. Data from the past flood incidences in Pakistan reveal that the country has lost millions of lives and also seen thousands of people displaced from their original communities due to floods [7].

Lack of data management technologies is considered to be the main cause of problems that exists in calculating the effects of the floods and other such disasters. Many researchers took over the task of data collection and analyzing techniques to tackle this problem. However, incomplete and segments of information from various regions of the country, did not present the accurate data about the damage and losses caused by flood. A country-wide meta-analysis was needed to get the true picture of the impacts of flood. Till this day, there is a gap in data management which makes it impossible to carry our predictive analysis or ensure that a country-wise flood analysis and prediction system could be implemented [8]. Another possible way to carry out estimation of disasters and increasing preparation is to establish provincial disaster management committees and risk reduction programs. Cases of disaster management and community resilience from Peshawar, Nowshera and adjoining areas reveal that the involvement of local authorities in enhancing community preparedness towards disasters can prove to be highly meaningful and yield better results in terms of minimizing flood related losses [9].

Many gaps have been identified in the disaster management and preparation strategies in Pakistan. Studies revealed that Pakistan do not have the infrastructure that is required to cope with floods. Apart from lack of disaster response technologies, there are policy gaps which add to the hardships faced by flood affected people. Deen [10] observed that the major reasons behind the continued suffering of the Pakistani communities due to floods can be linked to the failure of the Federal and Provincial Governments to coordinate with each other as well as the unpreparedness of the local authorities to deal with the disaster. These gaps are referred to as loopholes, which result in immense suffering of people in disastrous situations.

Massive destruction was recorded in different provinces of Pakistan during the 2010 floods. An estimated amount of 8.2 million people were directly or indirectly affected by floods. This included a major damage to the agriculture sector along with destruction of 300,000 houses. In Sindh, lives of nearly seven million people were affected while the death toll rose to 400. Gilgit-Baltistan, Azad Kashmir and some regions of Baluchistan also incurred losses, but the death toll in these areas was less as compared to Sindh [11]. The healthcare facilities of the country also suffered as 436 setting provided health related facilities were lost in the disaster [12]. The industries, businesses and farms lands suffered from direct as well as indirect losses as the supply chain of the entire country suffered due to losses in the raw materials which are produced in bulk, such as crops, cotton and staple foods [13]. With 2.9 million households being affected and a loss of almost 80% of the total food reserve of the country, the overall damages cost up to nearly 10 billion US dollars [14].

Van der Schrier [15] conducted a predictive analysis using data from the flood incidents of 2010 in Pakistan. This study was done to forecast future flood risks, as well as to analyse the causes and various climatic factors responsible for those disasters. One technique used in this study is called the "forced sensitivity method". In these experiments, similar weather conditions to that of 2010 floods were generated in the current weather. These conditions included five weather factors that were used to implement the algorithm. The results showed that if similar climate conditions as that of 2010 were applied in the present day, more severe catastrophic outcomes are anticipated due to global warming and extreme weather conditions. This points towards the threat of increased destruction by floods in the current climate conditions.

A detailed analysis of the floods that have occurred in the past needs to be done, to determine the flood prone areas and to gain an insight about future risks. This would help in forming strategies that will minimize the losses or ideally, prevent the occurrence of such disasters. Existing studies on the flood related events in Pakistan have focused on recording the losses and destruction caused by flood, along with the demographic data. Some researchers have studied the climatic and human related factors leading to floods, and have proposed new disaster management techniques. However, a gap still exists in implementation of these methods in real-time scenarios to verify their effectiveness. To increase disaster preparedness and responsiveness, the flood prone areas need to be identified and analysed regularly to forecast any future disasters, in order to take effective measures in a timely way.

5.1.5 Floods in Australia

Floods in Australia mostly occur along the rivers due to heavy rainfall. In urban areas, water overflowing from the drainage system in heavily populated areas can also lead to floods. Tropical cyclones can cause storm surges in low lying coastal areas. Rivers in Australia can be grouped in two categories, those that lie around the coast and drain straight to the ocean and those that drain large parts of the inland [16]. Different flood patterns are observed in both of these groups.

Riverine floods mostly occur in the broad uniform areas of central and western New South Wales and Queensland including some areas of North West Victoria and Western Australia. These floods onset slowly and lasts for a week or two and sometimes even months, resulting in massive loss of livestock, damage to agriculture lands, road and rail links along with a huge destruction in rural areas. This often leads to the isolation of whole communities residing in these areas.

A quick onset of floods is seen in the rivers that drain to the coast and in the mountain headwater regions of large rivers. This happens due to a quick flow of water in these regions as, the rivers, being steeper allow a faster flow of flood water. These floods last for just one or two days. However, they result in more damage and destruction as they build up quickly and leave no time to evacuate or to take preventive measures. Major towns and cities of Australia particularly lying in the East and South are affected by these floods.

Flash floods in Australia are a result of heavy rainfalls and intense thunderstorms. These floods can occur anywhere in Australia and pose great risks of loss of lives. People who enter the floodwaters either on foot or on vehicles are swept away. Apart from that, these floods can cause serious damage to property, infrastructure and lead to social disruption. The floods are a major issue in urban areas where the drainage systems are not able to handle the floodwater. The nature of landscape and steepness of the torrents in rural areas lead to a fast development of floodwater.

In Australia, the most significant floods occurred between 2010 and 2011. During this period, the monsoon rain and floods caused massive destruction, affecting about 78% of the entire state. The death toll rose to 33, out of which 21 died on the spot due to flash flooding [17]. Afterward, diseases and infections spread among the people, the standing flood water became a significant healthcare problem and caused more deaths. A huge loss of economy was also recorded as a result of floods in Queensland. Direct costs associated with the economic loss were estimated to be worth Australian $2 Billion. The indirect costs are estimated to be even higher than this.

Figure 5.2 illustrates the flood patterns in Australia over the years. The graphs clearly show that the average rainfall patterns have begun to fluctuate more since 1971 [18]. This reveals the continuously evolving weather of Australia during the last few decades. There have been a visible increase

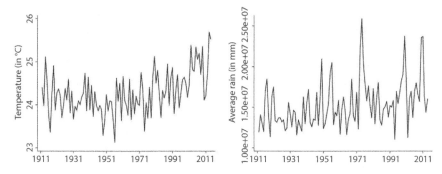

Figure 5.2 The pattern of temperature differences and average rainfall in Australia between 1911 and 2011 [18].

in temperature and the average rainfall in these years. These observations indicate the likelihood of more floods due to higher rate of rainfalls.

Various flood models have been proposed to analyse the risks of floods in Australia. These models rely on analysing floods with respect to the excess of infiltration and the capacity of soils to saturate water [19]. These relations have been investigated to determine flood risk ratios and to analyse floods using different models. However, the application of these models on static climates is yet to be explored and tested.

Flood analysis in the recent years has revealed that the volume of floods has particularly increased in the North-West region of Australia [20]. Weather related changes in Australia over a period of almost 2000 years have been investigated by a study. The hydro climatic changes in this region have been positively linked with instances of flash flooding [21]. Another report suggests that the high variability of the weather conditions of Australia and low population density makes it even harder to analyse flood risks. The understanding about the flood patterns and the flood risks is still quite low and there are gaps in research which need to be filled to ensure sustainability [22].

5.1.6   Why Floods are a Major Concern

Floods are natural disasters, which cause an immense loss of lives and damage to property, infrastructure and land. They pose a serious threat to the economy of any country as the destruction incurred by them and the post-disaster rehabilitation missions have cost billions of dollars in the past. The damages that have occurred due to floods make it necessary to work towards developing predictive models and strategies for overcoming the losses [23]. The major reason behind perceiving floods as among the most dangerous natural disaster is due to the loss of lives associated with it. According to the research, floods are among the natural disasters, which result in most loss of human lives. Floods are unpredictable. Most of the flood events in the past have happened suddenly and left no time for evacuation. Due to this uncertainty, the preflood preventive measures could not be successfully adopted and exercised in the past. Lack of awareness and preparation for coping with disastrous scenarios like floods, make it crucial to study the flood events that happened in the past, analyse their causes and build models to forecast the floods in advance so as to take the necessary measures to prepare or ideally, prevent these disasters. In developing countries like Pakistan, floods cause a huge damage to agriculture resources along with the loss of lives of people and animals. This results in huge economic loss. The developing countries suffer the most in face of such disasters, as the process of rehabilitation increase the burden on already feeble economies. This makes it an absolute necessity for these countries to conduct studies related to flood and determine the measures and strategies to reduce the loss.

5.2   Existing Disaster Management Systems

5.2.1   Introduction

This section aims to analyze the existing systems being used for disaster management. A critical analysis of these technologies is done to assess their effectiveness. The research data available for disaster preparedness and recovery at the global scale will be investigated. This includes the in-depth analysis of the technology and management systems used worldwide to manage floods and mitigate their ill-effects. The aim is to understand the coping and preparation strategies that are used around the world in order to deal with floods. Strengths and weaknesses of each technical solution being used, will be identified so as to formulate a system that will minimize those deficiencies. This section is organized as follows:

> Section 2.2 discusses the existing disaster management systems
> being used globally.
> Section 2.3 identifies the gaps in the current technology.

5.2.2   Disaster Management Systems Used Around the World

In the past few decades, natural disasters have increased significantly both in frequency and in severity. Between the years 2000 and 2005, on average

240 million people were affected by disasters. During this period, 80,000 fatalities were recorded on average and a damage worth of 80 Billion US Dollars was estimated. Disasters and the losses associated with them are on a rise across the globe due to a variety of factors:

1. Dramatic climate change
2. Agricultural practices contributing to an increased risk of disasters.
3. Increase in population leading to increased urbanization, food demands, production of industrial goods, causing an excessive exploitation of natural resources.

Due to increased vulnerability of the world to the threats of natural disasters, disaster management systems have become an important need of the hour. To better prepare for disasters, such systems should be developed, that can minimize the effects of any disastrous event. These systems should be built to facilitate disaster risk identification, preparedness and prevention and disaster response and recovery. This would help in timely detection and communication of any threats of flood present in an area, taking preventive measures to protect the people and property from destruction and respond to any such event by timely evacuations, locating and reaching out to stranded people. This would result in reducing the overall loss of human lives and resources, which they would have to face in case of absence of such system. Some countries raise their people's awareness regarding floods and focus on evacuation planning and emergency management for disaster response. Other work towards development of proper systems and models to predict, prevent and respond to disasters. Globally many systems are used for managing flood risks. In the subsequent sections, such systems are discussed in detail, along with the gaps associated with them.

5.2.2.1   Disaster Management Model

A disaster management model organizes various factors like human and material resources, finances and plans to analyse them easily and identify ways in which these factors can be manipulated to deal with a specific disaster. However, development of such system, do not guarantee the desired results as no two disasters have the same causes, intensity, pattern or outcomes [24]. Thus, these models need to be more flexible and should be able to incorporate changes effectively.

5.2.2.2   Disaster Risk Analysis System

In Malaysia, the annual rainfall rates are very high and flooding cannot be prevented merely by managing the rain water. To deal with this issue, Malaysia have established a disaster management committee which aims to assist people who are either directly or indirectly suffering from natural disasters. This committee aids in terms of humanitarian assistance, rescue operations and also financially to help people gain stability after being affected by disasters [25]. A flood delivery system was set up by this committee to provide relief services to flood affected people. However, the awareness about flood risks is still low among the people, as they consider such matters to be of interest to the government and not the nation. A pre-disaster risk analysis system for disaster preparedness have been developed by the committee to meet the nation's expectations [26]. Special funds are allocated by the government for disaster recovery and rescue activities which are used to plan and recover from the disasters [27].

5.2.2.3   Geographic Information System

The Geographic Information System (GIS) is also being implemented around the world for disaster management. This technology is used to view and analyse geographical locations and monitor the human-environment interaction. It is a powerful tool that generate maps, collects information, solve complex problems, visualize scenarios and propose solutions in case of a disaster. In face of a disaster, disaster management committees, and rescue workers need some critical information for decision making. This information includes data about the affected people and their whereabouts, resource availability, significant infrastructure, evacuation routes, and communication channels. Using this information, various factors like the quantity of relief items, medical aid, and location of fire stations can be determined by finding the number of expected evacuees. GIS also facilitates to online monitor the current work status for carrying out the recovery process. Adding data of the most recent disaster and the reaction of people can help in alerting the system and raising an alarm regarding a possible disaster [28]. These systems, however, cannot be used in the midst of an emergency as they rely heavily on the availability of data related to the disaster.

5.2.2.4   Web GIS

To provide an easy access to the geographical data, web GIS systems are proposed. Such systems work remotely over the internet, gather data about remote-access areas, and upload it over the web server for analysis by the users [29]. The databases used by web GIS can be accessed and analysed by multiple users at the same time. These systems have been enhanced to assist the overall analysis of risks. One such example is the Andean region's risk atlas, which is present online and provides details about the population, geographical conditions and hazards posed to the selected region [30].

5.2.2.5 Remote Sensing

Remote sensing involves identifying and monitoring the physical attributes of a region. This is done by analyzing the released and reflected radiation from the area under surveillance. These remotely sensed images are captured by specialized cameras and assist the researchers in acquiring information about the target area. This method has been used for flood prediction by monitoring the drainage systems and water bodies. The likelihood of occurrence of flood is identified by detecting the overflowing water. However, researchers have pointed out towards the difficulty of analysing all possible drainages due to their widespread presence and the difficulty in accessing the rough terrains spread across open fields and unused land regions [31].

Srilankan researchers used remote sensing to analyse different geographical locations in order to identify parameters and form a concrete dataset. This dataset could be further analysed for making flood related predictions. These datasets contain data about annual rainfall averages, the water discharge from the basins and population in a given area. The risk ratios from previous events of floods were also included to train the analysis systems in a more advanced manner [32]. In Nigeria future flood risks were predicted by obtaining high quality images using geospatial methods. The datasets included flood maps, data about river and land areas and description of depths of the water bodies. Together, these datasets were used to generate flood maps that could help in future disaster management and possible risk reduction [33].

5.2.2.6 Satellite Imaging

Government and businesses around the world acquire images of Earth, captured by imaging satellites. These images are further analysed to help identify risks of a particular disaster. The system used for analysis can be trained to recognise irregular patterns in the geographical images. Scientists have proposed the development of a community that works together for the development of a Spatial Data infrastructure which can help in identifying risks of disasters [34]. However, there are several limitations to the use of satellite imaging. Due to large land area of the Earth and high resolution images, the databases used in satellites are often quite huge. This makes the image processing relatively slow and time consuming, which may result in a delay in making decisions based on these images in emergency situations. Many times, the image quality is low due to noise, weather conditions and different barriers that may block the view of the target area.

5.2.2.7   Global Positioning System for Imaging

The Global Positioning System (GPS) is a radio navigation system based on satellites. It is a global navigation satellite system (GNSS) that transmits geolocation and time information to a GPS receiver located on or close to the Earth [35]. The GPS signals are relatively weak and are obstructed by obstacles like mountains and buildings.

The integration of GPS in disaster management systems has enabled the acquisition of geographical images for monitoring and monitoring. Evidence of GPS based analysis came from Turkey in an incidence of land sliding, where images captured through GPS were used for recognizing the disaster and identifying ways to mitigate the risks [36]. It was suggested that the same could possibly be used for identifying volcanic eruptions [37]. Recently, a flood risk map was developed using the data from the Haitian rivers. The methodology for this study relied on capturing GPS-based images and also images gathered through Unmanned Aerial Vehicles (UAV). The data collected through both of these methods were analysed to develop and refine the hydrological data of the target area [38]. It was concluded that flood risk maps can be developed with the combined use of appropriate modern technologies and local support from disaster prone areas was also deemed as necessary for development true risk representative maps.

5.2.3   Gaps in Current Disaster Management Technology

The current systems, being used for disaster management are based on predictive analysis and rely on geographical surveillance by satellites to manage floods. Several gaps have been identified in the existing technology. For example, there is lack of accuracy in the results achieved through GPS. The precision of the GPS can vary depending upon the time required for analysis and the number of antennas required for analysing an area may differ based on the area being scrutinized. The accuracy of GPS has been found to vary depending upon the type of motion in a given region. There is a delay in information processing in the case of circular movements or rapid changes in trajectory when a person or object is in the move [39]. In case of flood like emergency, systems relying on GPS technology, fail to provide the required information on time. This delay can result in more fatalities and economic loss. In satellite imaging systems, the overall processing time of images is increased due to large databases consisting of high resolution images. The quality of these images is highly affected by the barriers that exists between Earth and the satellite. Various weather conditions also influence the quality of the captured images. The results are affected by factors like noise, image orientation and illumination conditions. In the flood affected regions, these services cannot be availed due to unavailability of internet and telecommunication services owing to the destruction caused by flood. Such challenges need to be studied in detail to come up with a dedicated aerial imaging system, that is able to capture high quality images from the target area, map flooded regions and aid evacuations by locating the stranded people.

5.3 Advancements in Disaster Management Technologies

5.3.1 Introduction

This section is dedicated towards investigating the recent research and advancements in technology around the world for effective disaster management. The integration of Artificial Intelligence (AI) and machine learning to disaster management systems and the observed outcomes will be studied. To recover from disasters, there is a need to build a reliable system that can help in forecasting or prediction of such events, provide aid in communication from affected areas and produce maps to identify routes to reach the stranded people. The performance of existing systems based on imaging can be enhanced through the use of machine learning approaches. The machine learning algorithms provide the benefit of being more accurate, reliable and cost effective. The most common trends in using machine learning for making disaster related forecasts are highlighted. A comparison between the methods is done to assess the strengths and weaknesses of each model being reviewed.

This section is organised as follows:

Section 3.2 discusses the recent systems for disaster management that have incorporated AI and machine learning
techniques.

Section 3.3 explores the literature focused on the use of machine
learning in managing disasters and compares the selected
techniques.

Section 3.4 concludes the section.

5.3.2   AI and Machine Learning for Disaster Management

This section explores some most recent state-of-the-art techniques being
used for disaster management in various parts of the world. Artificial intelligence and machine learning technologies have already paved their way
for providing knowledge of upcoming disaster and its effective management protocols in different countries.

5.3.2.1   AIDR

In Nepal, during April 2015, an earthquake of 7.8 magnitudes hit at 21
miles east-southern coast of Lamjung. The standby task force was successful in mobilizing 3000 volunteers across the countries within 12 hours after
the quake. It was possible due to the revolutionized AI system in Nepal.
Volunteers in that area took to social media to upload and share crisis-
related photographs. Artificial Intelligence for Disaster Response (AIDR)
used those uploaded posts to determine the necessities of people based
on category such as urgent need, damage to infrastructure or even helps
regarding resource deployment.

5.3.2.2   Warning Systems

An earthquake of 8.3 magnitudes struck 29 miles from the Chilean city
of Illapel in September 2015. Deaths during the earthquake were prevented and reduced. The evacuation facilitated by effective communication got thousands of citizens out of the danger zone quickly. Also,
within minutes of the quake, a system of disaster warning sirens rang
through the impacted areas and nearby coasts. The mobile phones were
targeted with tsunami warning messages asking residents to evacuate
coastal areas.

5.3.2.3   QCRI

Qatar developed a tool known as the Qatar Computing Research Institute (QCRI) for disaster management. The tool was developed by Qatar Foundation to increase awareness and development of education and science in a community. For disaster management, QCRI aims to provide its services by increasing the efficiency of agencies and volunteer facilities. The tool has an AI system installed which helps in recognizing tweets and texts regarding any devastated area or crisis. The QCRI then provides an immediate solution to overcome the crisis. ("Using Artificial Intelligence for Emergency Management", 2018).

5.3.2.4   The Concern

The concern is a tool developed to analyze the disaster situation. The tool creates a comprehensive picture of the location during an emergency operation. The image is used by emergency centers to investigate the situation. The centers use those images to provide immediate response in the form of relief goods or other rescue efforts. The tool also helps in the creation of a planning module. The module helps in identifying and determining the areas prone to a disaster. The vulnerable areas can then be evacuated to avoid the loss of life. Up till now, 1Concenr has identified 163,696 square miles area. The tool has sheltered 39 million people. It also examined 11 million structures and found 14,967 faults among the construction. Thus, the program provides all the precautionary measures before a natural disaster hits. ("Using Artificial Intelligence for Emergency Management", 2018).

5.3.2.5   BlueLine Grid

BlueLine Grid was developed by one of the Police Commissioner of New York City. It serves as a platform of mobile communication for the assistance of rescue efforts during a catastrophe. The tool connects emergency workers, security teams and law enforcement organizations into a single network. The network could exchange data in the form of voice, text, location or any sort of group services. The platform was not just found effective for communication and collaboration, but it also encouraged the users to find public assistance by geographical proximity and area. Thus an immediate response system was created in New York City to overcome disaster and provide an immediate response to the hazardous situation. ("Using Artificial Intelligence for Emergency Management", 2018).

5.3.2.6   Google Maps

Recently, AI technology is evolving in India where Google is trying to predict floods and warn its users with the help of Google Maps and Google Search. AI system is trained by retrieving the data of rainfall records and flood imitation. Avoiding the traditional systems, the AI-based systems track the flood simulation with climate and rainfall incidence. Urban flooding can also be predicted with it. Research at the University of Dundee in the United Kingdom collected crowd-sourced data from twitter and other social media apps to check the rate of urban flooding. AI recognized the images and locations retrieved from social media to account for the incidence of urban flooding. Hence, a large number of applications are useful for disaster management involving AI and deep learning [40].

5.3.2.7   RADARSAT-1

RADARSAT-1 is a satellite developed by Canada to observe the Earth. The satellite uses synthetic aperture radar (SAR) for capturing accurate images for keeping the track of natural resources and monitoring the change in the global climate. The images taken by RADARSAT-1 are useful in many ways. It can be used in the fields of hydrology, forestry, geology and monitoring the ice and oceans. The data of RADARSAT-1 can also be analyzed for checking the before and after flood images and estimating the destruction occurred. SAR data has been utilized in the mapping and monitoring of hydrological parameters [41]. Flood mapping has been done with this useful technique. Various researchers utilized the threshold method to monitor the flood related changes by monitoring the return signals from open water bodies [42].

5.3.3   Recent Research in Disaster Management

In this section, we further investigate the literature to identify the recent approaches being adopted to use machine learning and AI for disaster management. Some recent research articles from well-known journals and conferences are selected and reviewed. The research highlights the trend of using statistical techniques along with machine learning models. Many researchers have proposed ensemble models and demonstrated and improved performance over individual results. The strengths and weaknesses of each technique are analyzed. Table 5.1 summarizes the selected machine learning techniques.

Table 5.1 Machine learning techniques for flood management.

No.	Technique	Result	Pros	Cons	Formula	Author
1	Integration of SAE with BPNN. Using K-means clustering for further improvement.	Deterministic Coefficient DC = 0.88	Integrated algorithm showed improved results over state-of-the-art techniques.	SAE-BP model has an imbalance of data distribution.	$z^{(l)} = f(p^{(l)})$	Liu et al.
2	Used BSA to calculate weights for each conditioning factor of flood, before classification using SVM.	96.48% success rate. 95.67% prediction rate.	Improved accuracy over individual results.	Possibility of getting misleading results due to high prediction power.	$W_i^+ = \ln \dfrac{P\{D|C\}}{\overline{P\{D|C\}}}$ $W_i^- = \ln \dfrac{P\{\bar{D}|C\}}{\overline{P\{\bar{D}|C\}}}$	Tehrani et al.
3	Combined FR with SVM for flood prediction.	Highest accuracy achieved by setting kernel width=0.1	Ability to manage huge dataset of geographic images and generate maps quickly.	Conditioning factors need to be analyzed to retain the most influential factors for mapping	$Z_j = \dfrac{z_j - z_{min}}{z_{max} - z_{min}}$	Mojaddadi et al.

(Continued)

Table 5.1 Machine learning techniques for flood management. (*Continued*)

No.	Technique	Result	Pros	Cons	Formula	Author
4	Implementation of eight machine learning and ensemble models for flood predictions.	Highest performance observed with BRT model. AUC = 0.975	Improved performance over individual methods	Changing the input data or future conditions may affect the accuracy.		Moghadam *et al.*
5	Experiments with ANN, boosted decision tree, decision forest, linear regression model and Bayesian linear model	Best accuracy achieved through Bayesian Linear Model	Proposed model can be implemented as a short-term flood detection system.	Experiments conducted with partial data and unidentified relevant variables.	$L_{TX33^*} = MI(L_{TX347}(T), V_{TX347}(T))$	Noymanee *et al.*

Artificial Neural Networks (ANN) have been commonly used for disaster prediction and displayed good results. These networks consist of three layers called Input, Hidden and Output layers. However, they have a limitation of being restricted to only one or two hidden layers. Liu *et al.* [43] integrated Stacked Autoencoders with Back Propagation Neural Network (SAE-BPNN). An autoencoder is an unsupervised network that mines the non-linear structures from images. A stacked autoencoder is built from a neural network that have sparse autoencoders, arranged in multiple layers. Each layer's output is applied as input to the next. To further improve the performance, K-means clustering was used to classify the data into different classes. Several SAE-BP modules were used, such that they could simulate their corresponding data classes. Results showed improved results using SAE-BP algorithm, as compared to all other benchmarks. Encoding for autoencoder is given as:

$$z^{(l)} = f(p^{(l)})$$

$$p^{(l+1)} = X^{(1,1)}z^{(l)} + x^{(l,1)}$$

Where $z_j^{(l)}$ is the activation function of the jth unit in layer (l) and also the output of this neural unit p_i^j is the input of this unit. X denotes the weights that links the units in different layers of the autoencoder.

Flood susceptibility mapping determines the areas that are most vulnerable to floods, based on multiple conditioning factors leading to flood incidents. Tehrany *et al* [44] used weights-of-evidence (WoE) model to determine the effect of a set of conditioning factors on flood events, using a bivariate statistical analysis (BSA). To calculate WoE, the positive and negative weights are determined.

$$W_i^+ = \ln \frac{P\{D \mid C\}}{P\{D \mid \bar{C}\}}$$

$$W_i^- = \ln \frac{P\{\bar{D} \mid C\}}{P\{\bar{D} \mid \bar{C}\}}$$

In above equations, ln is the natural log, P denotes the probability while variables like C, $\bar{C}$, D and $\bar{D}$ denotes the presence and absence of conditioning features. Using the acquired weights, these factors were classified again. They were then applied to an SVM model that determines the correspondence between each conditioning factor and flood occurrence. Results demonstrated improved performance over individual methods.

The performance issues of various machine learning models can be overcome through the integration of statistical methods. Tehrany *et al.* [45] proposed an ensemble system that uses SVM with frequency ratio (FR) to construct a spatial model for flood prediction. A statistical analysis was done using FR method to find a numerical value representing the relationship between occurrence of flood and classes of the conditioning factors. After finding FR for conditioning ratios, the weights were normalized between the range of zero and one using the following formula:

$$Z_j = \frac{z_j - z_{min}}{z_{max} - z_{min}}$$

where, Z_j denotes the normalized values of z_j, z_{min} and z_{max} denote the lowest and highest values of z_j respectively. The weights produced by this method are allotted to each of the conditioning factors which were used with the SVM model.

Using statistical methods along with machine learning for making flood related predictions have demonstrated an overall improved performance. Moghadam *et al.* [46] implemented eight machine learning and statistical models. Seven ensemble models were then proposed based on the individual implementation of these methods. They used Area Under Curve (AUC) as performance measure. In their experiments Boosted Regression Trees (BRT) showed the highest performance among other machine learning methods, individually with AUC = 0.975. Among ensemble methods, Emmedian model demonstrated the best performance with AUC = 0.976. This model is based on median of probabilities across predictions.

Existing machine learning models have been explored to tackle the problem of flood management. Jeerana Noymanee *et al.* [47] tested neural network, boosted decision tree, decision forest, linear regression model and Bayesian linear model to predict flood in the Pattani region. Among these, Bayesian linear model showed best performance and is recommended for prediction of floods. The upstream and downstream parts of a river were modeled using mathematical formulas. Following equations models the upstream part of a river:

$$L_{TX33^*} = Ml(L_{TX347}(T), V_{TX347}(T))$$

Where Ml is the machine learning action operator, L represents the water level, * is mark of predicted values, TX347 and TX33 are the station names given to different parts of the river and V is the rain variable.

5.3.4   Conclusion

In this section we reviewed the latest advancements in the use of technology for disaster management around the globe as well as discussed the recent research in this domain. Many countries have adopted AI and machine learning based techniques to deal with disasters. Recent research showed that the machine learning and AI models are increasingly being used for disaster management. Most of the these disaster management systems make predictions about disasters and provide insights about mitigating these risks. However, with the passage of time it has been understood that natural disasters like floods cannot be fully avoided or prevented. Despite the evident advancements in the forecasting systems, floods have continued to cause immense destruction across the world. This point towards the need to develop systems that focus on disaster response and relief activities to deal with the post-disaster situations. This includes systems that detect flood affected areas, determine rescue routes and transport services in these areas and aid in the evacuation of stranded people. A stable flood management system can still be a challenge to develop owing to the drastic changes in climate and the subsequent rise in the flood risks.

5.4   Proposed System

Despite the popularity of AI and machine learning models for disaster management and the wide range of on-going research in this area, the number of working algorithms for real-time flood risk management remains to be very low [48]. The limitations of the current disaster management systems point towards the need to develop a robust and reliable flood management model that is able to capture aerial images, generate map of flooded regions and locate affected people. To achieve this objective we propose a flood management model that uses image processing techniques along with machine learning to detect flooded areas from images and identify populated areas from them, so that the stranded people can be quickly identified and rescued. A detailed description of this methodology is provided in the next sections.

5.4.1   Image Acquisition Through UAV

Images captured through satellites often have low quality due to inherent noise present in remotely captured images, as well as various existing barriers between Earth and the satellite, such as clouds and flying objects, which can block the view of target area. Image processing through satellites is slow due to large size of image databases. This makes satellite imaging impractical to be used in emergency scenarios like floods. There is a need to implement an automated imaging system that uses high resolution spatial images, captured using a dedicated imaging device. This can be achieved through the use of UAVs, as they are able to work independently and capture high quality images from the target area. The limitations of satellite imaging methods can be reduced.by the use of UAV which are physically present at the site to capture high quality images. The captured images can be quickly sent to the server for further processing.

5.4.2   Preprocessing

Preprocessing is the first step in any image processing task. It is done to improve overall image quality and reduce noise. First, the images are converted to grayscale. The grayscale transformation is done to discard information that is not required for our analysis. In this model, the pixel's color information is not used for flood detection. Hence, they are transformed to grayscale to save the memory and processing time. After this, a noise filter should be applied to reduce noise and get a smooth image. This can be done using a median filter which is particularly useful for removing "salt and pepper" noise from images. It is a non-linear filter that removes noise while preserving the edges. It sorts all pixels present in a window according to their numerical value, then replaces the pixel being considered with the median pixel value. In case of windows of even size, the filter takes average of two middle values after sorting. Here, the output O will be given by:

$$O = \frac{i^{th} \, classified \, value + (i+1)^{th} \, classified \, value}{2}$$

5.4.3   Landmarks Detection

Landmark detection is the process of identifying objects like roads, bridges, houses and buildings from images. The landmarks indicate the populated areas in the image. By identifying the key landmarks in aerial images, the stranded people can be reached and rescued. Image processing techniques like edge detection and pixel based analysis can be used to successfully perform object detection on the input images. The next sections investigates the methods for recognising and extracting buildings and roads from images.

5.4.3.1   Buildings

In aerial images, buildings appear in the form of blocks, varying in size and colour. The four corner points of each block can be extracted using a corner detector like Harris Detector. Harris Stephen's algorithm is a combined edge and corner detector. It finds the difference in intensity for a displacement of (p,q) in all directions. This is given as below:

$$E(p,q) = \sum_{a,b} w(a,b)[I(a+p,b+q) - I(a,b)]^2$$

5.4.3.2   Roads

Roads in aerial images are considered to be curvilinear features. This indicates the need to adopt a suitable curvilinear feature detector like Carsten Steger [49]. This algorithm extracts the line position and derives its width (as shown in Figure 5.3). Other line detectors use a simple model for extraction and donot take into account the surrounding regions of a line.

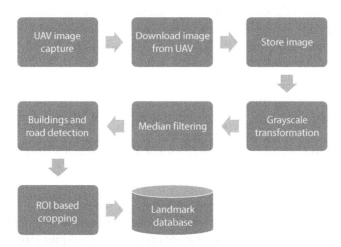

Figure 5.3 Landmarks extraction from images

In contrast, this model uses an explicit model for lines and their surroundings. This algorithm can also be used to detect features like rivers and railway tracks from the aerial images.

5.4.4   Flood Detection

Once, the landmarks are extracted, they can be compared to post-flood images to identify the occurrence of flood. For example, preflood and posflood images of a building that is damaged by flood will not be the same, hence they will not be matched by the algorithm. If the building is completely collapsed, it will not be detected in the post-flood image, hence indicating the occurrence of a disaster. Before and after flood images of other features like roads can also be compared and analysed.

5.4.4.1   Feature Matching

After identifying the key features in images, the next step will be to determine the occurrence of a flood like disaster. Once key points in an image are found and saved in a database, key points in a new source image can be compared to them. For this purpose, different feature matching algorithms can be adopted. Some of them are discussed in this section.

SURF Detector
The SURF detector uses a fast indexing step which can enhance the efficiency of the matching process. A descriptor contains the trace of the Hessian matrix for each point under consideration. This trace easily differentiates between a bright blob on a dark background and dark blob on a light background, for a typical point of interest, which is usually a blob-like structure. The major benefit of this technique is that it saves computation time by only considering the features having the same contrast for matching.

Brute Force Matching
This method selects each feature from the reference database and performs a comparison between this feature and other features having same contrast. This method, though simple to implement, can be slow if a large amount of features are present in the reference database.

FLANN Matching
The Fast Approximate Nearest Neighbors (FLANN) matching method was claimed to be faster than other feature matching techniques [50]. It incorporates the K-Nearest Neighbors algorithm with brute force matching.

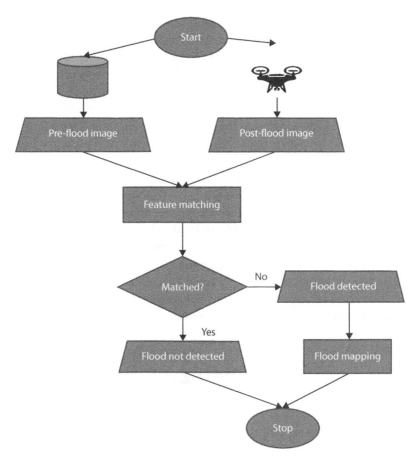

Figure 5.4 Flood detection using feature matching.

This reduces the overall matching time, as only a few features present in the neighborhood of a feature will be considered for comparisons.

5.4.4.2   *Flood Detection Using Machine Learning*

To build a more fast, robust and reliable model to detect flooded regions, a machine learning algorithm can be incorporated with landmark detection. A classifier can be trained using images from both before and after flood scenarios. A new image applied to the trained model will be classified as "flooded" or "non-flooded" by the trained prediction model. To achieve this objective, there is a need to find a suitable classifier for training. Selection of a classifier is done by considering a wide range of factors like ability to handle large datasets, robustness to the presence of irrelevant features or noise in the dataset, training time and classification time. The landmarks detected in the previous step will be cropped using Region of Interest (ROI) function and will be provided as input to the classifier for training. We propose the use of Artificial Neural Network for flood detection. The ANN classifier has the ability to learn by itself. Hence, the output is not only limited or dependent on the input training set. When exposed to real-time scenarios, they have the ability to quickly adapt and produce the output accordingly. This results in improved accuracy due to the self-learning behaviour of neural networks.

In literature, the ANN models have been regarded as the best ones for developing flood risk prediction models [51]. ANN have the ability to process complex flood variables and produce a highly accurate approximation of data sets, which makes it a highly suitable tool to develop an efficient flood prediction model. Studies have shown that ANNs have higher speed and accuracy than many of the conventional models and tools used previously [52].

A neural network consists of three layers called the input, output and hidden layers. Each layer consists of a network of interconnected neurons. The output neuron signal can be represented as:

$$O = h(net) = h\left(\sum_{j=1}^{k} w_j b_j \right)$$

Neuron output is represented by O, w_j represent the weighted vector, b is the input signal and $h(net)$ is the transfer function where net is a scalar product of weight and input with expression as:

$$net = (w_1 b_1) + (w_2 b_2) + \ldots + (w_n b_n)$$

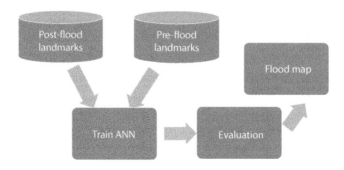

Figure 5.5 Flood detection using machine learning.

5.4.5   Conclusion

In this section, techniques for landmark detection from input aerial images have been discussed. A new model based on machine learning and image processing is proposed to detect flood from input images. Landmark detection is done to identify the populated areas, so that timely help can be provided to the people in that area. Methods to extract landmarks like buildings and roads from the images have been discussed. The detected landmarks can be further analysed to identify the occurrence of flood. Two methods have been proposed for this purpose. The image processing-based technique uses preflood and postflood images of landmarks and compares them. If the two landmarks match, this indicates absence of flood in that area. However if, in the post-flood image, the target landmark is damaged or collapsed, the two images will not match which indicates the occurrence of flood. To reduce false detections, all landmarks in the area should be analyzed before issuing a flood alert.

References

1. McCallum, I., Liu, W., See, L., Mechler, R., Keating, A., Hochrainer-Stigler, S., Szoenyi, M., Technologies to support community flood disaster risk reduction. *Int. J. Disaster Risk Sci.*, 7, 2, 198–204, 2016.
2. Ward, P.J., Jongman, B., Weiland, F.S., Bouwman, A., van Beek, R., Bierkens, M.F., Winsemius, H.C., Assessing flood risk at the global scale: Model setup, results, and sensitivity. *Environ. Res. Lett.*, 8, 4, 044019, 2013.
3. Huber, D.G. and Gulledge, J., *Extreme weather and climate change: Understanding the link, managing the risk*, Pew Center on Global Climate Change, Arlington, 2011.
4. Hirabayashi, Y., Mahendran, R., Koirala, S., Konoshima, L., Yamazaki, D., Watanabe, S., Kanae, S., Global flood risk under climate change. *Nat. Clim. Change*, 3, 9, 816, 2013.
5. Haraguchi, M. and Lall, U., Flood risks and impacts: A case study of Thailand's floods in 2011 and research questions for supply chain decision making. *Int. J. Disaster Risk Reduct.*, 14, 256–272, 2015.
6. Lenderink, G. and Van Meijgaard, E., Increase in hourly precipitation extremes beyond expectations from temperature changes. *Nat. Geosci.*, 1, 8, 511, 2008.
7. Sayed, S.A. and González, P.A., Flood disaster profile of Pakistan: a review. *Sci. J. Public Health*, 2, 3, 144–149, 2014.
8. Khalid, M.A. and Ali, Y., Analysing economic impact on interdependent infrastructure after flood: Pakistan a case in point. *Environ. Hazards*, 18, 2, 111–126, 2019.

9. Shah, A.A., Ye, J., Abid, M., Khan, J., Amir, S.M., Flood hazards: household vulnerability and resilience in disaster-prone districts of Khyber Pakhtunkhwa province, Pakistan. *Nat. Hazards*, 93, 1, 147–165, 2018.

10. Deen, S., Pakistan 2010 floods. Policy gaps in disaster preparedness and response. *Int. J. Disaster Risk Reduct.*, 12, 341–349, 2015.

11. Hashmi, H.N., Siddiqui, Q.T.M., Ghumman, A.R., Kamal, M.A., A critical analysis of 2010 floods in Pakistan. *Afr. J. Agric. Res.*, 7, 7, 1054–1067, 2012.

12. Hussain, A. and Routray, J.K., Status and factors of food security in Pakistan. *Int. J. Dev. Issues*, 11, 2, 164–185, 2012.

13. Polastro, R., Nagrah, A., Steen, N., Zafar, F., *Inter-agency real time evaluation of the humanitarian response to Pakistan's 2010 flood crisis*, DARA, Madrid, 2011.

14. Kreibich, H., Bubeck, P., Van Vliet, M., De Moel, H., A review of damage-reducing measures to manage fluvial flood risks in a changing climate. *Mitigation Adapt. Strategies Global Change*, 20, 6, 967–989, 2015.

15. Van der Schrier, G., Rasmijn, L.M., Barkmeijer, J., Sterl, A., Hazeleger, W., The 2010 Pakistan floods in a future climate. *Clim. Change*, 1–14, 2018.

16. Attorney-General's Department, Emergency Management Australia, Bureau of Meteorology, Floods, Warning, Preparedness and Safety, http://www.bom. gov.au/australia/flood/EMA_Floods_warning_preparedness_safety.pdf.

17. Peden, A.E., Franklin, R.C., Leggat, P., Aitken, P., Causal pathways of flood related river drowning deaths in Australia. *PLOS Curr. Dis.*, 1, 1–24, 2017.

18. Ulubaşoğlu, M.A., Rahman, M.H., Önder, Y.K., Chen, Y., Rajabifard, A., Floods, Bushfires and Sectoral Economic Output in Australia, 1978–2014. *Econ. Rec.*, 2019.

19. Johnson, F., White, C.J., van Dijk, A., Ekstrom, M., Evans, J.P., Jakob, D., Westra, S., Natural hazards in Australia: floods. *Clim. Change*, 139, 1, 21–35, 2016.

20. Ward, P.J., Jongman, B., Kummu, M., Dettinger, M.D., Weiland, F.C.S., Winsemius, H.C., Strong influence of El Niño Southern Oscillation on flood risk around the world. *Proc. Natl. Acad. Sci.*, 111, 44, 15659–15664, 2014.

21. Rouillard, A., Skrzypek, G., Turney, C., Dogramaci, S., Hua, Q., Zawadzki, A., Grierson, P.F., Evidence for extreme floods in arid subtropical northwest Australia during the Little Ice Age chronozone (CE 1400–1850). *Quat. Sci. Rev.*, 144, 107–122, 2016.

22. Johnson, F., White, C.J., van Dijk, A., Ekstrom, M., Evans, J.P., Jakob, D., Westra, S., Natural hazards in Australia: floods. *Clim. Change*, 139, 1, 21–35, 2016.

23. Najibi, N. and Devineni, N., Recent trends in the frequency and duration of global floods. *Earth Syst. Dyn.*, 9, 2, 757–783, 2018.

24. Othman, S.H. and Beydoun, G., Model-driven disaster management. *Inf. Manag.*, 50, 5, 218–228, 2013.

25. Chan, N.W., Impacts of disasters and disaster risk management in Malaysia: The case of floods, in: *Resilience and Recovery in Asian Disasters*, pp. 239–265, Springer, Tokyo, 2015.

26. Cloke, H.L. and Pappenberger, F., Ensemble flood forecasting: A review. *J. Hydrol.*, 375, 3-4, 613–626, 2009.
27. Khalid, M.S.B. and Shafiai, S.B., Flood disaster management in Malaysia: An evaluation of the effectiveness flood delivery system. *Int. J. Soc. Sci. Humanity*, 5, 4, 398, 2015.
28. Giardino, M., Perotti, L., Lanfranco, M., Perrone, G., GIS and geomatics for disaster management and emergency relief: A proactive response to natural hazards. *Appl. Geomat.*, 4, 1, 33–46, 2012.
29. Van Westen, C.J., Remote sensing and GIS for natural hazards assessment and disaster risk management, in: *Treatise on geomorphology*, vol. 3, pp. 259–298, 2013.
30. Andina, C., Atlas de las dinamicas del Territorio Andino. Poblacion y bienes expuestos a amenazas naturales. Communidad Andina, Comité Andino para la Prevención y Atención de Desastres, CAPRAD, 2009.
31. Youssef, A.M., Pradhan, B., Hassan, A.M., Flash flood risk estimation along the St. Katherine road, southern Sinai, Egypt using GIS based morphometry and satellite imagery. *Environ. Earth Sci.*, 62, 3, 611–623, 2011.
32. Samarasinghea, S.M.J.S., Nandalalb, H.K., Weliwitiyac, D.P., Fowzed, J.S.M., Hazarikad, M.K., Samarakoond, L., Application of remote sensing and GIS for flood risk analysis: A case study at Kalu-Ganga River, Sri Lanka. *Int. Arch. Photogramm. Remote Sens. Spat. Inf. Sci.*, 38, Pt 8, 110–115, 2010.
33. Ojigi, M.L., Abdulkadir, F.I., Aderoju, M.O., Geospatial mapping and analysis of the 2012 flood disaster in central parts of Nigeria, in: *8th National GIS Symposium*, April 2013, Dammam, Saudi Arabia, pp. 1067–1077, 2013.
34. Manfré, L.A., Hirata, E., Silva, J.B., Shinohara, E.J., Giannotti, M.A., Larocca, A.P.C., Quintanilha, J.A., An analysis of geospatial technologies for risk and natural disaster management. *ISPRS Int. J. Geo-Inf.*, 1, 2, 166–185, 2012.
35. *Global Positioning System Standard Positioning Service Performance Standard: 4th Edition, September 2008*, Archived (PDF) from the original on April 27, 2017. https://www.gps.gov/technical/ps/2008-SPS-performance-standard.pdf
36. Hastaoglu, K.O. and Sanli, D.U., Monitoring Koyulhisar landslide using rapid static GPS: A strategy to remove biases from vertical velocities. *Nat. Hazards*, 58, 3, 1275–1294, 2011.
37. Calcaterra, S., Cesi, C., Di Maio, C., Gambino, P., Merli, K., Vallario, M., Vassallo, R., Surface displacements of two landslides evaluated by GPS and inclinometer systems: a case study in Southern Apennines, Italy. *Nat. Hazards*, 61, 1, 257–266, 2012.
38. Joseph, A., Gonomy, N., Zech, Y., Soares-Frazão, S., Modelling and analysis of the flood risk at Cavaillon City, Haiti. *La Houille Blanche*, 2, 68–75, 2018.
39. Terrier, P. and Schutz, Y., How useful is satellite positioning system (GPS) to track gait parameters? A review. *J. Neuroeng. Rehabil.*, 2, 1, 28, 2005.
40. Joshi, N., How AI Can And Will Predict Disasters. Retrieved from https://www.forbes.com/sites/cognitiveworld/2019/03/15/how-ai-can-and-will-predict-disasters/#7ad844dd5be2, 2019.

41. Martinis, S., Twele, A., Voigt, S., Towards operational near real-time flood detection using a split-based automatic thresholding procedure on high-resolution TerraSAR-X data. *Nat. Hazards Earth Syst. Sci.*, 9, 2, 303–314, 2009.

42. Liu, Z., Huang, F., Li, L., Wan, E., Dynamic monitoring and damage evaluation of flood in north-west Jilin with remote sensing. *Int. J. Remote Sens.*, 23, 18, 3669–3679, 2002.

43. Liu, F., Xu, F., Yang, S.A., Flood forecasting model based on deep learning algorithm via integrating stacked autoencoders with BP Neural Network. *2017 IEEE Third International Conference on Multimedia Big Data*, 2017.

44. Tehrany, M.S., Pradhan, B., Jebur, M.N., Flood susceptibility mapping using a novel ensemble weights-of-evidence and support vector machine models in GIS. *J. Hydrol.*, 512, 332–343, 2014.

45. Tehrany, M.S., Pradhan, B., Jebur, M.N., Flood susceptibility analysis and its verification using a novel ensemble SVM and frequency ratio method, in: *Stoch Environ Res Risk Assess*, 29, 4, 1149–1165, 2015.

46. Moghadam, H.S., Valavi, R., Shahabi, H., Chapi, K., Shirzadi, A., Novel forecasting approaches using combination of machine learning and statistical models for flood susceptibility mapping ensemble support vector machine and frequency ratio method. *J. Environ. Manage.*, 217, 1–11, 2018.

47. Noymanee, J., Nikitin, N.O., Kalyuzhnaya, K.V., Urban Pluvial Flood Forecasting using Open Data with Machine Learning Techniques in Pattani Basin. *Procedia Comput. Sci.*, 119, 288–297, 2017.

48. Martinis, S., Kersten, J., Twele, A., A fully automated TerraSAR-X based flood service. *ISPRS J. Photogramm. Remote Sens.*, 104, 203–212, 2015.

49. Steger, C., An unbiased detector of curvilinear structures. *IEEE Trans. Pattern Anal. Mach. Intell.*, 20, 2, 113–125, 1998.

50. Muja, M. and Lowe, D.J., Fast approximate nearest neighbors with automatic algorithm configuration. *Science*, 340, 2009. http://citeseerx.ist.psu.edu/viewdoc/download?doi=10.1.1.160.1721&rep=rep1&type=pdf

51. Sulaiman, J. and Wahab, S.H., Heavy rainfall forecasting model using artificial neural network for the flood-prone area, in: *IT Convergence and Security 2017*, pp. 68–76, Springer, Singapore, 2018.

52. Abbot, J. and Marohasy, J., Input selection and optimization for monthly rainfall forecasting in Queensland, Australia, using artificial neural networks. *Atmos. Res.*, 138, 166–178, 2014.

6

Temporal Color Analysis of Avocado Dip for Quality Control

Homero V. Rios-Figueroa[1]*, Micloth López del Castillo-Lozano[2], Elvia K. Ramirez-Gomez[2] and Ericka J. Rechy-Ramirez[1]

[1]Research Center in Artificial Intelligence, University of Veracruz, Sebastian Camacho, Xalapa, Veracruz, Mexico
[2]Institute of Basic Sciences, University of Veracruz, Xalapa, Veracruz, Mexico

Abstract

Avocado dip changes color rapidly. The color on an avocado dip is a key feature to assess its esthetic and nutritious property. For this reason, we perform a research on temporal color analysis of avocado as quality control. The dip is subjected to microwave energy of 0.56 kJ/g to inactivate the enzyme that causes change of color. The color of the dip is monitored through time using digital image analysis. The results confirmed that after vacuum packing, refrigeration at 5°C, and 32 days, the dip under microwave treatment reported better color than a control sample.

Keywords: Color analysis, avocado, image analysis, microwave treatment

6.1 Introduction

The industrialization and sale of avocado are very important for many countries, specifically for Mexico. One of the products that has avocado is avocado dip (AD), which is mostly consumed fresh. However, because of the the high cost of avocado, its consumption is limited in other parts of the world. One way to increase its consumption is to industrialize AD.

Computer vision systems have been used for evaluating quality control and safety for various processes in the food industry (e.g., to classify and

---

*Corresponding author: hrios@uv.mx

Muthukumaran Malarvel, Soumya Ranjan Nayak, Surya Narayan Panda, Prasant Kumar Pattnaik and Nittaya Muangnak (eds.) Machine Vision Inspection Systems (Vol. 1): Image Processing, Concepts, Methodologies and Applications, (147–158) © 2020 Scrivener Publishing LLC

check size, shape, color, and level of ripeness of different fruits and food preparations) [1–7]. Consequently, computer vision and color analysis play a key role on the assessment of laboratory procedures in the industrialization of the AD. For example, a study [8] has analyzed the enzymatic browning of sliced and pureed avocado using fractal kinetics derived only from L* component after converting the images from RGB to $L^*a^*b^*$ color space. Nevertheless, the authors did not investigate the color change under microwave conditions. In contrast, our study analyzes the change of color in $a^*–b^*$ space which is less sensitive to illumination changes.

Another study [9] investigated the effect of microwave treatment on enzyme inactivation and quality change of defatted avocado puree. In contrast, our study works directly on fresh avocados and puree without defatting.

6.2   Materials and Methods

Figure 6.1 shows the block diagram of our methodology, which is composed of the following stages:

- Dip preparation. First, the avocado dip is prepared from Hass avocado.
- Microwave treatment. Second, the avocado dip is treated for 60 seconds with microwaves, using a standard oven to get

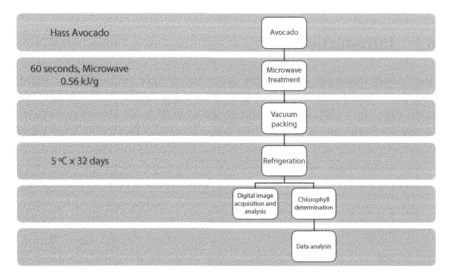

Figure 6.1 Diagram of the methodology.

0.56 kJ/g. During the heating, the dip attained a temperature of around 90°C. To stop the effect of the microwave, the temperature is suddenly dropped using ice.

- Vacuum packing. Then, the dip is vacuumed packed.
- Refrigeration. Finally, the dip is refrigerated at 5°C for 32 days.
- Analysis. A sample is obtained for analysis every 4 days. Specifically, digital image acquisition and chlorophyll determination are performed. Details regarding the chlorophyll determination can be found in the study of Ramirez-Gomez [10].

6.3   Image Acquisition

Matlab 2015, image acquisition toolbox and image processing toolbox, was used for image acquisition and processing.

Images are acquired using a standard USB camera, which returns images in the YUY2 color space. These images were transformed to red–green–blue (RGB) space.

The experimental setup is shown in Figure 6.2. It is important to remark that a designed cylindrical container for placing the avocado dip was made in order to reduce noise on images coming from lighting environment.

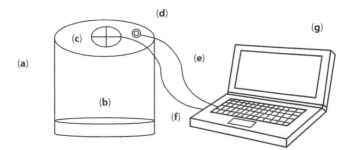

Figure 6.2 Diagram of the image acquisition setup with connection to a laptop. (a) The body of the cylindrical container is made of a nonreflecting white plastic. (b) The base where the avocado dip is placed. (c) The hollow where the cylinder USB camera is screwed. (d) The hollow where a USB cable comes out to power the illumination leds. (e) The cable for powering the leds that connects to a USB port from the laptop. (f) The cable that powers the USB camera and gets the images to the laptop (g) using a USB port.

6.4   Image Processing

As mentioned earlier, color is highly important to determine the freshness of the avocado dip. The image processing to analyze the avocado dip color was performed as follows:

- First, for each image, the average color (r_a, g_a, b_a) is computed in RGB color space by components:

$$r_a = \left(\sum_{i=1}^{N} r_i\right)\Big/N, g_a = \left(\sum_{i=1}^{N} g_i\right)\Big/N, b_a = \left(\sum_{i=1}^{N} b_i\right)\Big/N$$

  where (r_i, g_i, b_i) is i^{th} pixel in the image, and N is the total number of pixels in the image.
- Second, to obtain invariance of color to illumination changes, the average color in the RGB space is transformed to the $L^*a^*b^*$ color space.
- Finally, scatter plot diagrams and bivariate frequency histograms were generated to study the color distribution of each image in a^*-b^* space (see Figures 6.5–6.8).

6.5   Experimental Design

Two experimental designs were performed to analyze color changes on avocado dip under different conditions.

6.5.1   First Experimental Design

To analyze the color on the avocado dip, image colors of avocado dip samples were computed in RGB color space. The timeline analysis of the samples was of 48 hours. A color analysis was performed at 0, 4, 24, and 48 hours. These samples were processed using two treatments:

- Sample A. The avocado-dip samples did not go under microwave treatment and vacuum packing.
- Sample B. Avocado-dip samples went under microwave treatment and vacuum packing.

6.5.2   Second Experimental Design

To analyze the evolution of avocado dip in a longer period, a timeline analysis of 32 days was used. In this experimental design, image colors of avocado dip samples were transformed from the RGB space to the $L^*a^*b^*$ space, so that the color evolution can be analyzed with independence of illumination. The (a^*, b^*) components keep the color without influence from the luminance, L^* component. These samples were processed using two treatments:

- Sample A. Avocado dip packed in vacuum and kept in refrigeration for 32 days.
- Sample B. Avocado dip packed in vacuum and kept in refrigeration for 32 days. Additionally, microwaves were applied with 0.56 kJ/g.

6.6   Results and Discussion

6.6.1   First Experimental Design (RGB Color Space)

The results that follow are for avocado dip without refrigeration and without vacuum packing.

Figures 6.3 and 6.4 show the avocado dips of sample A (i.e., avocado dip without microwave treatment) and sample B (i.e., avocado dip was subjected to microwave treatment), respectively. Regarding sample A, it can be seen that the avocado dip color only stayed green at the 0 hour. It changed to brown color after 4 hours from its treatment. On the other hand, it can be noticed that the avocado dip color of sample B remained green after 24 hours from its treatment. Consequently, microwave treatment (sample B) kept the green avocado dip color for 24 hours more than treatment without microwaves (sample A).

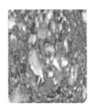

Figure 6.3 Avocado dip samples without microwave treatment taken at 0, 4, 24, and 48 hours.

Figure 6.4 Avocado dip samples with microwave treatment taken at 0, 4, 24, and 48 hours.

6.6.2   Second Experimental Design ($L^*a^*b^*$ Color Space)

Figure 6.5 shows the color evolution in a^*–b^* space without microwave treatment, whereas Figure 6.6 displays the results with microwave treatment. The results show that using the proposed microwave energy, 0.56 kJ/g, avocado dip is preserved greener than the control sample for all the

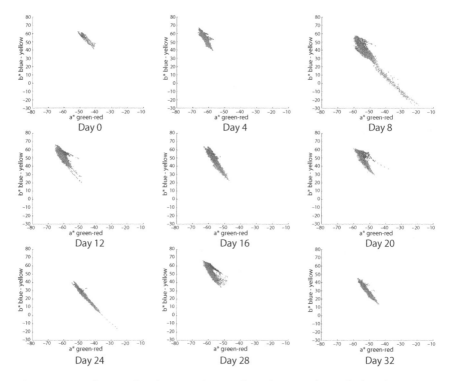

Figure 6.5 Distribution color plots in a^*–b^* space for each image of avocado dip. The horizontal axis of each plot is the a^* dimension, which varies from green to red. The vertical axis of each plot corresponds to b^* dimension, which varies blue to yellow. The color of each plotted pixel is located in coordinates (a^*, b^*), and for graphical purposes the displayed color is the corresponding (r, g, b) value. These plots correspond to images from avocado dip with refrigeration at 5°C, vacuum packing, and without microwave treatment. The images are displayed from left to right from day 0 to day 32 with an interval of 4 days.

times tested, with no refrigeration, and with refrigeration, 5°C, under vacuum packing.

Moreover, it can be seen that color in the a^*–b^* space of the sample B (subjected to microwave, Figure 6.6) is almost always more to the left and above than the sample A (control sample, Figure 6.5). This means that, almost always, its color is greener to yellower, more to the left in the a^* dimension (green–red), and more up in the b^* dimension (blue–yellow). This reflects the actual color of avocado dip that has a mixture of green–yellow coloration.

Figures 6.7 and 6.8 show an alternative display of color distribution for each image analyzed in a^*–b^* space. These plots show the joint probability distribution $P(a^*,b^*)$ of random variables a^* and b^*. In this case, $P(a^*,b^*)$ is

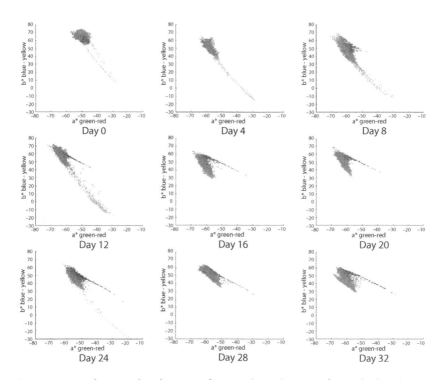

Figure 6.6 Distribution color plots in a^*–b^* space for each image of avocado dip. The horizontal axis of each plot is the a^* dimension, which varies from green to red. The vertical axis of each plot corresponds to the b^* dimension, which varies from blue to yellow. The color of each plotted pixel is located in the coordinates (a^*, b^*), and for graphical purposes, the displayed color is the corresponding (r, g, b) value. These plots correspond to images from avocado dip with refrigeration at 5°C, vacuum packing and with microwave treatment with 0.56 kJ/g. The images are displayed from left to right from day 0 to day 32 in increments of 4 days.

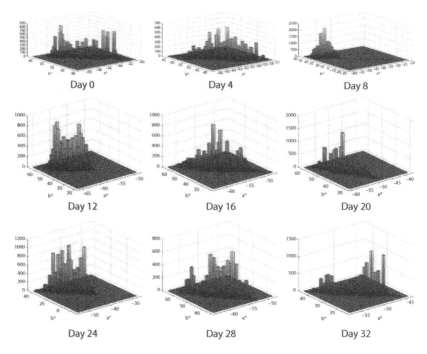

Figure 6.7 Bivariate frequency histogram for a^*–b^* space for each image of avocado dip. The horizontal plan is formed by a^* and b^* axes. The vertical axis is the frequency for each (a^*, b^*) value. The corresponding images of avocado are without microwave treatment.

represented by an unnormalized bivariate histogram. In each plot, the horizontal plane corresponds to the Cartesian product of the intervals, where each random variable, a^* and b^* vary. Random variable a^* varies in the range $[-100, 100]$, corresponding to the variation from color green to color red. Whereas random variable b^* varies in the range $[-100, 100]$, corresponding to the variation from color blue to color yellow. The vertical axis represents the frequency in the bivariate histogram. The height/value of each histogram bar at coordinates $(a^* = a_x, b^* = b_y)$ is equal to the number of pixels that simultaneously attain the color value $(a^* = a_x, b^* = b_y)$. The color of the bars in the bivariate histogram is represented using a "heat" color map which varies in the colors: blue, light blue, green, orange, and yellow, in correspondence from lower to higher frequencies. For instance, if a few pixels obtain a pair of values $(a^* = a_x, b^* = b_y)$, in the histogram, for that point, it will be represented with a short blue bar. In contrast, if many pixels obtain a particular combination of pair of values, the histogram on that position will display a large bar which has painted all the mentioned colors in the heat map, and in the highest part of the bar, it will have a yellow color.

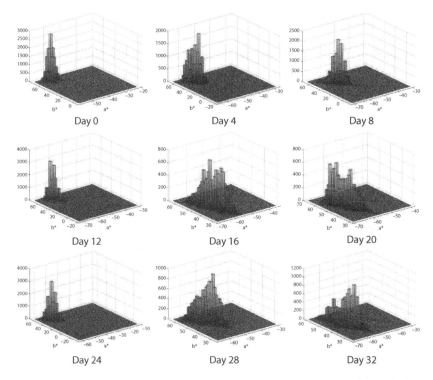

Figure 6.8 Bivariate frequency histogram for a^*-b^* space for each image of avocado dip. The horizontal plan is formed by a^* and b^* axes. The vertical axis is the frequency for each (a^*, b^*) value. The corresponding images of avocado are with microwave treatment.

Figure 6.7 displays the evolution of the bivariate frequency histogram in the a^*-b^* color space from day 0 to day 32 of the corresponding images for the control sample of avocado dip without microwave treatment.

Figure 6.8 displays also the evolution of the bivariate frequency histogram in the a^*-b^* color space for the same period of time, but in this case, the sample of the avocado dip received microwave treatment with 0.56 kJ/g.

Additionally, it is important to remark that the designed cylindrical container is useful to have a controlled illumination setting. Moreover, because of the use of computer vision monitoring in the a^*-b^* space, color invariance to illumination is preserved in a practical way using a standard USB camera. This experimental setting could be of value for laboratories studying the preservation of color for avocado dip under different treatments and for other food science experiments that need to monitor color through time.

6.7   Conclusion

This study presented an experimental setup for analyzing the color of avocado dip through time subjected to laboratory conditions. The analysis was based on color transformations using image processing/computer vision. Images were taken with a standard USB camera and transformed to $L^*a^*b^*$ space because the a^*b^* components have color invariance to illumination. Avocado-dip samples were analyzed under two experimental designs using different treatments: i) avocado-dip samples with microwave versus avocado-dip samples without microwave; and ii) avocado-dip samples packed in vacuum and kept in refrigeration for 32 days versus avocado-dip samples packed in vacuum, kept in refrigeration for 32 days, and with microwaves applied with 0.56 kJ/g. These treatments were analyzed in order to determine which ones maintain the color longer through time. Sample images were taken every 4 days during the timeline of the experiment. This study showed that avocado dip subjected to microwave energy of 0.56 kJ/g, with vacuum packing, and refrigeration at 5 °C, in an interval time of 32 days, preserved the green-yellow color tones longer than a reference sample without microwave treatment.

References

1. Zhang, B., Gu, B., Tian, G., Zhou, J., Huang, J., Xiong, Y., Challenges and solutions of optical-based nondestructive quality inspection for robotic fruit and vegetable grading systems: A technical review. *Trends Food Sci. Technol.*, 81, 213, 2018.
2. Moreda, G.P., Muñoz, M.A., Ruiz-Altisent, M., Perdigones, A., Shape determination of horticultural produce using two-dimensional computer vision—A review. *J. Food Eng.*, 108, 245, 2012.
3. Zhang, Y., Wanga, S., Ji, G., Phillips, P., Fruit classification using computer vision and feedforward neural network. *J. Food Eng.*, 143, 167, 2014.
4. Liu, Y., Pu, H., Sun, D., Hyperspectral imaging technique for evaluating food quality and safety during various processes: A review of recent applications. *Trends Food Sci. Technol.*, 69, 25, 2017.
5. Mery, D. and Pedreschi, F., Segmentation of colour food images using a robust algorithm. *J. Food Eng.*, 66, 353, 2005.
6. Steinbrenera, J., Poschb, K., Leitner, R., Hyperspectral fruit and vegetable classification using convolutional neural networks. *Comput. Electron. Agric.*, 162, 364, 2019.

7. Calvo, H., Moreno-Armendáriz, M.A., Godoy-Calderón, S., A practical framework for automatic food products classification using computer vision and inductive characterization. *Neurocomputing*, 175, 911, 2016.

8. Quevedo, R., Ronceros, B., Garcia, K., Lopéz, P., Pedreschi, F., Enzymatic browning in sliced and pureed avocado: A fractal kinetic study. *J. Food Eng.*, 105, 210, 2011.

9. Zhou, L., Tey, C.Y., Bingol, G., Bi, J., Effect of microwave treatment on enzyme inactivation and quality change of defatted avocado puree during storage. *Innov. Food Sci. Emerg. Technol.*, 37, 61, 2016.

10. Ramirez-Gomez, E.K., Digital image analysis of avocado dip treated with microwaves. Master thesis in Food Science, University of Veracruz, Mexico, 2019, (in Spanish).

7

Image and Video Processing for Defect Detection in Key Infrastructure

Hafiz Suliman Munawar

University of New South Wales (UNSW), Sydney, Australia

Abstract

In addition to causing damage to vehicles, road defects are one of the main causes of vehicle accidents which lead to loss of human lives. Many methods of detecting defects have been introduced over the years to reduce the consequences of these defects. One of these methods is image processing. Use of image and video processing has many applications in medicine, science, agriculture, and defect detection in structures. It has been used for defect detection on roads because timely detection and analysis of defect is very important for road serviceability and safety of the people.

Detection of a defect by image processing broadly follows some of the basic steps which include feature extraction, edge detection, morphological operators, and training of data. Different approaches are used for various kinds of defect detection and analysis which have replaced the manual inspection method of roads saving time and resources. This chapter discusses the basic steps involved in defect detection using image processing along with existing systems that use machine learning and artificial intelligence for the detection of defects from a distance. To write this chapter, papers on the topic of image and computer vision-based defect detection systems have been consulted.

Keywords: Image and video processing, defect detection, infrastructure, pavement cracking, puddle detection, deep learning

Email: h.munawar@unsw.edu.au

Muthukumaran Malarvel, Soumya Ranjan Nayak, Surya Narayan Panda, Prasant Kumar Pattnaik and Nittaya Muangnak (eds.) Machine Vision Inspection Systems (Vol. 1): Image Processing, Concepts, Methodologies and Applications, (159–178) © 2020 Scrivener Publishing LLC

7.1   Introduction

According to the latest report from the World Health Organization (WHO), around 1.35 million people have lost their lives in fatal road accidents. The number of deaths due to accidents increased from 1.2 million to 1.35 million in 3 years. Apart from the huge death count, the number of nonfatal injuries is getting much bigger every year which affects the health and well-being of survivors, as well as their families. Road accidents are the prime killer of people aged 5 to 29 years [1]. These causalities indirectly affect the economic growth of a country. According to a study conducted by The World Bank, a 10% reduction in road accidents can increase the Gross Domestic Product (GDP) by 3.6% in 24 years [2]. Developed countries are also affected by the issues of road accidents, but this a major problem in developing countries because of law and order situations and poor conditions of roads. Developed countries pay great attention to these issues and are trying to minimize the number of traffic accidents by using advanced techniques for detecting defects on roads. Underdeveloped countries lack these resources, and much attention is not given to the road conditions, which leads to a lot of traffic-related issues. Countries, like Iran, showed that the poor condition of roads contributed to almost 36% in the occurrence of traffic accidents [3]. Although there are many reasons which cause road accidents, like reckless driving, faulty vehicles, disobeying laws, a major issue among them is of the poor condition of roads and bridges. Many useful and advanced techniques have been applied to provide facilities to drivers and help minimize the risk of accidents. Roads are exposed to numerous attacks, such as meteorological conditions, base erosion, earthquakes, and most importantly, traffic. To reduce the threats caused by traffic accidents, road conditions should be properly monitored and reported at earliest for taking timely measures.

Previously, the detection of road defects was done manually by the road inspectors who had to drive on the road and collect visuals from the place which were then later measured and characterized to determine the required operation. This method is not only time-consuming but it is also a very tedious task to manage such a large data [4]. Once the problem was identified, fixing it would take time which also creates problems for the usual traffic. To solve these issues, newer technologies were incorporated to elevate the road conditions and to make improvements in road safety. With the growing use of image processing techniques and machine learning models in various fields of technological advancements, these techniques are now also being used to detect defects in surfaces. These techniques can detect defects in glass structures, ceramic tiles, pipes, solar wafers, and concrete. This ability of defect detection helps in early diagnosis of the problem and enhancements can be made in the structures to prevent any major disaster. This chapter mainly focuses on the use of image processing and machine learning tools for defect detection in roads and bridges which helps in minimizing road accidents up to some extent. Various kinds of defects are discussed along with their reasons and ways to reduce them are described in this chapter.

Different types of defects and failures which arise on roads and bridges mainly include cracks, water puddles, and potholes. Timely detection of these issues is essential for maintaining the reliability and structural health monitoring of the roads. All of these issues are individually addressed to know what causes such drawbacks. Various technologies that are used to prevent issues are also reviewed. Although many advanced methods have been developed to correctly detect the defects in roads and warn the drivers but it still needs a lot of attention and improvement.

7.2   Reasons for Defective Roads and Bridges

There are several reasons for the poor conditions of roads and bridges out of which the major reason is the use of faulty material and weak concrete, which is unable to bear the harsh conditions and heavy burden of bigger vehicles. After some time of being constantly exposed to these conditions, road conditions start to worsen. Another issue which mainly occurs during the rainy season is inadequate drainage of water. Water keeps standing on the road which is not only a problem in itself but also wears out the road condition by gradually weakening the concrete that results in potholes. The composition of the road is mainly of asphalt which is joined together by asphalt binder, many defects occur because of the inability of asphalt binder to contract and expand with the changing temperature which results in cracking on the roads. Countries that have very harsh weather conditions and receive snowfall often are affected by the frost on roads. As frost heave is harmful to the concrete material which softens the base, reducing the load bearing ability of the roads. Apart from the issue in concrete material, there are also issues of inefficient workmanship which during the time of road construction, which leads to an improper surface finish of the road that easily breaks after some time. Delay in the maintenance of the roads and lack of proper check on authorities is among the biggest issues in the construction field. These issues are not given their due and timely attention which leads to even bigger potholes and cracks that lead to a long time being required for fixing issues, resulting in inconvenience for the population.

7.3   Image Processing for Defect Detection

To deal with road defects, many machine learning and image processing technologies have been used to provide the best facilities to the drivers. Many of these applications are installed in the vehicle and detect the defects on the roads from a distance, which alert the driver and minimize the chances of accidents. Previous methods of defect detection on road were time-consuming. Therefore, much importance was given to improve the techniques of image processing that can provide information about defects on the roads in a quick and efficient manner. In these methods, the image of the concrete surface is taken and sent to the system which analyses characteristics like width, height, and area of the defect. For further improvements, a robot-based inspection of the roads has also been used which uses the concepts of machine learning. The major issue which arises during the defect analysis through machine learning and image processing is the presence of noise and the randomness in the shapes of the defects. All the image-based systems have some basic steps that are followed to ensure correct detections, an overview of the image-based detection system is presented in Figure 7.1.

For understanding the basics of image processing techniques that are implied for defect detection and different types of defects on the roads, this section will discuss the types of defects and the technologies used to detect the particular defect along with some basic steps required in image processing.

7.3.1   Feature Extraction

The quality of all the image and video-based systems depends on how efficiently it extracts useful data and discards the extra or irrelevant information. The most important step of image and video processing is the extraction of data that contains information without any loss so that it gives results with precision and accuracy. As the image-based systems use data sets for their training and learning, every image contains thousands to a million pixels and contains a lot of unnecessary data. Various methods of feature extraction are applied to the raw images which reduce the dimensionality of the image and save the computational time and resources.

Some of the basic feature extraction methods are edge detection, noise and background, image segmentation, principal component analysis (PCA), and speeded-up robust features (SURF) [37]. For even advanced methods of extraction, optical flow [38], a histogram of oriented gradients, Histogram Chain Codes [39], and wavelet-based approaches are used [37].

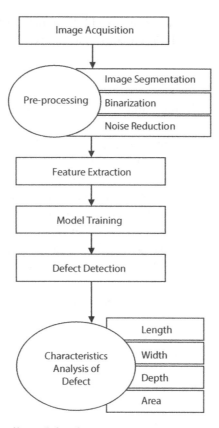

Figure 7.1 Overview of basic defect detection.

7.3.2 Morphological Operators

Morphological operations are widely used in image processing techniques for the removal of flaws in the images. These operations are applied to the image by selecting a small matrix whose size and shape significantly affect the results. Different kinds of morphological operations include dilation which adds pixels to the boundary, erosion which shrinks the boundary pixels, opening and closing which opens and fills up the gaps in the required region, respectively [40].

Morphological operators are used in the applications of defect detection as the input images of this application contains a lot of imperfections and errors and need to be resolved before further processing of the image. Defects possess very random characteristics in terms of their shape and size, so it is necessary to use the operations extremely carefully, such that the flaws in the raw data can be removed fully which leads to correct training of the model and exhibition of accurate results.

7.3.3   Cracks Detection

Most of the concrete bridges and roads show early age cracking in concrete which occurs immediately after their construction. Early detection of cracks is a major maintenance task as timely detection helps in taking appropriate steps and prevents major disasters. As soon as the cracks are formed in the concrete water and corrosive agents seep through these cracks to react with the undersurface materials and steel, an increase in the destruction of the roads and bridges occur, which requires costly maintenance. Many different kinds of cracks occur in concrete structures, which include alligator cracking, block cracking, edge cracks, and joint reflector cracks. The classification of these cracks is important to find the breaking point in the structure [5]. As there are various kinds of cracks, they also have randomness in shape, which makes them even more difficult to detect and analyze.

For an efficient and fast detection of cracks in concrete, a system based on image processing techniques was developed by Kaseko, which integrated conventional image processing techniques with the artificial neural network (NN) models by using video images. This method of defect detection comprised of image segmentation, extraction of features, breakdown of the image into tiles, and classifying the type of cracks. Though this technique successfully differentiated in major different kinds of cracks, it still needed further improvement and higher-resolution images [6]. Some other crack detection techniques that were used took the image of the cracked surface and detected the crack characteristics, like width and length by crack analysis [7]. However, improvement in their performance was much needed which was addressed in [8], which corrected the uneven brightness of the background area in the obtained image by using morphological techniques. For accurate information of crack characteristics, an artificial NN-based pattern recognition was proposed, and better results were obtained.

Typical algorithms of crack detection include edge detection, thresholding, and morphological operations which are used in many approaches for detection visually distinct cracks. Detection of cracks becomes very difficult in an automated manner because of notable visual clutter. Therefore, the use of machine learning proved to be more efficient as compared with the hand-tuned parameters [9]. An example of crack detection through image processing is shown in Figure 7.2.

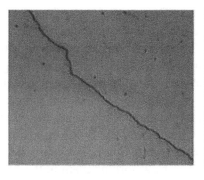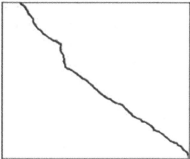

Figure 7.2 Crack detection [8].

7.3.4 Potholes Detection

Potholes are even bigger issues than the presence of cracks because they cause major harm to vehicles in addition to being the cause of other issues like water puddles in the rainy season. Potholes create a lot of inconvenience for the travelers, and it is even a bigger problem in developing countries where the roads are not of the best quality. Detection of potholes is comparatively easy than cracks in real time and proper timely action can be taken by the driver. Various reasons that contribute toward the formation of potholes are heavy traffic, the load exerted on the concrete and lack of timely maintenance. These cracks allow water and toxins to react with asphalt which eventually results in bigger potholes.

Potholes detection can be done in two ways, either by developing a device which can be installed in vehicles and perform road scan and send alert signal to the driver, and he can avoid them in time or by using a device that logs the position of potholes with Global Positioning System (GPS) and that data can be shared with general public by incorporating it with Google maps. Both systems use the basic techniques of image processing and machine learning which provides accuracy up to some extent but needs further improvements. In [10], a system for detection of potholes and road signs by image processing was developed by Danti *et al.* This system detected the pothole by using the distinguished black color of the hole and stated that application of a black and white threshold would easily highlight the pothole. To further improve the performance of these techniques, another system that used image thresholding by the use of a histogram shape-based algorithm was developed by Koch *et al.* Morphological thinning and elliptical regression algorithms were applied to separate background pixels from the area of interest [11]. A detailed survey provides specifics of the existing system applied to defect detection specifically focusing on pothole detection. The pros and cons of image processing methods used in pothole detection are reviewed at length [12].

Method of pothole detection by [13] used only image processing without using machine learning, GoPro camera was used to take sample images as it removes the errors that occur due to blurred images. Regions with potholes were extracted from the given image and a Gaussian filter was used to remove the noise in the images. Edge detection is the major and most important part of the analysis which was done by using a simple canny edge detector producing a black and white image. The canny detector was dilated to remove unwanted edges by absorbing them in the outer boundary and leaving the contour visible. The designed system had fairly fast execution speed which made it possible to detect potholes in vehicles traveling at a speed of less than 60km/h. Figure 7.3 shows the method of detecting potholes using a Canny edge detector.

7.3.5 Water Puddles Detection

The presence of water puddles on the road is dangerous to the vehicles and is also a cause of many accidents. Therefore, awareness about these defects

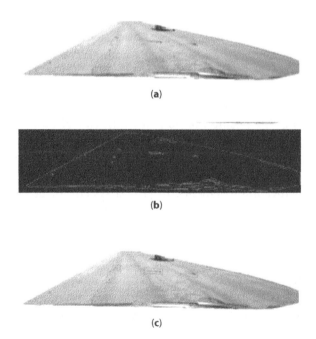

(a)

(b)

(c)

Figure 7.3 Potholes detection. (a) Input image, (b) Detection, (c) Output image [13].

on roads is much needed for the safety of the travelers. For the detection of water puddles and wet roads, two main approaches are used; one of which is the use of near-infrared (NIR), and the other is microwave radar.

Using the method of NIR, an idea of detecting ice and wet areas on-road using temperature variations from the exothermic reaction was presented. These methods showed poor results on water and were expensive for commercial use [14, 15]. The use of bistatic radars was also incorporated in the detection of water puddles, for which the model of dual-polarized radar at 24 GHz and 77 GHz for detection of water and ice that works by detecting low friction areas was given, and it showed better results than NIR [16].

In later developments, the use of a camera was introduced to detect wet areas on-road using red, blue, and green (RGB) or hue, saturation, and brightness (HSB) information, which was not enough for characterizing a water body as their color distribution varies greatly [17]. For addressing this issue, the idea of using a stereo camera to obtain images was given and two different approaches to detect damp regions and water puddles were presented because they have different characteristics. Detection of water bodies comprised of hypothesis generation and hypothesis verification, features were extracted from the images obtained from the stereo camera and the data was trained by support vector mechanism (SVM) that margins the dry area from wet puddle detection was done by using the random sample consensus (RANSAC) that randomly selects samples from the data set and applies the least square method for estimation of model parameters. Inliers and outliers are separated by applying a threshold which helps in evaluating the model parameters [18]. An example of a water puddle and its detection is shown in Figure 7.4 and Figure 7.5 respectively.

7.3.6 Pavement Distress Detection

Detection of pavement defects has come a long way with providing many facilities to people and commercial use. With the growth of technology in

Figure 7.4 Water puddles [18].

Figure 7.5 Water puddles detection [18].

image processing and availability of higher-resolution cameras, this field gained much popularity and accuracy, such that some models can even identify 1mm cracks. Currently, pavement defects are detected by two methods; one is used by public agencies which is a typical manual type while the other is used by private vendors and is semi-automatic. Manual approaches are much time consuming so semi-automatic approaches are widely used which obtain defect information by using different algorithms [19, 20].

For further refinement in this field, civil infrastructure defect detection with the integration of computer vision is evolving as a whole research field that is constantly working to evolve the methods and overcome the limitations. Many of the artificial NN algorithms were incorporated to train the system and achieve better accuracy. It was proposed to work with a crack detection method that used unsupervised learning along with supervised learning for the detection of multiple cracks in the image [21]. Discrete and multiscale wavelet resolution transformations also caught much attention for detection purposes. In later stages, NNs were used for the cracks classification and showed much better performance than traditional classifiers. Use of Deep Convolutional Neural Network (DCNN) for the detection of defects gained much attention and a method of VGG-16 model with pretrained weights on ImageNet was proposed by Gopalkrishnan *et al.* [19]. Deep learning methods require a fairly large data set for training purposes, such as has been used in this method. The model had 144 million parameters contained in 16 layered deep convolutional NNs and was significantly insensitive toward color and texture variations. Results obtained from this model were significantly good with higher values of true positives and true negatives and even proved to be cost-efficient because simple augmentation methods like scaling, mirror, and rotation were used [19]. Pavement distress and the detection of the defect are shown in Figure 7.6.

After discussing different types of road defects, it is clear that all of the defects require a particular system for their detection and analysis. Though all defects may not be as severe as to cause major problems and may only

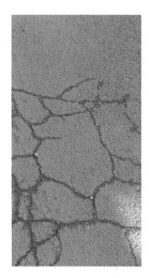 

Figure 7.6 Pavement distress detection [22].

Table 7.1 Structural defects and severity scales [23].

Defect types	Negligible	Moderate	Critical
Cracking	<0.8 mm	0.80-3.20 mm	>3.20 mm
Potholes	<10 mm diameter	10-50 mm (diameter)	50-75 mm (diameter)
Water puddles	No drop, wet surface	Active flow <30 drips per minute	Active flow >30 drips per minute

require a quick action for maintenance. A comparison of the defects and the scales of their severity are given in Table 7.1.

7.4   Image-Based Defect Detection Methods

The use of image-based techniques increased tremendously in various fields, including technology, medicine, agriculture, and defect detection, because it is a versatile method in addition to being cost-efficient. Defect detection is important for the safety of travelers and to provide them inconvenience free travel routes. For many similar reasons, various methods for defect detection were proposed by researchers. Some of the image-based methods, and their uses will be discussed in this section. Classifying the defect detection by image-based techniques broadly includes threshold-ing techniques, edge detection, wavelet transform, and machine learning techniques.

7.4.1   Thresholding Techniques

Thresholding is a simple way of splitting the image into the foreground and background. The region of interest (ROI) for any image is formed by the foreground, and all the further processing techniques are applied only on ROI. This splitting of image pixels helps in reducing the complexity and computation of the data which otherwise takes more time and resources. Binarization of image is crucial and dependent on the thresholding of the system. For a proper binarized image, an appropriate threshold value is needed. Thresholding techniques are divided into two categories, local thresholding techniques and global thresholding techniques [22]. Some local thresholding techniques are applied in the images obtained for crack detection, among which, the intensity thresholding is an efficient and widely used method. Primitively, histogram-based and iterated clipping methods have been used for enhancing the images but they were unable to handle the input obtained from the frequently changing environment [23, 24]. In recent years, the idea of using a dynamic optimization method for segmentation was suggested. Though this method has high computa-tional cost but was useful in obtaining data from low signal to noise ratio (SNR) images [25]. Some of the local thresholding techniques are Niblack's techniques, T.R Singh's technique, Sauvola's technique, and Bernsen's tech-nique [26]. Adaptive binarization has also been used for the thresholding purpose which is similar to the Sauvola technique but runs faster like the Otsu method [27].

7.4.2   Edge Detection Techniques

Edge detection is a widely and most commonly used technique for the detection of contours and boundaries. The points at which the bright-ness of the image changes sharply form an edge of the object. Some of the important edge detectors are canny edge detector, Sobel edge detector, and fuzzy edge detectors which have little variations in their operation. After noise reduction and image smoothing, a bidimensional empirical mode decomposition algorithm was used for the application of the Sobel edge detector [28]. In another method, morphological and median filters were applied for noise reduction and crack detection. Although edge detection has many advantages, they are incapable of complete crack detection. Canny edge detector was used by Zhao to detect edges in the pavement but the canny operators are unable to detect weak edges so Mallet wavelet transform was used to overcome this issue and the process proved to be less time consuming and more effective [29].

7.4.3 Wavelet Transform Techniques

Wavelet transform techniques decompose the signal into a mathematical function that analyzes the incoming image and converts it into a set of mathematic expressions. The use of the transform reduces the storage space for the images which helps in increasing the process performance. These transforms have been utilized in defects and cracks detection in the pavement. Subsequently, separation of noise and background for the road distress is done by using wavelet coefficients [30]. Two-dimensional continuous wavelet transforms are also used for the creation of multiscale complex coefficient maps which help in constructing maxima location maps for crack detection. Though these transforms greatly help in space-saving, great care is needed while applying them so that user data does not get compressed. Also, the transforms are not good in handling cracks with high curvature and low continuity [31].

7.4.4 Texture Analysis Techniques

Texture analysis is very important for defect detection as the concrete is highly textured and contains randomness. Texture analysis has four major categories which are;

- i. Statistical method,
- ii. Structural methods,
- iii. Model-based methods,
- iv. Transform based methods.

These approaches differ from each other mainly by the method of textural feature extraction [32]. Crack detection in pavements can be done by texture classification using local binary pattern operators that easily differentiate cracks and background [33]. Roads and bridges are the crucial components for transportation and need to be in perfect conditions for safe traveling of the public. Although both of these structures are concrete, their texture and composition are slightly different from each other so they are also individually addressed by the researchers to ensure correct results. Cracks in bridges are detected by the use of SVM and wavelet feature methods that provided fairly good detection results but needed improvement by incorporating unmanned aerial vehicles (UAV) [34].

7.4.5   Machine Learning Techniques

Machine learning is being used for many purposes in different fields of science because it is a subdomain of artificial intelligence (AI) that has the distinguishability of learning and improving automatically by experience. Machine learning involves development of such computer programs that are able to access and learn about the given data and make predictions or decisions based on it. Machine learning techniques have been used in defect detection. These techniques take the input image of the concrete structure and divide it into subimages [31]. Features are extracted from these subimages to form a vector and use them for the training of the model which helps in the classification of the cracks. Back Propagation (BP) NN using the set of moment invariants as the feature has also been used for distinguishing the types of defects in the road or bridge [35]. Another method is using statistical values, like mean and standard deviation, for crack detection. This was later refined by using a curve detector, and Bayesian classifier was given [21]. Extending the use of machine learning in defect detection, many classifiers have been incorporated to ensure better performance. Adaboost is the first boosting algorithm that provided successful results and has been used in defect detection to reduce the number of images for the inspection [36]. Some of the basic feature extraction methods are edge detection, noise and background, image segmentation, Principal Component Analysis (PCA) and Speeded-Up Robust Features (SURF) [37]. For even advanced methods of extraction, optical flow [38], a histogram of oriented gradients, Histogram Chain Codes [39], and wavelet-based approaches are used [40].

7.5   Factors Affecting the Performance

Numerous factors affect the performance of an image-based system that gathers data from structures that exhibit randomness in their characteristics and has a chance of error because of the rapidly changing environment. For image-based models that are installed in the vehicle or any other place, take the input image and analyze it based on its training. Major factors that can affect the performance of these systems are described in this section.

7.5.1 Lighting Variations

With changing weather conditions, the lighting conditions vary greatly which affects the image quality for the image-based system. On a rainy day, the values of pixels in the image vary greatly from an extremely sunny day for the same area, and it will affect the performance of the system because of the abrupt change in pixel values. In addition to this, shady areas also exhibit different characteristics than a brighter place and the image quality will also be affected by this change. Both of these factors need to be addressed while designing any model of defect detection on roads [11].

7.5.2 Small Database

All the NN models and especially CNN models require a very large data set for the training of the system. If a model is trained on a smaller database, it may not retrieve all the relevant features from the image which results in the wrong detection or maybe no detection at all in some cases. For this reason, the training database of the models should be fairly large containing millions of images with a lot of variations such that correct detection of the defect can be ensured.

7.5.3 Low-Quality Data

If the images in the database contain a lot of errors and flaws, it will result in wrong parameter training and incorrect detection of the defect. Brightness and contrast values of the pixel vary greatly with a small change in the input image. Values of the pixels need to be normalized before passing it for the training. Proper filtering and noise removal from the image is necessary for the image-based systems so that the results produced are accurate.

7.6 Achievements and Issues

The use of image processing and machine learning has gained tremendous importance in the field of road defect detection and reduced human effort for the manual inspection of roads and provided road safety to the travelers. This section discusses some of the achievements in this field in addition to the issues and challenges that still exist in the technology requiring improvements.

7.6.1   Achievements

The use of image and computer vision-based methods in the defect assessment and detection has come a long way providing many facilities and ease to people. Currently, the existing methods are successful in automating the detection, localization and measuring the defects in concrete. These systems are also used in the inspection of bridges and tunnels because of their high resolution, which was not possible before. The use of automated software has replaced the manual inspection method of defects on the road that required a lot of time and man force.

In addition to the provision of facilities to the construction vendors, they have greatly facilitated the drivers by providing information to them about the defects on the road. This helps reduce the chances of accidents on a great scale and also provides an inconvenience-free travel route to the people.

7.6.2   Issues

As all of the used computer vision methods rely on the acquired data given to them, there is still a great chance of errors in the incoming images which leads to incorrect detection of the defects. The performance of these systems is greatly affected by factors like camera distance and placement as a slight change can lead to the wrong detection or no detection. Environmental factors also play a huge role in the performance of these systems, images acquired on a sunny day will vary from the images obtained on a cloudy or rainy day because of the lightning variations and it causes issues for the system that are based on the acquired images.

Recent methods of machine learning depend on the training data for the creation of robust classifiers which need supervised learning that requires labor and is prone to errors. When a public scene is monitored, it also has issues related to people's privacy, so it is recommended to refrain from taking people's images and videos.

7.7   Conclusion

Defect detection on roads and bridges using the techniques of image processing and machine learning have exhibited tremendous benefits as they have greatly helped in reducing the number of accidents and provided trouble-free routes to the drivers. Many of these systems have been used to inspect the condition of roads which results in the timely detection of any defects and help in the maintenance of roads. These systems have replaced the manual methods of road inspection which required a lot of time and resources in addition to the man force. Roads exhibit different kinds of defects which include cracks, potholes, puddles and patches which greatly differ from each other in characteristics so every defect needs particular detection systems which have been discussed in this chapter.

Though the application of image processing methods for detecting defects proved to be of much greater importance and provided many facilities, still they are faced with certain issues and factors that negatively affect the performance of the system, calling for further improvements. Image-based defect detection systems should be available on a larger scale with proper installment in vehicles for the general public so that they can benefit from the systems, leading to a reduction in the number of accidents and ensuring safer travelling.

References

1. World Health Organization (WHO). Global status report on road safety 2018 (2018). Geneva, Switzerland, WHO, 2019.
2. Bank, T.W., *The High Toll of Traffic Injuries: Unacceptable and Preventable*, The World Bank, USA, 2018.
3. Esmaeili, A., Khalili, M., Pakgohar, A., Determining the road defects impact on accident severity; based on vehicle situation after an accident, an approach of logistic regression. *International Conference on Statistics in Science, Business and Engineering (ICSSBE)*, Langkawi, Malaysia, IEEE, 2012.
4. Cord, A. and Chambon, S., Automatic road defect detection by textural pattern recognition based on AdaBoost. *Comput.-Aided Civ. Infrastruct. Eng.*, 27, 244–259, 2012.
5. Sun, Y., Salari, E., Chou, E., Automated pavement distress detection using advanced image processing techniques. *IEEE International Conference on Electro/Information Technology*, Windsor, ON, Canada, IEEE, 2009.
6. Kaseko, M.S. and Ritchie, S.G., A neural network-based methodology for pavement crack detection and classification. *Transp. Res. Part C Emerg. Technol.*, 1, 4, 275–291, 1993.
7. Ito, A., Aoki, Y., Hashimoto, S., Accurate extraction and measurement of fine cracks from concrete block surface image. *28th Annual Conference of the Industrial Electronics Society*, IECON 02, Sevilla, Spain, IEEE, 2002.
8. Lee, B.Y., Kim, Y.Y., Yic, S.T., Kimd, J.K., Automated image processing technique for detecting and analysing concrete surface cracks. *Struct. Infrastruct. Eng.*, 9, 6, 567–577, 2013.
9. Prasanna, P., Dana, K.J., Gucunski, N., Basily, B.B., La, H.M., Lim, R.S., Parvardeh, H., Automated crack detection on concrete bridges. *IEEE Trans. Autom. Sci. Eng.*, 13, 2, 591–599, 2014.

10. Danti, A., Kulkarni, J.Y., Hiremath, P., An image processing approach to detect lanes, pot holes and recognize road signs in Indian roads. *International Journal of Modeling and Optimization*, 2, 6, 658–662, 2002.

11. Koch, C. and Brilakis, I., Pothole detection in asphalt pavement images. *Adv. Eng. Inf.*, 25, 3, 507–511, 2011.

12. Bello-Salau, H., Aibinu, A.M., Onwuka, E.N., Dukiya, J.J., Onumanyi, A.J., Image processing techniques for automated road defect detection: a survey. *11th International Conference on Electronics, Computer and Computation (ICECCO)*, Abuja, Nigeria, IEEE, 2014.

13. Nienaber, S., Booysen, M., Kroon, R., Detecting potholes using simple image processing techniques and real-world footage. *South African Transport Conference*, Pretoria, 2015.

14. Riehm, M., Gustavsson, T., Bogren, J., Jansson, P.E., Ice formation detection on road surfaces using infrared thermometry. *Cold Reg. Sci. Technol.*, 83–84, 71–76, 2012.

15. Jonsson, P., *Remote sensor for winter road surface status detection*, SENSORS, Limerick, Ireland, 2011.

16. Viikari, V., Varpula, T., Kantanen, M., Automotive radar technology for detecting road conditions. Backscattering properties of dry, wet, and icy asphalt. *European Radar Conference*, Amsterdam, Netherlands, IEEE, 2008.

17. Rankin, A. and Matthies, L., Daytime water detection based on color variation. *IEEE/RSJ International Conference on Intelligent Robots and Systems*, Taipei, Taiwan, IEEE, 2010.

18. Kim, J., Baek, J., Choi, H., Kim, E., Wet area and puddle detection for advanced driver assistance systems (ADAS) using a stereo camera. *Int. J. Control Autom. Syst.*, 14, 1, 263–271, 2016.

19. Gopalakrishnan, K., Khaitan, S. K., Choudhary, A., & Agrawal, A. . Deep Convolutional Neural Networks with transfer learning for computer vision-based data-driven pavement distress detection. *Constr. Build. Mater.*, 157, 322–330, 2018. https://doi.org/10.1016/j.conbuildmat.2017.09.110

20. Oliveira, H. and Correia, P.L., Identifying and retrieving distress images from road pavement surveys. *15th IEEE International Conference on Image Processing*, San Diego, CA, USA, IEEE, 2008.

21. Oliveira, H. and Correia, P.L., Automatic road crack detection and characterization. *IEEE Trans. Intell. Transp. Syst.*, 14, 1, 155–168, 2012.

22. Singh, O.I., Sinam, T., James, O., Taiyenjam, R., Local contrast and mean based thresholding technique in image binarization. *Int. J. Comput. Appl. Technol.*, 51, 6, 4–10, 2012.

23. Kirschke, K.R. and Velinsky, S.A., Histogram-based approach for automated pavement-crack sensing. *J. Transp. Eng.*, 118, 5, 700–710, 1992.

24. Oh, H., Garrick, N.W., Achenie, L., Segmentation algorithm using iterative clipping for processing noisy pavement images, in: *International Conference on Imaging Technologies: Techniques and Applications in Civil Engineering, (ASCE)*, Second International Conference Engineering Foundation; and

Imaging Technologies Committee of the Technical Council on Computer Practices, American Society of Civil Engineers. 1998.

25. Tsai, Y.C., Kaul, V., Mersereau, R.M., Critical assessment of pavement distress segmentation methods. *J. Transp. Eng.*, 136, 1, 11–19, 2010.

26. Firdousi, R. and Parveen, S.R., Local Thresholding techniques in image binarization. *International Journal of Engineering And Computer Science*, 3, 3, 4062–4065, 2014.

27. Shafait, F., Keysers, D., Breuel, T., Efficient implementation of local adaptive thresholding techniques using integral images. *Document Recognition and Retrieval XV, 15th Document Recognition and Retrieval Conference, part of the IS&T-SPIE Electronic Imaging Symposium*, San Jose, CA, USA, 2008.

28. Ayenu-Prah, A.Y. and Nii, A.O., Evaluating pavement cracks with bidimensional empirical mode decomposition. *J. Adv. Signal. Process*, 1, 1–7, 2008.

29. Zhao, H., Qin, G., Wang, X., Improvement of canny algorithm based on pavement edge detection. *3rd International Congress on Image and Signal Processing*, Yantai, China, IEEE, 2010.

30. Zhou, J., Huang, P.S., Chiang, F.P., Wavelet-based pavement distress detection and evaluation. *Opt. Eng.*, 45, 2, 2006.

31. Zou, Q., Cao, Y., Li, Q., Mao, Q., Wang, S., CrackTree: Automatic crack detection from pavement images. *Pattern Recognit. Lett.*, 33, 3, 227–238, 2012.

32. Bharati, M.H., Liu, J.J., MacGregor, J.F., Image texture analysis: methods and comparisons. *Chemometr. Intell. Lab. Syst.*, 72, 1, 57–71, 2004.

33. Hu, Y. and Zhao, C.X., A local binary pattern based methods. *Journal of Pattern Recognition Research*, 1, 140–147, 2010.

34. Bu, G., Chanda, S., Guan, H., Jo, J., Blumenstein, M., Loo, Y., Crack detection using a texture analysis-based technique for visual bridge inspection. *Electron. J. Struct. Eng.*, 14, 1, 41–48, 2014.

35. Nguyen, T.S., Avila, M., Begot, S., Automatic detection and classification of defect on road pavement using anisotropy measure. *17th European Signal Processing Conference*, Glasgow, UK, IEEE, 2009.

36. Cord, A. and Chambon, S., Automatic road defect detection by textural pattern recognition based on AdaBoost. *Comput.-Aided Civ. Infrastruct. Eng.*, 27, 4, 244–259, 2012.

37. Koch, C., Georgieva, K., Kasireddy, V., Akinci, B., Fieguth, P., A review on computer vision-based defect detection and condition assessment of concrete and asphalt civil infrastructure. *Adv. Eng. Inf.*, 29, 2, 2015.

38. Halfawy, M.R. and Hengmeechai, J., Optical flow techniques for estimation of camera motion parameters in sewer closed-circuit television inspection videos. *Autom. Constr.*, 38, 39–45, 2014.

39. Nguyen, T.H., Zhukov, A., Nguyen, T.L., *On-road defects detection and classification*, Artificial Intelligence Science and Technology (AIST), Shanghai, China, 2016.

40. Srisha, R. and Khan, A., Morphological operations for image processing: understanding and its applications, in: *Proc. 2nd National Conference on VLSI, Signal processing & Communications NCVSComs*, 2013.

8

Methodology for the Detection of Asymptomatic Diabetic Retinopathy

Jaskirat Kaur[1]* and Deepti Mittal[2]

[1]Jaskirat Kaur, Assistant Professor, Department of Research and Development, Chandigarh Group of Colleges, Mohali, Punjab, India
[2]Deepti Mittal, Associate Professor, Department of Electrical and Instrumentation Engineering, Thapar Institute of Engineering and Technology, Patiala, Punjab, India

Abstract

Diabetic retinopathy, an asymptomatic problem of diabetes, is one of the leading sources of blindness worldwide. The primary detection and diagnosis can decrease the incidence of severe vision loss due to diabetes. Therefore, the present study was conducted to design an experiment in order to diagnose symptomless clinical stages of diabetic retinopathy, i.e., progressive diabetic retinopathy and nonproliferative diabetic retinopathy subjectively and objectively. The diagnostic confirmation of diabetic retinopathy depends on the reliable detection and classification of bright lesions, such as exudates and cotton wool spots, and dark lesions, such as: microaneurysms and hemorrhages, present in retinal fundus images. However, variations in the retinal fundus images make it difficult to discriminate dark and bright lesions in the existence of landmarks, like blood vessels and optic disk. Thus, it is essential to remove any spurious and false areas caused by anatomical structures before the segmentation of retinal lesions. In addition, to design an efficient computer-aided diagnostic method, a benchmark composite database, having variable characteristics, such as position, dimensions, shapes, and color is required. Keeping all these facts in mind, a composite experimental methodology is designed in this study for an effective analysis of the computer-aided solution for the diagnosis of diabetic retinopathy.

Keywords: Diabetic retinopathy, fundus images, retinal images, lesions, blood vessels, methodology

---

Corresponding author: jaskiratkaur17@gmail.com

Muthukumaran Malarvel, Soumya Ranjan Nayak, Surya Narayan Panda, Prasant Kumar Pattnaik and Nittaya Muangnak (eds.) Machine Vision Inspection Systems (Vol. 1): Image Processing, Concepts, Methodologies and Applications, (179–196) © 2020 Scrivener Publishing LLC

8.1   Introduction

Retinal abnormalities comprise an important public health issue having high occurrence in developing countries. Retinal abnormalities are broadly classified as systemic and nonsystemic. Systemic retinal abnormalities spread in the entire body and affect multiple organs in the body, whereas nonsystemic retinal abnormalities are ocular manifestations that originate and reside in retina. This study is focused on designing an experiment for the analysis of systemic retinal abnormality related to diabetes. Among a variety of retinal abnormalities, diabetes is one of the severe retinal abnormalities. Diabetes has several adverse effects on numerous parts of the body, such as eyes, nervous system, heart, kidneys, and other organs, but the first most likely to be affected is the retina, hence, the patient's sight. In addition, prolonged diabetes is the foremost cause of irreversible vision loss, accounting for almost 15% of all blindness cases [1]. Diabetic retinopathy (DR), a retinal abnormality of diabetes mellitus, is the prime cause of vision impairment worldwide. According to International Diabetes Federation, the rise in occurrence of diabetes affects 451 million people globally and is estimated to affect vision of about 693 million people by 2045 [2]. Rapidly rising rate of obesity, sedentary lifestyles, and lack of physical activity are the prime contributing factors of an increased prevalence of diabetes. A survey conducted by International Diabetes Federation estimated that around 49.7% diabetic cases worldwide were undiagnosed and left untreated, leading to complications, such as blindness, kidney failure, heart disease, stroke, and so on [3]. Globally, diabetes is the seventh leading cause of death in the year 2016. India tops the list of countries with the highest number of diabetics in 2017 and represented 49% of the world's diabetes burden with an estimated 72 million cases, a figure expected to almost double to 134 million by 2025 [4].

Diabetic retinopathy is a chronic abnormality which is characterized by the presence of single or multiple retinal lesions like micro aneurysms (MA), hemorrhages (HEM), exudates (EXU), and cotton wool spots (CWS). Mainly DR can be categorized as nonproliferative DR (NPDR), progressive DR, and proliferative DR. Nonproliferative DR advances from mild stage to moderate and severe stages [5]. Mild NPDR is characterized by the presence of even one micro aneurysms. Moderate NPDR is characterized by the collective presence of few hemorrhages, hard exudates, and cotton wool spots, whereas these lesions are present in large number in severe NPDR. Additionally, the only sole appearance of exudates determines the presence of progressive DR. Proliferative DR, an advanced stage identified by the development of new vessels in varying parts of retinal fundus image, may lead to irreversible vision loss. Also, the treatment at this stage turned out to be less effective. Individuals affected with non-proliferative DR and progressive DR usually show no distinctive symptoms and mostly does not affect vision until a proliferative stage of DR is reached. In brief, vision impairment through DR is stage-dependent and the vision is least affected when retinopathy is diagnosed at early stage. It is, therefore, significant to diagnose DR at an initial symptomless clinical stage. One major challenge in the process of diagnosing DR is to diagnose the severity level of DR correctly. Therefore, the present study is focused on the designing of experiment for the diagnosis of symptomless clinical stages of DR, i.e., progressive DR and nonproliferative DR.

8.2   Key Steps of Computer-Aided Diagnostic Methods

Generally, the computer-aided diagnostic methods for the detection of DR are based on five steps that are shown in Figure 8.1.

(i)   Retinal image database: Several types of open-source retinal image databases are available online that are used by researchers to evaluate the methods. However, because of their lack of completeness with respect to DR screening, few researchers have developed and used clinically

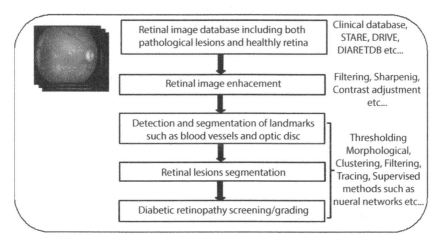

Figure 8.1 The architecture of computer-aided diagnostic method for the detection and grading of DR.

acquired databases along with open-source databases to evaluate the robustness of their designed methods with respect to variability in retinal images.

(ii) Retinal image enhancement: The key issues in fundus imaging are nonuniform illumination, presence of artifacts, and blur. Image enhancement involves filtering, sharpening, and local and global contrast improvement without destroying the significant information that is useful for diagnosis.

(iii) Detection and segmentation of anatomical structures: In this step, landmarks, namely, blood vessels and optic disk are identified, segmented, and separated from the background. The resulting image is then used for retinal lesions identification and classification.

(iv) Retinal lesions segmentation: In this step, bright and dark lesions are detected, segmented, and distinguished from each other by specifically designed method.

(v) Diabetic retinopathy detection (screening) and grading: In this step, various classification methods are applied to classify retinal images with suspected lesions into various grades of DR.

(vi) Retinal image enhancement: The key issues in fundus imaging are nonuniform illumination, presence of artifacts and blur. Image enhancement involves filtering, sharpening, and local and global contrast improvement without destroying the significant information that is useful for diagnosis.

(vii) Detection and segmentation of anatomical structures: in this step, landmarks namely, such as blood vessels and optic disk are identified, segmented, and separated from background. The resulting image is then used for retinal lesions identification and classification.

(viii) Retinal lesions segmentation: In this step, bright and dark lesions are detected, segmented, and distinguished from each other by specifically designed method.

(ix) Diabetic retinopathy detection (screening) and grading: In this step, various classification methods are applied to classify retinal images with suspected lesions into various grades of DR.

Some of the computer-aided diagnostic methods do not involve grading of DR and solely discriminate images as normal and pathological. In such methods, precise retinal lesions segmentation is not carried out, and only the presence or absence of lesion is obtained.

8.3   DR Screening and Grading Methods

Numerous computer-aided diagnostic methods have been developed for disease detection from various body using medical images, such as mammograms, ultrasound, Electrocardiogram (ECG), Magnetic Resonance Imaging (MRI), fundus, and so on [6–15, 27–29]. The identification and detection of various anatomical structures is necessary to judge the severity level of DR. As a result, numerous computer-aided diagnostic methods were proposed for the detection of DR using these methods. Such computer-aided diagnostic methods are summarized in Table 8.1 [16–26].

Pires *et al.* screened retinal images with DR solely based on the presence or absence of lesions. They detected various dark and bright lesions using bag-of-visual words, semisoft coding and max pooling techniques [17]. The authors though did not classify the kind of lesion spotted and evaluated only the presence or absence of the DR. The method reported the area under the ROC curve of 94.2%. Whereas Mookiah *et al.* proposed a similar DR screening method to discriminate between healthy and unhealthy retinal image using feature extraction and reported an AUC of 94.17% [18]. Welikala *et al.* applied 4D feature vector to feed an SVM classifier and recognized only the severe stage of DR with sensitivity/specificity of 91/96, respectively [19]. Prakash *et al.* classified retinal images into five severity grades of DR by using dual-stage classification using NN-SVM and achieved an accuracy of 80% [20]. However, these approaches were computationally expensive. Roychowdhury detected dark and bright retinal lesions using 30 sets of optimized features [21]. They applied hierarchical classification approach to eliminate the false positives and then final classification of dark and bright lesion structures is carried out. Per-image sensitivity of 100% and low specificity of 53.16% demonstrate the incapability of the approach to detect normal images as healthy during classification process. Akram *et al.* proposed a three-step method consisting of preprocessing, extraction of candidate lesions, feature set formulation, and final classification for grading the severity of DR [22]. The method combines m-Medoids modeling using Gaussian mixture model in an ensemble to form a hybrid classifier. The proposed system achieved per-image and per-lesion sensitivity/specificity/accuracy of 99.17/97.07/98.5 and 96.41/93.86/94.88, respectively. However, the process of hybridization of classifiers demonstrates it to be a computationally expensive. The DR screening system

Table 8.1 Brief detail of state-of-the-art related to DR screening.

Author (Ref.)	Method used	Task	Number of retinal images	Performance measures (%)
Pires [17]	• Bag of visual words • Semisoft coding • Max pooling Techniques	Detection of lesions related to DR	1077 (DR1) 520 (DR2) 1200 (MESSIDOR)	AUC = 94.20
Mookiah [18]	• Multiresolution analysis • Feature ranking framework • Wavelet transform	Differentiated between normal and diabetic retinal images	340 (Clinical)	(Image-based) Acc = 94.17 SN = 92.81 SP = 96.27
Welikala [19]	• Dual classification • SVM classifier • Genetic algorithm	Detection of only proliferative DR	45 (MESSIDOR) 15 (Clinical)	(Region-based) SN = 91.38 SP = 96.00 (Image-based) SN = 100 SP = 97.50
Prakash [20]	• Morphological operations • Region growing method and SVM	Graded images into mild, moderate, severe NPDR and PDR	10 (Clinical)	(Image-based) SN = 80 SP = 100 ACC = 90

(Continued)

Table 8.1 Brief detail of state-of-the-art related to DR screening. (*Continued*)

Author (Ref.)	Method used	Task	Number of retinal images	Performance measures (%)
Akram [21]	• m-Mediods-based approach • Gaussian mixture model • Hybrid classifier	Graded images into mild, moderate and severe NPDR	89 (DIARETDB) 40 (DRIVE) 81 (STARE) 1200 (MESSIDOR)	(Image-based) SN = 99.17 SP = 97.07 ACC = 98.52 (Lesion-based) SN = 96.41 SP = 93.86 ACC = 94.98
Wong Li Yun [22]	• Back propagation neural network	Graded images into mild, moderate, severe NPDR and PDR	124 (Clinical)	(Image-based) SN = 91.7 SP = 100 PPV = 84
Mishra [23]	• K nearest neighbor classifier	Detected severity level based on identification of limited number of lesions	Not mentioned	Not evaluated
Verma [24]	• Random forest classifier	Detection of mild, moderate and sever NPDR based on identification of limited number of lesions	65 (STARE)	ACC = 87.50

(Continued)

Table 8.1 Brief detail of state-of-the-art related to DR screening. (*Continued*)

Author (Ref.)	Method used	Task	Number of retinal images	Performance measures (%)
Ahmad Fadzil [25]	• Gaussian Bayes classifier • CLAHE-based enhancement	Detected only no DR and severe NPDR/PDR	256 (Clinical)	(Image-based) SN = 84 SP = 97 ACC = 95
Sohini Roychowdhury [26]	• Gaussian mixture Model • K nearest neighbor • Support vector machine	Graded images into four stages of DR	1200 (MESSIDOR)	(Image-based) SN = 100 SP = 53.16 AUC = 90.4
Figueiredo [16]	• Hessian multiscale analysis • Cartoon and texture decomposition	Detected patients with the presence or absence of DR	2870 (DR images) 42900 (Normal images)	(Patient-based) SN = 95.32 SP = 65.05

SN, sensitivity; SP, specificity; Acc, accuracy; AUC, area under the curve.

developed by Yuna *et al.*, identified four stages corresponding to normal retina, moderate and severe nonproliferative DR, and proliferative DR in 124 retinal fundus images [23]. Classification of these four stages was achieved using a three-layer feed forward network. The authors reported a sensitivity/specificity of 91.7/100. However, the major limitation of this method is that the authors used the limited number of test images used for training the classifier which makes it unsuitable for practical applications. A similar approach based on DR-related features was proposed by Mishra *et al.* [24]. Four stages of severity related to DR were identified using a KNN classifier. However, the authors did not calculate the performance parameters making the method incapable to demonstrate the accuracy. Verma *et al.* classified retinal images into normal, moderate and severe nonproliferative DR stages by quantifying blood vessels and hemorrhages [25]. The authors reported the classification accuracy of 87.5% for pathological images using random forests classifier. However, the method did not segment other lesions necessary for the precise classification of NPDR. Recently, Figueiredo *et al.* applied a wavelet and multiscale image analysis-based thresholding method for the segmentation of dark and bright lesions and resulted in collective per-image sensitivity/specificity of 95/70, respectively [16]. The method was also evaluated for detecting the presence or absence of DR in a patient and resulted in an average sensitivity/specificity of 95.32/65.05, respectively. However, the technique proposed diverse binary detectors to detect diverse types of lesions, such as isolated dots, clusters of dotted lesions, and large/medium lesions. Likewise, distinct mathematical settings for each type of retinal lesion demonstrate that the method is incapable for practical applications.

The studies on DR screening and grading methods have some shortcomings, such as (i) most of the state-of-the-art screening methods rely on the detection of specific retinal lesion, whereas diagnostic interpretation for DR involves the detection of all dark and bright lesions; (ii) limited number of methods have been designed to grade DR after elimination of anatomical structures. A better grading system can be designed with the segmentation of retinal lesions related to DR after removal of spurious responses generated from anatomical structures; (iii) there have been only a few methods in the literature to provide objective performance parameters calculated on sufficient number of images, therefore, their generalization capability is uncertain; and (iv) there have been only a few attempts in literature devoted to the classification of retinal images into different severity levels of DR based on quantitative evaluation of dark and bright retinal lesions. Therefore, it is challenging to identify the severity levels of nonproliferative DR in retinal fundus images for general clinical use.

8.4   Key Observations from Literature Review

Based on the critical review of the literature, the following observations have been made:

- Literature related to blood vessels segmentation indicates that different filtering, morphological, supervised, thresholding-based methods are commonly used for the segmentation of retinal blood vessels. Hybrid models using thresholding and supervised methods provide the idea of multiscale implementation and have shown good segmentation results for pixelwise classification of blood vessel and nonblood vessel structures. The connectivity in geometrical structure of blood vessels was not preserved in most of these hybrid approaches. Thus, this research gap related to the proper connectivity of segmented blood vessels should be taken care of in the designed methods.

- A comprehensive literature survey on optic disk detection and segmentation reveals that the blood vessels convergence-based methods are best suitable for optic disk detection. The efficiency of precise location of optic disk using blood vessels convergence-based method needs to be improved by extracting and then incorporating other optic disk-related features, such as its contour, circularity, and blood vessel crossings of optic disk.

- Exudates segmentation methods (specially designed for the detection of progressive DR) and bright lesions segmentation methods, as proposed in literature, have their own advantages and disadvantages. It was also observed that after extensive literature review, the combination of two or more methods, to utilize the advantages of each method, aids in reducing false positives due to spurious responses during segmentation of exudates. Also, most of the previous work segment the exudates without elimination of anatomical structures, and so result into overlapping responses. Therefore, to increase accuracy and preciseness of the segmentation of exudates, adaptive quantization, and dynamic thresholding-based methods needs to be combined after the segmentation and elimination of anatomical structures.

- Extensive literature available on bright and dark lesions segmentation methods indicates that geometrical and morphological features are common in providing differentiation among various retinal lesions to detect nonproliferative DR cases. Even though these features have shown good results in segmentation of retinal lesions, still there is a need for improvement. That improvement can be obtained by the inclusion of diverse type of features, such as shape, size, intensity, and texture, to improve the accuracy of computer-aided diagnostic system.

- Presently, most of the methods available in literature use open-source benchmark databases comprising of clear retinal images to develop and test computer-aided diagnostic methods. An individual open-source retinal image database is designed for specific purpose, such as e-Optha EX database, consisting of only exudates is mainly designed for the evaluation of methods for exudates segmentation. Therefore, evaluation of DR detection methods on such databases is not justified. Although few researchers have combined various open-source databases to remove this ambiguity, but still clinically acquired images which are encountered by ophthalmologists in day-to-day practice should also be the part of the database. Therefore, in order to maintain diversity of retinal images, with respect to type of lesions, field of view, number of patients, machine settings, and so on, a composite database comprising both clinically acquired retinal fundus images with the available open-source benchmark retinal image databases needs to be considered. Also, the evaluation of DR detection methods on a large composite database would ensure their generalization capability.

8.5 Design of Experimental Methodology

It is required to design an experiment in an appropriate way to accomplish research gaps effectively. The design of the experimental methodology proposed in the present study is described in this section. Figure 8.2 depicts the flowchart of the design of the experimental methodology. The steps carried out in the designing of the methodology are described below.

(i) Development of Retinal Images Database:
- Fundus images database for the present study is acquired from two sources: open-source and clinically

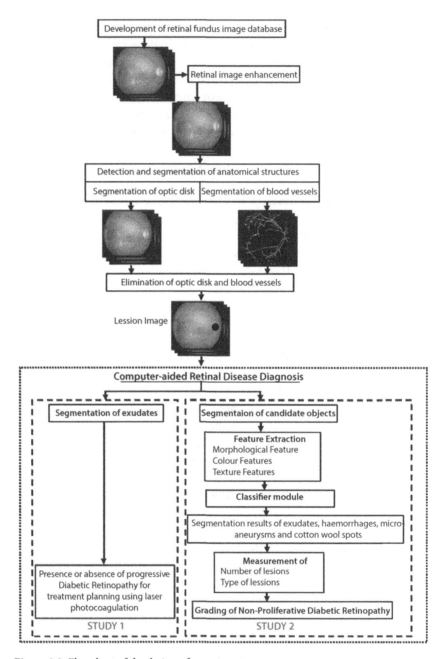

Figure 8.2 Flowchart of the design of experiment.

acquired. Two thousand and one hundred six retinal fundus images are acquired from six open-source benchmark databases, which are available online, and 2942 retinal fundus images are acquired clinically. Clinical retinal fundus image database is developed over a span of two and a half years to carry out the experiments. The database, as acquired from a reputed eye hospital, comprises normal and pathological retinal images. The inspiration behind to collect and use retinal image data from various sources is to make the proposed computer-aided DR detection method independent of image acquisition variability and to make a fair evaluation of effectiveness of the proposed method.

(ii)   Retinal Image Enhancement:
   –   An enhancement method for retinal fundus images is developed as per the requirement of ophthalmologists. The ophthalmologists require (a) the removal of artifacts due to nonuniform illumination inherited in retinal images up to an extent that an artifact removal method should not deteriorate the information hidden behind the artifacts, (b) the reduction of blurring in retinal images for better visualization of details, and (c) an overall good contrast of retinal fundus images to reduce the fatigue associated with visualization of retinal lesions hidden in dark background of retinal images. With all these considerations, retinal image enhancement method needs to be designed for better visual quality as compared to the original retinal fundus images.

(iii) Segmentation and Elimination of Landmarks:
   –   In this step, landmarks, namely, blood vessels and optic disk are identified, segmented and separated from background. The resulting image, termed as lesion image, is then used for retinal lesions identification and classification. The detection and elimination of landmarks aid in reducing the spurious responses in the further processing steps designed for retinal lesion identification, such as detection of bright and dark lesions, from the retinal fundus image.

Experimental methodology for computer-aided diagnostic methods in this work is designed for the detection of two diseases related to DR, i.e., progressive DR and nonproliferative DR.

(iv) Detection of Progressive DR (Study 1):

- Bright retinal lesions, such as exudates, are one of the earliest and most prevalent signs of the onset of chronic DR termed as progressive DR. The ophthalmologists' segment and treat exudates to cease the progression of retinopathy from reaching vision-threatening complications. Therefore, to identify the presence of progressive DR in retinal images, bright lesions, namely, exudates, are segmented. The designed method must reliably segment exudates, irrespective of associated heterogeneity, bright, and faint edges. The precise detection of exudates is further used for treatment planning of progressive DR where the physicians need to determine the exact area of exudates to make it exposed to the laser for photocoagulation.

(v) Detection and Grading of Nonproliferative DR (Study 2):

- Experienced ophthalmologists judge the severity level of NPDR to cease DR at an initial symptomless clinical stage and to diagnose other retinopathies as diabetic macular oedema and diabetic macular ischemia. The grading of severity level of NPDR is based on the interpretation of dark and bright lesions present in retinal image. Therefore, effective detection, segmentation, and categorization of retinal lesions needs to be carried out to grade nonproliferative DR. Finally, computer-aided severity level detection method needs to be designed for the diagnosis of early stage of nonproliferative DR. The method should grade the severity level of nonproliferative DR by objective quantification of dark and bright retinal lesions detected in the previous step.

8.6 Conclusion

The experimental methodology to accomplish research gaps related to detection of DR has been presented in this study. Its important constituents are design of experiment, collection of open-source databases, development of clinical retinal images database, and benchmarking of retinal images database. In the first subsection, the introduction related to systemic retinal abnormalities, specifically DR, has been presented. The key steps of computer-aided diagnostic methods and the available computer-aided DR grading and screening methods are presented in detail in the subsequent sections. Based on the critical review of the literature, an experimental methodology is designed which gives the framework for the diagnosis of DR objectively and subjectively. The designing steps that are needed to be carried out are retinal image enhancement, anatomical structures detection and elimination, retinal lesion detection, and classification of progressive DR and nonproliferative DR.

References

1. Sarah, W., Gojka, R., Anders, G., Richard, S., Hilary, K., Global Prevalence of Diabetes: Estimates for the year 2000 and projection for 2030. *Diabetes Care*, 27, 5, 1047–1053, 2004.
2. Cho, N.H. *et al.*, IDF Diabetes Atlas: Global estimates of diabetes prevalence for 2017 and projections for 2045. *Diabetes Res. Clin. Pract.*, 138, 271–281, 2018.
3. International Diabetes Federation, Diabetes Complications [Online]. Available: https://www.idf.org/aboutdiabetes/what-is-diabetes/complications.html. [Accessed: Jan. 10, 2018].
4. FIRSTPOST. https://www.firstpost.com/india/diabetes-is-indias-fastest-growing-disease-72-million-cases-recorded-in-2017-figure-expected-to-nearly-double-by-2025-4435203.html.[Accessed: Dec. 3, 2017].
5. Chu, J. and Ali, Y., Diabetic retinopathy: a review. *Drug Dev. Res.*, 2, 4, 226–237, 1989.
6. Singh, V.P., Srivastava, S., Srivastava, R., Effective mammogram classification based on center symmetric-LBP features in wavelet domain using random forests. *Technol. Health Care*, 25, 4, 709–727, 2017.
7. Chaudhuri, S., Chatterjee, S., Katz, N., Nelson, M., Goldbaum, M., Detection of blood vessels in retinal images using two dimensional matched filters. *IEEE Trans. Med. Imaging*, 8, 263–269, 1989.
8. Manikandan, M.S. and Dandapat, S., Multiscale entropy based weighted distortion measure for ECG coding. *IEEE Signal Process Lett.*, 15, 829–832, 2008.
9. Thakur, A. and Anand, R.S., A Local statistics based region growing segmentation method for ultrasound medical images. *International Journal of Signal Processing (IJSP)*, 1, 2, 141–146, 2004.
10. Bremner, J.D., Randall, P., Vermetten, E., Staib, L., Magnetic resonance imaging-based measurement of hippocampal volume in posttraumatic stress disorder related to childhood physical and sexual abuse: a preliminary report. *Biol. Psychiatry*, 41, 1, 23–32, 1997.

11. Winkel, R.R. *et al.*, Mammographic density and structural features can individually and jointly contribute to breast cancer risk assessment in mammography screening: a case-control study. *BMC Cancer*, 16, 1, 1–12, 2016.
12. Alahmer, H. and Ahmed, A., Computer-aided Classification of Liver Lesions from CT Images Based on Multiple ROI. *Procedia Comput. Sci.*, 90, 80–86, 2016.
13. Mittal, D., Kumar, V., Saxena, S.C., Khandelwal, N., Kalra, N., Neural network based focal liver lesion diagnosis using ultrasound images. *Comput Med Imaging Graph*, 35, 4, 315–323, 2011.
14. Pathak, A.N. and Sunkaria, R.K., Multiclass brain tumour classification using SVM. *Int. J. Comput. Appl.*, 97, 23, 34–38, 2014.
15. Shrivastava, V.K., Londhe, N.D., Sonawane, R.S., Suri, J.S., Computer-aided diagnosis of psoriasis skin images with HOS, texture and color features: a first comparative study of its kind. *Comput. Methods Programs Biomed.*, 126, 98–109, 2016.
16. Figueiredo, I.N., Kumar, S., Oliveira, C.M., Ramos, J.D., Engquist, B., Automated lesion detectors in retinal fundus images. *Comput. Biol. Med.*, 66, 47–65, 2015.
17. Pires, R., Jelinek, H.F., Wainer, J., Valle, E., Rocha, A., Advancing bag-of-visual-words representations for lesion classification in retinal images. *PLoS One*, 9, 6, 1–12, 2014.
18. Mookiah, M.R.K., Chua, C.K., Min, L.C., Ng, E.Y.K., Laude, A., Computer aided diagnosis of diabetic retinopathy using multi-resolution analysis and feature ranking frame work. *J Med Imag Health In*, 3, 4, 598–606, 2013.
19. Welikala, R.A. *et al.*, Genetic algorithm based feature selection combined with dual classification for the automated detection of proliferative diabetic retinopathy. *Comput Med Imaging Graph*, 43, 64–77, 2015.
20. Prakash, N.B., Selvathi, D., Hemalakshmi, G.R., Development of algorithm for dual stage classification to estimate severity level of diabetic retinopathy in retinal images using soft computing techniques. *International Journal of Electrical Engineering and Informatics*, 6, 4, 717–739, 2014.
21. Roychowdhury, S., Koozekanani, D., Parhi, K., DREAM: Diabetic Retinopathy Analysis using Machine Learning. *IEEE J. Biomed. Health. Inf.*, 18, 1717–1728, 2014.
22. Usman Akram, M., Khalid, S., Tariq, A., Khan, S.A., Azam, F., Detection and classification of retinal lesions for grading of diabetic retinopathy. *Comput. Biol. Med.*, 45, 1, 161–171, 2014.
23. Yuna, W.L., Acharyab, U.R., Venkatesha, Y.V., Cheec, C., Minb, L.C., Ngd, E.Y.K., Identification of different stages of diabetic retinopathy using retinal optical images. *Inf. Sci. (Ny).*, 178, 106–121, 2008.
24. Mishra, P.K., Sinha, A., Teja, K.R., Bhojwani, N., Sahu, S., Kumar, A., A computational modeling for the detection of diabetic retinopathy severity. *Bioinformation*, 10, 9, 556–561, 2014.
25. Verma, K., Deep, P., Ramakrishnan, A.G., Detection and classification of diabetic retinopathy using retinal images, *Proceedings on Annual IEEE India*

Conference of Engineering Sustainable Solutions INDICON-2011, IEEE Xplore, 2011.

26. Fadzil, M.A., Izhar, L., Nugroho, H., Nugroho, H., Analysis of retinal fundus images for grading of diabetic retinopathy severity. *Med. Biol. Eng.*, 49, 6, 1–8, 2011.

27. Nayak, S.R., Khandual, A., Mishra, J., Ground truth study of fractal dimension of color images of similar textures. *J. Text. I.*, 109, 1159–1167, 2018.

28. Sivakumar, S., Nayak, S.R., Kumar, A., Vidyanandini, S., An empirical study of supervised learning methods for breast cancer diseases. *International Journal of Light and Electron Optics*, 175, 105–114, 2018.

29. Nayak, S.R. and Mishra, J., Analysis of medical images using fractal geometry. *Histopathological Image Analysis in Medical Decision Making*, Chapter 8, 181–201, 2018.

Offline Handwritten Numeral Recognition Using Convolution Neural Network

Abhisek Sethy[1]*, Prashanta Kumar Patra[1] and Soumya Ranjan Nayak[2]

[1]Department of Computer Science and Engineering, College of Engineering & Technology, BPUT, Odisha, India
[2]Amity School of Engineering and Technology, Amity University, Uttar Pradesh, India

Abstract

In this current digital age of world, character recognition (CR) has been done through various machine learning algorithms. And it considered to be one the most challenging segment of pattern recognition. In addition to the above context, offline handwritten character is the most challenging one as compared with the printed one. Despite various algorithms that were harnessed on various handwritten scripts, it can be possible to have more feasibility solution and high recognition rate. Here, in this paper, we have focused on the handwritten numerals of Odia and Bangla scripts. To overcome the ambiguities that arise in handwritten, one has been resolved using the Convolutional Neural Network (CNN). Here we have suggested a state-of-the-art CNN-based approach for recognition of multiple handwritten numerals of both the scripts and clearly shown how effectively it has been used for evaluating the discriminate features from the original image and later leads to report high recognition rate. At the simulation level, we have listed up variance nature of the individual's images, and through CNN, a high recognition rate is achieved, which is quite helpful in building the automatic recognition system for handwritten numerals to have solution for real-time problems.

Keywords: Character Recognition (CR), Handwritten Character Recognition (HCR), Convolutional Neural Network (CNN)

*Corresponding author: abhisek052@gmail.com

Muthukumaran Malarvel, Soumya Ranjan Nayak, Surya Narayan Panda, Prasant Kumar Pattnaik and Nittaya Muangnak (eds.) Machine Vision Inspection Systems (Vol. 1): Image Processing, Concepts, Methodologies and Applications, (197–212) © 2020 Scrivener Publishing LLC

9.1   Introduction

Handwritten character recognition (HCR) has been one of the active research areas of pattern recognition [1]. Various conventional and latest machine learning approaches have been used in the recognition system. An automatic recognition system is one of the arts of conversion of differently sized character documents into digital formats and which may lead to various aspect of application, such as operation related to banking, postal, and so on. Despite various research being performed for handwritten and printed scripts [2], satisfactory recognition of various handwritten are yet to be reported. Among such scripts, English [3], Chinese [4], Arabic [5], and Japanese [6], and so on. These handwritten characters are considered more challenging compared with the printed one because of their similar orientation, shape, and size. Because of these varieties in writing skill of different individuals, it has added more complex to the structure of handwritten characters, which leads to confusion in proper recognition of characters. In the context of any automatic ideal OCR system, the crucial part is to have well-defined benchmark data sets along with a proper feature extraction procedure. This procedure must identify discriminant features from the characters, symbols, and words. Selection of classifier is another important aspect which has a significant impact on the recognition accuracy. Recognition of handwritten characters is quite challenging as on printed ones because of the following reasons:

- The handwritten characters of various writers were not only not identical but also most of them vary in different aspects, such as size and shape.
- Such a wide range of writing styles of individual character added more complexity in recognition task. In addition, some similarities among the character in shapes, the overlaps, and the interconnections of the neighboring characters further complicate the character recognition problem.

Here, this paper adopts a procedure to establish a recognition system for handwritten Odia and Bengali numerals. Usually, in the recognition system, handwriting recognition usually consists of various stages among the preprocessing, feature extraction, classification, and postprocessing included. Among feature extraction and classifier design, there are two major steps in any recognition system [7]. To have a proper recognition system, we have harnessed the convolutional neural networks (CNN) [8] to the handwritten Odia and Bangla numerals. The main advantage of implementation of CNN-based approach is that it does not require any feature hand-crafted feature vector. It has such architecture that it is capable to create the feature vector from the training sample of handwritten images. It is completely an unsupervised one. It is quite capable of extracting its own feature vector from the trained characters samples, and they had also provided additional advantage to skip the preprocessing of the image and was very much helpful in extracting the feature of handwritten characters of new scripts for which it is possible to collect at least some training samples with ground truth [9]. Usually, some approaches they have assumed may exist in CNN [10] trained data set for character problems, and we have to only forward the new samples to the train CNN one and perform the recognition task. In this paper, we have to perform multilingual script recognition of numerals, such as Odia and Bangla numerals. All simulations were done over benchmark database that were collected from various research institute across the globe. In the next section, we have listed up the literature survey and then proposed a model for recognition of handwritten numerals of both Bengali and Odia numerals [40].

9.2   Related Work Done

In such field of handwritten numerals, recognition of a good number of works has been reported in both printed and offline in the past years by various researcher across various corners of the globe [2, 6]. The Odia and Bangla scripts were generated from the Brahmi script and some part Devanagari script. These scripts are the official language of the state Odisha and West-Bengal and the most ancient regional language of India. Both of these are basically spoken in the eastern zone of India mainly in state Odisha, West-Bengal, Bihar, Gujarat, and so on. Chatterjee et al. [11] and Sinha et al. [12] have initially shown interest in the recognition system of Devanagari scripts. Pal et al. [13] have performed over Odia scripts and suggested a probabilistic approach for recognition system along with the importance of curvature feature of the individuals. And also received 94.6% as the recognition rate through the neural network classifier. Some writer identification was using neural network as was done by Desai [14]. They have listed up 94.6% recognition rate for Gujarati handwritten digits. Some researchers also make an application orient approach, such as Kundu & Chen [15], who have reported the HMM approaches for postal words recognition and they have listed 88.2% recognition accuracy over the data sets. Later on, some gradient-based approach was proposed by Roy et al. [16] and termed them as histogram approach. They have calculated feature vector along four directions, such as horizontal, 45-degree slant, vertical, and 135-degree slanted. In addition, they have shown the significance of neural network and quadratic classifier, and for those, they have achieved 90.38% and 94.81% recognition rate with a rejection of 1.84% and 1.31%, respectively, achieved. Apart for all, some Fourier transformation-based approaches were suggested by Mishra et al. [17]. They had considered the cosine transformation and wavelet transformation over the Odia numerals. Average recognition rates of 92% and 87.50% were noted.

An evolutionary-based approach was depicted by Dash et al. [18]. They had implemented a stock-well-based approach over the handwritten numerals. To validate what they proposed, they had adopted a 10-fold validation, and all simulation analyses were done in zone-based ones and 99.1% recognition rate reported. In following subsequent year again Dash et al. in [19] make an analysis over various transformation-based approaches and listed up their differences, such as Slantlet transform based, Stockwell transform based, and Gabor-wavelet-based transformation. Here, the main focus is on the nonredundant nature of the individuals and this has achieved a very good recognition rate over the handwritten samples. Some researchers mainly focused on the preprocessing steps, like Sethy et al. [20], who suggested Binarization of the individual digits and added some Fourier transformation analysis over the handwritten sets as cosine transformation to the handwritten numerals and successfully reported the desired feature vector. Later, they have reported that 80.2% and 90% recognition rates were achieved.

In addition to such methodologies, some orthogonal-based approach also listed up by Mohapatra et al. [21]. They have shown the variant and in-variant nature of the numerals and a recognition rate of 98.5% was achieved. In next years, some statistical-based feature, like Grey level Co-occurrence Matrix (GLCM), was introduced by Sethy et al. [22]. Here, they have shown decision-based classification through a random forest tree. Once again, Sethy et al. [23] proposed an improved version of histogram analysis, which included the rectangle components as R-HOG. These rectangle histograms were reported in the feature selection part, and dimensional reduction was performed through principal component analysis (PCA) [24] over high-dimensional feature vector. The highest Pc scores were reported as the key feature set, and the remaining work were done by SVM and Quadratic classifiers, respectively. An extreme learning-based approach was reported by Das et al. [25]. In this approach, they maintained a single hidden layer neural network for the recognition of handwritten numerals. Some work also reported on both the Bengali numerals and character by Das and Pramanik [26]. They have reported the significance on convex hull feature of the numerals. Rubby *et al.* [27] focused on the Bengali handwritten numerals and harnessed the CNN-based approach for recognition. Here, they have taken Ekush and CMATERdb data set and achieved 97.73% and 95.01%, respectively. Once again in the following year, Rubby *et al.* [28] have suggested a lightweight CNN for recognition of Bangla handwritten characters which consists vowels and consonants. Once again [41], Sethy *et al.* have also performed some feature reductional concept through PCA and Kernel PCA over various handwritten data sets. They have also shown the significance of radial basis function-based neural network and angular symmetric axis constellation [42, 43] for the recognition system. With regard to pattern recognition analysis, fractal dimension examination plays a prominent role in feature evaluation. This work has described the related factors, such as spatial resolution, region of interests, texture feature, color metric for similar texture, and so on [44–53].

9.3   Data Set Used for Simulation

In this paper, we implemented the recognition system for handwritten Odia and Bangla numerals. All the simulations were carried over with standard databases collected from various research institutes, such as Bangla numerals collected from NIT, Rourkela by Das *et al.* [25], the numeral database has been collected from IIT, BBSR by Puhan *et al.* [18] and another Odia numeral database collected from ISI Kolkata by Bhattacharya *et al.* [35]. In the abovementioned numeral data set, we have collected 10 numerals starting from 0 to 9, which are suggested in Figure 9.1, Figure 9.2, and Figure 9.3, respectively, representing handwritten character data set. In order to have proper setup for the data sets, we have categorized the level from 0 to 9.

0	1	2	3	4	5	6	7	8	9

Figure 9.1 Sample of handwritten Odia numeral database of IIT, BBSR.

0	1	2	3	4	5	6	7	8	9

Figure 9.2 Sample of handwritten Bangla numeral database of NIT, Rourkela.

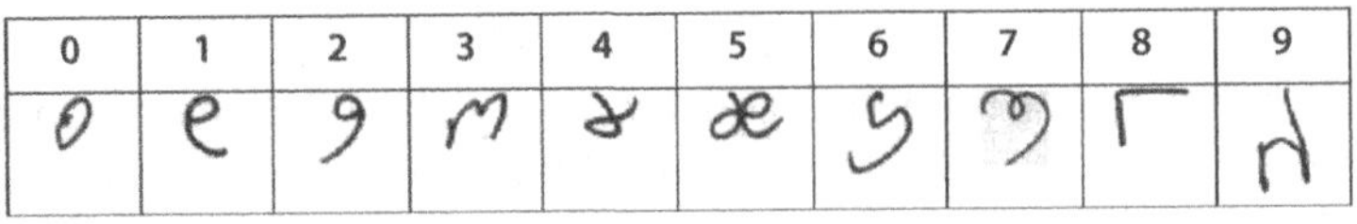

0	1	2	3	4	5	6	7	8	9
𝜃	ℓ	9	𝓂	⅄	æ	5	♡	𝖦	𝗇

Figure 9.3 Sample of handwritten Odia numeral database of ISI, Kolkata.

Table 9.1 Overall statistic of the handwritten numeral data set.

Standard database collected	No. of categories of classes	Training count	Testing count	Total
Odia Numeral Database of IIT, BBSR	10	4000	1000	5000
Bangla Numeral Database of NIT, Rourkela.	10	3345	1000	4345
Odia Numeral Database of ISI, Kolkata.	10	4970	1000	5970

We have also mentioned a well-defined training and testing ratio of data for implementation of the recognition system as shown in Table 9.1.

All the handwritten numerals data sets are maintained with proper training and testing ratio so that it will in robust frame of implementation of the handwritten numerals as shown below in Table 9.1. All these handwritten samples were collected from various age groups, starting from 5 to 50 years, and all were presented into database format for research purpose.

9.4 Proposed Model

In any recognition system, it is important to have a well-defined data set and in addition, involved preprocessing criteria to get a less noisy image, leading to a high recognition rate. Meanwhile, CNN [31] is an effective architecture which has its own preprocessing steps and variations among the individuals. In this proposed CNN, an inherent methodology is provided and data for normalized one are given, before that we have made a standard size of 32×32 for each image size, which act as the input to the network. Basically, CNN is a widely used visual processing and it provides highest optimized way to process any 2-D image for which it is capable to train on its own and produce the desired feature vector. Moreover, it says the variation listed and it helps generate a connection which is sparse in nature and that has to connect with the weights. In another way, we can also suggest that though it follows a gradient-based approach and will produce a low error [32]. Mainly, this CNN architecture consists of many layers as one output layer acts to input the next layer and is quite helpful to predict the desired output. In addition, there is also some limitations to the network related to the parameters and variants, to over fit such situation, we have trained a single network at first with larger sample space along with various iteration values. Here, in the proposed work, we have taken three different benchmark data set where each have 10 categories that have already been discussed in Table 9.1. In this paper, we have used an architecture similar to the well-known LetNet-5 architecture and trained about 4000 for Odia IITBBSR, 3345 for Bangla numerals, and 4970 for ISI Kolkata numeral data set. We have made a constrain in the fine tuning to report a high recognition rate in this 10-class problem. The architecture explained in the study of LeCun *et al.* [34] have implemented a bangle numeral database and reported a 95.84% recognition rate through proper training CNN [33], where we have obtained about 87%. There are times that we have to avoid the overtraining issue because the characters deep learning can also be introduced, as suggested by Theano [35]. All these have been done in python library which was proposed in [36, 37]. It is quite helpful in optimizing and evaluating mathematical expressions effectively to multidimensional arrays.

The overall architecture of CNN that we have implemented is explained in Figure 9.4 and Figure 9.5, respectively. As an initial step, we have included various layers, and some feature map was also performed using some kernel functions. In this CNN approach, the first layer is C1 and the convolution layer having six feature maps which is calculated using 5*5 kernels upon input of image of size 32*32. In next two set of convolution along with some sampling done through single hidden layer and at last a perceptron is achieved represented in Figure 9.4(a). Layer C1 depicts 28×28 feature set maps to prevent connections of inputs from falling off the boundary. Layer S2, which is the first subsampling shown in Figure 9.4(b), provides six feature maps each with a size of 14×14, it also supports max pooling using a 2×2 kernel on the output of C1 layer. Net at C3 is the second convolution layer shown in Figure 9.5(a). Here, at this layer, a 12 × 12 feature map is retrieved by overlapping 5× 5 kernels at output layer of S2. Layer S4 is the second subsampling layer shown in Figure 9.5(b) and produces 2×12 feature map each with a size of 5 × 5 and used max pooling over 2×2 kernel on the output of C3 layer. Finally, we have obtained nearly 300 features at layer F5 each with a size of 5*% through 12 kernels shown in Figure 9.5(c), respectively. In a subsequent step, this CNN-based approach is helpful in producing higher levels of feature from each

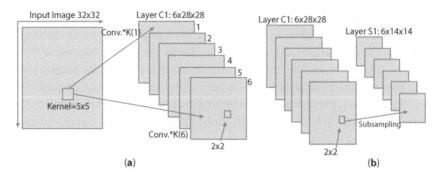

Figure 9.4 (a) Input an image to layer C1, (b) forwarding the value from layer C1 to layer S2.

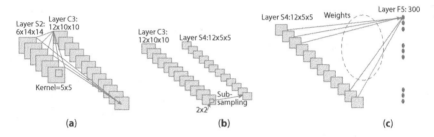

Figure 9.5 (a) Forwarding from layer S2 to layer C3, (b) forwarding from layer C3 to layer S4, (c) forwarding from layer S4 to layer F5.

input image data set at layer F5 and used them for training purpose to support vector machine with RBF kernels. To have proper simulation setup, we used scikit-learn [29, 30] toolbox under python environment, and the values of certain parameters C and γ are also done based on grid values respectively.

9.5   Result Analysis

To have a proper implementation of the proposed system, the respective handwritten characters have listed the CNN-based approach over the images and reported the feature vector and introduced some Kernel function. Here, we have included two handwritten numeral data sets of Odia Numerals and one set of Bangla numerals; all these are of 10 classes, containing 5000, 4345, and 5970 overall of sample of data. The recognition accuracies obtained on the respective test sets are comparable with the state-of-the-art recognition accuracies on each of them, and numerals are processed with abovementioned algorithms perfectly. In overall basis, here, we have listed various training and testing accuracies, as shown in

Table 9.2 Training and Testing Accuracy over the three data sets.

Handwritten data set name	Training loss	Val. loss	Training accuracy	Val. accuracy	Test data set	Test accuracy
Odia Numeral	0.012	.014	98.3	97.71	Odia Numeral Database of IIT, BBSR	98.3
Bangla Numeral	0.0814	0.01120	97.37%	96.81%	Bangla Numeral Database of NIT, Rourkela.	97.1%
Odia Numeral	0.0138	0.01396	98.81%	98.40%	Odia Numeral Database of ISI, Kolkata.	98.6%

Table 9.2. It also shows the loss and recognition rate achieved through various stages of the model. In addition, we have listed up the recognition rate at various numbers of hidden neurons, such as 2000, 3000 up to 11000. By doing such, we are able to note down various changes in the recognition rate as depicted in Figure 9.6, Figure 9.7, and Figure 9.8 below.

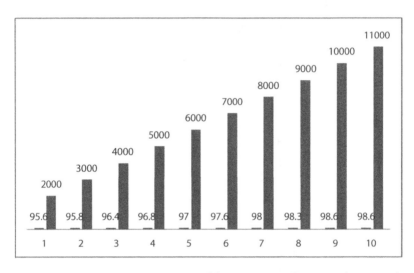

Figure 9.6 Various Recognition rate reported for IIT BBS Handwritten Odia Numeral Data set.

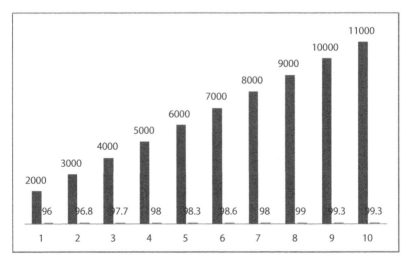

Figure 9.7 Various Recognition rate reported for ISI Kolkata Handwritten Odia Numeral Data set.

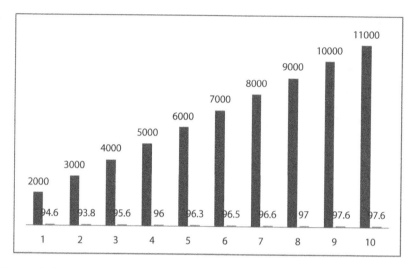

Figure 9.8 Various recognition rates reported for NIT Rourkela handwritten Bangla numeral data set.

9.6   Conclusion and Future Work

In this paper, we have attempted a new approach for handwritten numeral recognition. To achieve such, we had considered the CNN-based approach and depicted how effectively it helps in the recognition system. The main aim is that it is capable of creating its own feature for each individual and preprocessing is also achieved through it. Proper training and testing of the data are required to make the system robust. As CNN-based approach consists of multilayer, we have focused each and every input-output layer and maintained a well-defined training and test ratio among the data sets. We have also shown how the number of hidden neuron is helpful in calculating the complexity of the proposed model. As an outcome CNN-based approach, we have obtained 98.6% for IIT BBS handwritten numerals, 97.6% for NIT, RKL Bangla Numerals, and 99.3% for ISI Kolkata Odia numerals, respectively. Apart from it, we have also shown some details of recognition rate with respect to proposed work and inputted in tabular format as shown in Table 9.3 below. We have achieved very good recognition rate over benchmark handwritten data set. Apart from its various invented machine learning approaches, such as direction-based, extreme learning based can be applied to such problem domain. Further, other techniques are to be explored for better recognition accuracy. This convolution-based approach can also be very much helpful in fractal analysis [43].

Table 9.3 Recognition Rate reported by existing method with current method.

Authors	Reported data set	Feature extraction techniques used	Reported classifier	Reported recognition rate (%)
In [13] Pal *et al.*	ISI Kolkata Handwritten Odia Characters	Curvature Feature values	Modified Quadratic Classifier	94.6 %
In [17] Mishra *et al.*	NIT, RKL Handwritten Odia Characters	DCT and DWT	Support Vector Machine (SVM)	92%, 87.5 %
In [20] Sethy *et al.*	ISI Kolkata Handwritten Odia Numerals	Binarization and DCT	BPNN	80.2%, 90%
In [24] Sethy *et al.*	NIT, RKL Handwritten Odia Characters	DWT, PCA	BPNN	94.8%
In [40] Bhomik *et al.*	ISI Kolkata Handwritten Odia Numerals	Stroke calculation along Horizontal and Vertical	Neural Network (NN)	95.89%, 90.50%
we author	IIT, BBS Odia Numeral NIT, RKL Bangla Numeral ISI KOL, Odia Numeral	CNN	CNN	98.6% 97.6% 99.3%

References

1. Mantas, J., An overview of character recognition methodologies. *Pattern Recognit.*, 19, 6, 425–430, 1986. https://doi.org/10.1016/0031-3203(86)90040-3.
2. Arica, N. and Yarman-Vural, F.T., An overview of character recognition focused on off-line handwriting. *IEEE Trans. Syst. Man Cybern. Part C (Appl. Rev.)*, 31, 2, 216–233, 2001. https://doi.org/10.1016/0031-3203(86)90040-3.
3. Srihari, S.N., Cohen, E., Hull, J.J., Kuan, L., A system to locate and recognize ZIP codes in handwritten addresses. *IJRE*, 1, 37–45, 1989. https://digital.ijre.org/index.php/int_j_res_eng/article/view/311.
4. Tsukumo, J. and Tanaka, H., Classification of handprinted Chinese characters using nonlinear normalization and correlation methods, in: *[1988 Proceedings] 9th International Conference on Pattern Recognition*, May, Rome, Italy, IEEE, pp. 168–171, 1988.
5. Amin, A. and Al-Sadoun, H.B., Hand printed Arabic character recognition system, in: *Proceedings of the 12th IAPR International Conference on Pattern Recognition, Vol. 3-Conference C: Signal Processing (Cat. No. 94CH3440-5)*, vol. 2, October, Jerusalem, Israel, IEEE, pp. 536–539, 1994, 10.1109/ICPR.1994.577012.
6. Yamada, H., Yamamoto, K., Saito, T., A nonlinear normalization method for handprinted Kanji character recognition—line density equalization. *Pattern Recognit.*, 23, 9, 1023–1029, 1990. https://doi.org/10.1016/0031-3203(90)90110-7.
7. Plamondon, R. and Srihari, S.N., Online and off-line handwriting recognition: a comprehensive survey. *IEEE Trans. Pattern Anal. Mach. Intell.*, 22, 1, 63–84, 2000. 10.1109/34.824821.
8. Simard, P.Y., Steinkraus, D., Platt, J.C., Best Practices for Convolutional Neural Networks Applied to Visual Document Analysis. *Proceedings of International Conference on Document Analysis and Recognition*, Edinburgh, UK, IEEE, pp. 958–962, 2003. 10.1109/ICDAR.2003.1227801.
9. LeCun, Y., Bottou, L., Bengio, Y., Haffner, P., Gradient-based learning applied to document recognition. *Proc. IEEE*, 86, 11, 2278–2324, 1998.
10. Ciresan, D. and Meier, U., Multi-column deep neural networks for offline handwritten Chinese character classification, in: *International Joint Conference on Neural Networks (IJCNN)*, IEEE, pp. 1–6, 2015.
11. Sethi, I.K. and Chatterjee, B., Machine recognition of constrained hand printed Devanagari. *Pattern Recognit.*, 9, 2, 69–75, 1977. https://doi.org/10.1016/0031-3203(77)90017-6.
12. Sinha, R.M.K. and Mahabala, H.N., Machine recognition of Devanagari script. *IEEE Trans. Syst. Man Cybern.*, 9, 8, 435–441, 1979.
13. Pal, U., Wakabayashi, T., Kimura, F., A system for off-line Oriya handwritten character recognition using curvature feature, in: *10th international conference on information technology (ICIT)*, 2007 December, Orissa, India, IEEE, pp. 227–229, 2007.

14. Desai, A., Gujarati handwritten numeral optical character recognition through neural network. *Pattern Recognit.*, 43, 2582–2589, 2010. https://doi.org/10.1016/j.patcog.2010.01.008.

15. Kundu, Y.H. and Chen, M., Alternatives to variable duration HMM in handwriting recognition. *IEEE Trans. Pattern Anal. Mach. Intell.*, 20, 11, 1275–1280, 2002.

16. Roy, K., Pal, T., Pal, U., Kimura, F., Oriya handwritten numeral recognition system, in: *Eighth International Conference on Document Analysis and Recognition (ICDAR'05)*, Seoul, South Korea, IEEE, pp. 770–774, 2005.

17. Mishra, T.K., Majhi, B., Panda, S., A comparative analysis of image transformations for handwritten Odia numeral recognition, in: *2013 International Conference on Advances in Computing, Communications and Informatics (ICACCI)*, Mysore, India, IEEE, pp. 790–793, 2013.

18. Dash, K.S., Puhan, N.B., Panda, G., Handwritten numeral recognition using non-redundant Stock well transform and bio-inspired optimal zoning. *IET Image Proc.*, 9, 10, 874–882, 2015.

19. Dash, K.S., Puhan, N.B., Panda, G., On extraction of features for handwritten Odia numeral recognition in transformed domain, in: *2015 Eighth International Conference on Advances in Pattern Recognition (ICAPR)*, Kolkata, India, IEEE, pp. 1–6, 2015.

20. Sethy, A. and Patra, P.K., Off-line Odia handwritten numeral recognition using neural network: a comparative analysis. *International Conference on Computing, Communication and Automation (ICCCA)*, IEEE, pp. 1099–1103, 2016.

21. Mohapatra, R.K., Majhi, B., Jena, S.K., Classification of handwritten Odia basic character using Stock well transform. *Int. J. Appl. Pattern Recognit.*, 2, 3, 235–254, 2015. https://doi.org/10.1504/IJAPR.2015.073854.

22. Sethy, A., Patra, P.K., Nayak, D.R., Gray-level co-occurrence matrix and random forest based off-line Odia handwritten character recognition. *Recent Pat. Eng.*, 13, 2, 136–141, 2019. https://doi.org/10.2174/1872212112666180601085544.

23. Sethy, A. and Patra, P.K., R-HOG Feature-Based Off-Line Odia Handwritten Character Recognition, in: *Examining Fractal Image Processing and Analysis*, IGI Global, pp. 196–210, 2020.

24. Sethy, A., Patra, P.K., Nayak, D.R., Off-line handwritten Odia character recognition using DWT and PCA, in: *Progress in Advanced Computing and Intelligent Engineering*, Springer, Singapore, pp. 187–195, 2018. https://doi.org/10.1007/978-981-10-6872-0_18.

25. Das, D., Nayak, D.R., Dash, R., Majhi, B., An empirical evaluation of extreme learning machine: application to handwritten character recognition. *Multimed. Tools Appl.*, 1–29, 2019. https://doi.org/10.1007/s11042-019-7330-0

26. Das, N. and Pramanik, S., Recognition of Handwritten Bangla Basic Character and Digit Using Convex Hall Basic Feature. *International Conference on Artificial Intelligence and Pattern Recognition (AIPR-09)*, 380–386, 2009.

27. Rabby, A.S.A., Haque, S., Abujar, S., Hossain, S.A., EkushNet: Using Convolutional Neural Network for Bangla Handwritten Recognition. *Procedia Comput. Sci.*, 143, 603–610, 2018. https://doi.org/10.1016/j.procs.2018.10.437.

28. Rabby, A.S.A., Haque, S., Islam, S., Abujar, S., Hossain, S.A., BornoNet: Bangla Handwritten Characters Recognition Using Convolutional Neural Network. *Procedia Comput. Sci.*, 143, 528–535, 2018. https://doi.org/10.1016/j. procs.2018.10.426.

29. Pizzi, N. J., Pedrycz, W., Aggregating multiple classification results using fuzzy integration and stochastic feature selection. *Int. J. Approx. Reason.*, 51, 8, 883–894, 2010. https://doi.org/10.1016/j.ijar.2010.05.003.

30. Mishra, T.K., Majhi, B., Sa, P.K., Panda, S., Model Based Odia Numeral Recognition using Fuzzy Aggregated Features. *Front. Comput. Sci. Springer*, 916–922, 2014. https://doi.org/10.1007/s11704-014-3354-9.

31. Bhattacharya, U. and Chaudhuri, B.B., Databases for research on recognition of handwritten characters of Indian scripts, in: *Eighth International Conference on Document Analysis and Recognition (ICDAR'05)*, Seoul, South Korea, IEEE, pp. 789–793, 2005.

32. Hu, B., Lu, Z., Li, H., Chen, Q., Convolutional neural network architectures for matching natural language sentences, in: *Advances in neural information processing systems*, Springer, pp. 2042–2050, 2014.

33. Matsugu, M., Mori, K., Mitari, Y., Kaneda, Y., Subject independent facial expression recognition with robust face detection using a convolutional neural network. *Neural Netw.*, 16, 5-6, 555–559, 2003. https://doi.org/10.1016/ S0893-6080(03)00115-1.

34. LeCun, Y., Bottou, L., Bengio, Y., Haffner, P., Gradient-based learning applied to document recognition. *Proc. IEEE*, 86, 11, 2278–2324, 1998.

35. Bhattacharya, U., Shridhar, M., Parui, S.K., Sen, P.K., Chaudhuri, B.B., Offline recognition of handwritten Bangla characters: an efficient two-stage approach. *Pattern Anal. Appl.*, 15, 4, 445–458, 2012. https://doi.org/10.1007/ s10044-012-0278-6.

36. Torvalds, L., http://deeplearning.net/software/theano, 2015.

37. Bergstra, J., Breuleux, O., Bastien, F., Lamblin, P., Pascanu, R., Desjardins, G., Turian, J., Warde-Farley, D., Bengio, Y., A CPU and GPU math expression compiler, in: *Proceedings of the Python for scientific computing conference (SciPy)*, vol. 4, No. 3, 2010.

38. Bastien, F., Lamblin, P., Pascanu, R., Bergstra, J., Goodfellow, I., Bergeron, A., Bouchard, N., Warde-Farley, D., Bengio, Y., Theano: new features and speed improvements, 1–10, 2012. *arXiv preprint arXiv:1211.5590*.

39. http://scikit-learn.org/, 2010.

40. Bhowmik, T.K., Parui, S.K., Bhattacharya, U., Shaw, B., An HMM based recognition scheme for handwritten Oriya numerals, in: *9th International Conference on Information Technology (ICIT'06)*, Bhubaneswar, India, IEEE, pp. 105–110, 2006.

41. Sethy, A., Patra, P.K., Nayak, S.R., Jena, P.M., Symmetric Axis Based Off-Line Odia Handwritten Character and Numeral Recognition, in: *3rd International Conference on Computational Intelligence and Networks (CINE)*, Bhubaneswar, India, IEEE, pp. 83–87, 2017.

42. Sethy, A. and Patra, P.K., Off-line Odia Handwritten Character Recognition: An Axis Constellation Model Based Research. *International Journal of Innovative Technology and Exploring Engineering (IJITEE)*, vol. 8, 9S2, 788–793, 2019.

43. Sethy, A., Patra, P.K., Nayak, S.R., Jena, P.M., Symmetric Axis Based Off-line Odia Handwritten Character and Numeral Recognition. *International Journal of Informatics and Communication Technology*, vol. 07 (2), pp. 96–104, 2018.

44. Nayak, S.R., Mishra, J., Palai, G., Analysing Roughness of Surface through Fractal Dimension: A Review. *Image Vision Comput.*, 89, 21–34, 2019. https://doi.org/10.1016/j.imavis.2019.06.015.

45. Nayak, S.R., Mishra, J., Khandual, A., Palai, G., Fractal Dimension of RGB Color Images. *International Journal for Light and Electron Optics*, vol. 162, pp. 196–205, 2018. https://doi.org/10.1016/j.ijleo.2018.02.066.

46. Nayak, S.R., Mishra, J., Palai, G., A modified approach to estimate fractal dimension of gray scale Images. *International Journal for Light and Electron Optics*, vol. 161, pp. 136–145, 2018. https://doi.org/10.1016/j.ijleo.2018.02.024.

47. Nayak, S.R., Khandual, A., Mishra, J., Ground truth study of fractal dimension of color images of similar textures. *J. Text. Inst.*, 109, 1159–1167, 2018. https://doi.org/10.1080/00405000.2017.1418710.

48. Nayak, S.R. and Mishra, J., A Modified Triangle Box-Counting with precision in Error fit. *J. Inf. Optim. Sci.*, 39, 1, 113–128, 2018. https://doi.org/10.1 080/02522667.2017.1372155.

49. Nayak, S.R., Mishra, J., Palai, G., An extended DBC approach by using maximum Euclidian distance for fractal dimension of color images. *International Journal for Light and Electron Optics*, vol. 166, pp. 110–115, 2018. https://doi.org/10.1016/j.ijleo.2018.03.106.

50. Nayak, S.R., Padhy, R., Mishra, J., A new extended differential box counting method by adopting unequal partitioning of grid for estimation of fractal dimension of digital images. *Computational Signal Processing and Analysis*, vol. 490, pp. 45–57, 2018. https://doi.org/10.1007/978-981-10-8354-9_5.

51. Nayak, S.R. and Mishra, J., Fractal Dimension of Gray Scale images, in: *Progress in Computing, Analytics and Networking*, vol. 710, pp. 225–234, 2018. https://doi.org/10.1007/978-981-10-7871-2_22.

52. Nayak, S.R. and Mishra, J., Analysis of Medical images using Fractal Geometry, in: *Histopathological Image Analysis in Medical Decision Making*, Chapter 8, pp. 181–201, 2018.

53. Nayak, S.R., Mishra, J., Mohan Jena, P., Fractal analysis of image sets using differential box counting techniques. *Int. J. Inf. Technol.*, 10, 1, 39–47, 2018. https://doi.org/10.1007/s41870-017-0062-3.

A Review on Phishing—Machine Vision and Learning Approaches

Hemamalini Siranjeevi[1], Swaminathan Venkatraman[2*]
and Kannan Krithivasan[3]

[1]Department of Computer Science and Engineering, Srinivasa Ramanujan Centre,
SASTRA Deemed University, Kumbakonam, India
[2]Discrete Mathematics Laboratory, Department of Mathematics, Srinivasa
Ramanujan Centre, SASTRA Deemed University, Kumbakonam, India
[3]Department of Mathematics, SASTRA Deemed University, Thanjavur, India

Abstract

Phishing is a criminal act wherein fraudsters acquire users' sensitive information. Criminals create a lot of phishing websites to lure users into traps that seize their credentials. Many countermeasures have evolved, but they fail because of high false prediction rates. This review presents a detailed report on some of the attempts toward avoiding, detecting, and preventing phishing. The literature has documented the role of training and education on the reduction of phishing victims. It also shows that out of all the methods used for identifying phishing websites, visual methods demand high computational power.

Keywords: Phishing, identity-theft, fraud-detection, fake websites, illegitimate user

10.1 Introduction

Online transactions have encountered an enormous loss of about £21.6 million in the first half of 2012, which is an increase of 28% compared with 2011. India's loss amounts to $225 million in 2013, says RSA's

---

Corresponding author: swaminathan@src.sastra.edu

Muthukumaran Malarvel, Soumya Ranjan Nayak, Surya Narayan Panda, Prasant Kumar Pattnaik and Nittaya Muangnak (eds.) Machine Vision Inspection Systems (Vol. 1): Image Processing, Concepts, Methodologies and Applications, (213–230) © 2020 Scrivener Publishing LLC

Fraud report 2013. About 46,747 phishing attacks created a loss of nearly \$453 million during December 2014, according to a report by RSA. Users' Identity information viz., PIN, password, passcode, Credit/ Debit card number are fetched through a website that often imitates a legitimate site.

Anti-phishing techniques undergo regular updations to quench the financial thirst of the criminals [1]. So, there is still no complete solution that has high accuracy [2]. Abdelhamid et al. [3] concluded that because phishing Identification tries to categorize a given test webpage as phishy (illegitimate), valid (legitimate), and suspicious, it can be considered as a classification problem. As soon as the browser loads the website, the classifier can use rules to identify highly contributing features to determine the website type.

10.2 Literature Survey

Some of the feature-based machine learning approaches to detect phishing websites are (a) content-based approaches using Lexical URL, (b) Heuristics-based procedures, (c) URL Blacklists (d) Whitelists, (e) CANTINA-based, and (f) image-based approaches. In general, it takes nearly half a day to enlist a new malicious website in the URL blacklist. So, the existing Blacklists cannot handle further Phishing attacks [4].

Phishers directly copy web pages to deceive users. They trick the users into using fake Website-URLs. Barraclough et al. [5] used the idea of designing five inputs and extracting consistent features with the help of phishing techniques. These 5 inputs contributed to a sum of 288 elements, namely, legitimate site rules (1) contributing 66 extracted features, user-behavior profile (2), providing 60 functions; Phish tank (3), adding 72 features, user-specific site (4), providing with 48 elements and Pop-ups from e-mail (5) containing 42 characteristics. They trained and tested the phishing detection model using the 288 features obtained. Huang et al. [6] found that 288 was optimal because of the stability it could offer. The phishing features selected should be such that they allow the deployment of evolutionary antiphishing techniques and strategies.

10.2.1 Content-Based Approaches

Zhang et al. [7] proposed CANTINA, a TF-IDF-based technique to index legitimate pages. Another content-based approach proposed by

Mavrommatis and Provos [8] checked if the frames are misplaced and if Obfuscated java scripts are present. Afroz *et al.* [9] used Fuzzy Hashing to identify phishing sites efficiently. Le *et al.* [10] concentrated only on URL features to identify phishing websites.

10.2.2   Heuristics-Based Approaches

Phishing attempts are alive only for 48 hours and are highly elusive, thus, necessitating evolutionary methods to handle phishing. Shahriar and Zulkernine [11] automated testing process using five heuristics to identify websites as legitimate or phishing. Juan and Chuanxiong [12] detected phishing by comparing the similarity of the two websites after compressing. The challenge in the Heuristic-based strategy is that data sets are aged. Martin *et al.* [13] and Aburrous *et al.* [14] claim that a phishing website is alive for only about 48 hours, making it elusive. Regularly updating information from phishing databases can be helpful.

10.2.3   Blacklist-Based Approaches

Blacklists maintained on user's machines, or a server can scrutinize every request from the browser. Users may identify Malicious URLs through voting and add them to the blacklists. Xiang *et al.* [2] created an Antiphishing toolbar utilizing Blacklist IE8 to distinguished phishing sites with the help of page properties. They used input feed provided by PhishTank, which is updated regularly. Sheng *et al.* [15] used Blacklists. However, they could identify only 20% of pages in 0-hour. Fifty percent to 80% of the pages were displayed only after 12 hours. Google Safe browsing detected phishing URLs using a predefined list of fake URLs. Microsoft IE9 Antiphishing Protection and SiteAdvisor (McAfee 1997) could identify malware attacks like Spyware, Trojan horse, etc. It calculated threat rating using the history of URLs visited. But, SiteAdvisor couldn't identify newly created threats. Verisign (Symantec 2000) could recognize "clones" of websites. Netcraft Toolbar (1995) used Blacklist, which consists of fraud websites identified by Netcraft along with the location. Usage of web browser activated this toolbar. Sheng *et al.* [15] and Xiang *et al.* [2] found that Blacklist-based verification of URL done by humans is very slow in recognizing new attempts of phishing. If the features chosen by anti-phishing approaches are defective, the accuracy will not be reliable. Thus, blacklist-based solutions lack precision, leading to inadequacy in online transactions. Barraclough *et al.* [5] devised an alternative solution using a system that integrated Neural

Network and Fuzzy Logic with five inputs. Such a system would provide approximations using the fuzzy If...then rules and offer higher-level reasoning. Raw data can be handled using Neural Network.

10.2.4   Whitelist-Based Approaches

Trusted websites get into the whitelist after every successful attempt by the user. Such a system treats all other sites as untrusted. Automated Individual WhiteList (AIWL) proposed by Juan and Chuanxiong [12] traced every login attempt of a user through the Naïve Bayes algorithm and saved after repeated success logic for a specific website, thus, they detected and prevented users from malicious websites.

PhishZoo by Afroz et al. [9] used fuzzy hashing techniques to build the profiles of trusted websites. They used a combination of several metrics to identify websites.

10.2.5   CANTINA-Based Approaches

CANTINA was proposed in 2007 by Zhang et al. [7]. Xiang et al. [2] suggested an improvement of CANTINA, i.e., CANTINA+, wherein they utilized the features with machine learning using Document Object Model, Search engines, etc., to enable machine learning to detect phish. It is a content-based technique that uses the method of TF-IDF proposed by Thabtah et al. [16]. Term Frequency—Inverse Document Frequency (TF–IDF) was used to assign weights and count the frequency of words to calculate their importance. CANTINA+ goes one step further, by selecting the top 5 TF-IDF, and input it to the search engine, after adding it with the URL. If the web page is among the first 30 results, then it is Legitimate, else Phishy. In this paper, the authors supplemented TF-IDF with other features like Age of Domain, Suspicious URL, and Dots in the URL, etc. to reduce the errors. The limitation of this approach is TF-IDF is not suitable for Legitimate websites with images and hidden text since the type of web page may be identified with hidden text.

10.2.6   Image-Based Approaches

Wenyin et al. [17] suggested a plan based on visual similarity, using three metrics viz., Block level, Layout, and Style. Dhamija and Tygar [18] enabled a remote server to prove its identity to the user, with the help of agreed Discrete Image through Dynamic Security Skins. The users verify the legitimacy of the webpage by comparing the image fetched from the server with the expected image. The disadvantage of this system is that the users should decide the credibility of the website. The user has to look for signs that the visited site is a spoof website. It suggests a revolution in the web infrastructure itself.

10.3   Role of Data Mining in Antiphishing

Enhanced Multi-label Classifiers based Associative Classification (eMCAC), proposed by Abdelhamid [19], discover rules from a set of classes associated with single label data that other current AC algorithms are unable to induce. This algorithm minimizes the number of extracted rules, thereby generating rules with multiple class labels from single data sets. Hamid and Abawajy [20] suggested using profiling and clustering techniques to detect email-borne phishing. They created and clustered profiles using the characteristics of phishing emails as feature vectors. Using these complete profiles were generated for e-mails. Ahmadinejad and Fong [21] assessed how API extensions of SNSs could launch inference attacks. They also evaluated inference attacks and other attacks based on them. Alam *et al.* [22] proposed two new techniques, called Annotated Control Flow Graph (ACFG) and Sliding Window of Difference and Control Flow Weight (SWOD-CFWeight), to identify metamorphic malware using behavioral signature. This approach proved to be efficient, despite changes in compilers, optimizations, operating systems, and obfuscations. Alazab [23] extracted features of malware that simulated Windows Application Programming Interface (API) calls using mining and machine learning methods to detect malware behaviors. Chang and Chang [24] help online auction users detect fraudsters by developing a systematic method to discover fraudulent strategies from proven cases of online auction fraud. Fraudulent behavior can be any one of Aggressive, Classical, Luxury, and Low-profiled. The proposed method identifies whether an account is fraudulent or legitimate, and also the behaviors statuses. On judging an account as having one of the fraudulent behavior statuses, the user can observe his next move to check for deceptive flipping behavior strategies before making a final trading decision. Chatzipoulidis *et al.* [25] proposed a risk prediction methodology to measure zero-day risk. Chena and Sharma [26] suggested Educational campaigns to improve end-user knowledge to encounter cyber threats and mitigate the rate of being attacked. By joining WebTrust, TRUSTe, and BBBOnline, which are some of the privacy seal programs, a social networking site may try to gain user trust. Participation in these seal programs signifies that a social networking site has met the recognized industry privacy requirements and consequently restores user trust [27]. Furthermore, privacy protection policies and privacy-aware system architecture and site designs may be adopted by vendors as well. Liao *et al.* [28] studied the role of educating people about privacy, social awareness, trust, etc. The determinants of transaction intentions for inexperienced versus experienced shoppers were identified and have significantly contributed much to e-commerce. Crossler *et al.* [29] studied Behavioral InfoSec research, a growing area of research. Greenleaf and Park [30] analyzed the innovative and international aspects of privacy principles in Korean law and compared it with Asian jurisdictions. The authors concluded that Korean law was comparatively stronger in Asia. Liébana-Cabanillas *et al.* [31] determined which variables were significant in electronic banking and found that social, economic, demographic, financial, or behavioral factors were important using machine learning techniques. Herzberg [32] discussed indicators based on bookmarks to identify phishing, Lee *et al.* [33] examined the effect of the misleading claims offered by vendors selling devices such as smartphones and tablets, on Korean Internet banking. Computers & Security has continuously been consolidating phishing reports. Schultz [34] reported an average increase of 25% in the number of phishing sites per month between July and October. The Gartner Group reported a loss of USD 1.2 billion in the financial year of 2005. Schultz [35] reported that the US military and certain US agencies were about to initiate attacks to test how well federal employees conform to e-mail security policies. Mohammad *et al.* [36] suggested that adaptability is a mandatory feature of a successful phishing detection model. It should also restructure and respond to the changing environment of phishing websites.

Parsons *et al.* [37] examined unaddressed potential variables in phishing research, namely, the priming of participants and the diversity of e-mails used, based on an analysis of an empirical study. This analysis found that informed participants were unbiased. Instead, they differentiated phishing e-mails easily than uninformed participants. The study proved that knowledge about phishing had improved their response to phish. This finding implies that employees under time or productivity constraints may make poor security decisions. It also demonstrates that the category of the e-mail, the sender, and intention affect the performance in a phishing study. Rughiniş and Rughiniş [38] identified five types of end-users: "explorer," "reactive," "prudent," "lucky," and "occasional" using K-means cluster analysis. This analysis will be helpful for understanding end-users' security orientations.

Zhang *et al.* [39] used four variants of algorithms to classify 3,000 websites of Chinese origin as phishy or legitimate. SMO algorithm scored better among the four. Yan *et al.* [40] designed CoverPad to improve leakage resilience.

10.3.1   Phishing Detection

Chen *et al.* [41] used text extraction with hybrid data mining to assess how severe the phishing attacks were. Nishanth *et al.* [42] found out that the method suggested byAnkaiah and Ravi [43] provided better imputation than the method proposed by Chen *et al.* [41]. They found that patterns in past incidents can be used to predict and avoid future events, thus reducing the financial loss occurring as a result of phishing. Damage can be a result of one of Direct, Indirect, or opportunity cost. Gowtham and Krishnamurthi [44] used two preliminary screening modules, namely the Preapproved Site Identifier and the Login Form finder, to reduce false positives and another module, namely, Web page feature generator to extract 15 features from web pages, with FPR of 0.42% and 99.6%. Han *et al.* [45] suggested protecting users from Pharming attacks using "Automated Individual White-list". Besides, the author was also able to defend their credentials. He *et al.* [46] used a combination of CANTINA, Anomaly method, and PILFER method with some modifications to convert a web page into 12 features. An SVM classifier extracted the identity of the web pages based on the elements and categorized it was legitimate or phishy. Barraclough *et al.* [5] used a total of 288 features consolidated from new inputs like User-behavior profile, Rules of legitimate Site, and the user's frequently visited sites, PhishTank, phish that arises from e-mails, etc. The author utilized an Inference scheme that combined Neural network with Fuzzy logic to discover illegitimate sites. Kazemian and Ahmed [47] used methods such as K-means clustering algorithm and Affinity Propagation and three supervised machine learning methods viz., KNN, SVM, and Naïve Bayes Classifier. There was a significant improvement in the accuracy rates of up to 98%. They used online learning, which allows training without "old training data." Ramanathan and Wechsler [4] employed NLP and Machine learning to discover the organization that the phishing attacker is trying to impersonate. They found (i) Named entities using CRF, (ii) Topics using LDA, and built a model to discover the impersonated entity. Then they communicated it to the body for corrective action. Ramesh *et al.* [48] detected phishing websites and identified the target and arrives at the target domain set. They recognized the legitimacy of the site using the TID algorithm and Third-party DNS lookup on this set. This method detects the newest webpages hosted in any language. Limitations are it can't identify phishing webpages hosted on compromised domains because of S1, S2, S3. Accuracy of prediction changes with keywords extracted from suspicious pages, so keywords obtained need to identify the document uniquely. Detection of phishing pages across many languages comes at the cost of language-independent keyword extraction. TF-IDF retrieves document frequency of the term. Search engine results and DNS lookup are used to identify the target. So speed is dependent on the search engine. Shahriar and Zulkernine [11] proposed testing of Cross-site scriptings, like the injection of scripts based on reliability testing. Finite State Machine is used to describe the test website, which is then used to capture the submission of inputs and corresponding responses, and then eight heuristics are developed. They used form-based features, state, and submission responses to establish the heuristics for testing the websites. Lakshmi and Vijaya [49] employed Machine-learning for prediction and supervised learning (Multilayer perceptron, Decision tree induction Naïve Bayes Classifier) for exploring results. They used 200 URLs. A decision tree classifier was found to perform well. Wenyin *et al.* [50] constructed a Semantic Link Network from a given suspicious web page and discovered the target using reasoning based on the predefined rules. They used PhishTank data of 1000 illegitimate webpages and data of 1000 legitimate webpages. The method showed false-negative of 16.6% and false-positive of 13.8%. The authors contributed to discovering the target and application of SLN, considering relations such as Link, Search, and text. Four convergent situations are specified. Li *et al.* [51] proposed detection based on the Transductive Support Vector Machine (TSVM), which uses the distribution information of the unlabeled samples. This approach is in contrast to SVM, which uses only poor representative labeled samples. Web image features extracted based on the Document Object Model.

10.3.2   Phishing Prevention

Rahman and Anwar [52] concluded that unless passwords are protected, precautions like firewalls and filters installed by users will be at a loss. Almasizadeh and Abdollahi [53] proposed a new approach for the quantitative security analysis of computer systems. Bose and Leung [54] identified that banks needed to improve the accessibility of anti-phishing measures because such information is comparatively scarce. Carminati *et al.* [55] suggests a threefold profiling approach, BANKSEALER, that tries to mitigate the deficiency of old data by differentiating the behavior of new transactions from ones that have already been learned by the system. Chen *et al.* [56] proposed a system that examines drive-by download web attacks through only-user requests, neglecting crawler requests, because efficient filtering is necessary to process user requests efficiently. Das and Samdaria [57] proposed an SSL/TLS security feature for user authentication through tokens. The author showed that the proposed solution is secure, efficient, and user-friendly in comparison to other similar approaches. Dosis *et al.* [58] proposed a solution for enhancing digital forensics through ontologies to represent and integrate evidence, thereby reducing human intervention in digital forensics. Virvilis *et al.* [59] examined the security features offered in web browsers on iOS, Android, and desktop (Windows) platforms and found that most browsers, especially those for mobile devices provide limited protection against such threats. The authors proposed and evaluated a countermeasure, which can be used to significantly improve the level of protection offered to the users, regardless of the web browser or platform they are using. Khalid *et al.* [60] found that common security measures for individuals and privacy protection technologies as important antecedents affecting users' decision to choose a software firewall. Lai *et al.* [61] studied identity theft to provide useful information for consumers, government agencies, e-commerce industries, and so on. Gouda *et al.* [62] proposed how Single-Password Protocol (SPP) secures user entry across multiple servers through one single password, thus preventing phishing attacks. Ojo and Ige [63] proposed Forenlog Analyzer to support human analysts that want to generate reports that will substantiate prima facie cases against computer intruders. Evaluation with different intrusion logs illustrates the significance of patterns and uncertainty for supporting the extraction of criminal evidence against intruders. Vos *et al.* [64] investigated the effect of trust on e-commerce and found which security measures can mitigate perceived risks. The author identified the relationships between quality, loyalty, satisfaction, and trust in the domain of e-commerce. The author also analyzed how well electronic service met the value and loyalty expectations of customers. Layton and Watters [65] found that tangible costs are very significant in their own right concerning Data breaches. Luo *et al.* [66] applied HSM to victimization by phishing and found how to make employees abstain from phishing attempts. Contena *et al.* [67] identified the likely occurrence of risk by involving 736 people and dividing them groups viz., explorative, and confirmatory factor analysis. Vishwanath *et al.* [68] found that urgency cues in most phishing e-mails stimulated the users to get deceived. The author also found that frequent media use had a strong influence on an individual getting deceived.

10.3.3   Training and Education

Arachchilage and Love [69] suggested a theoretical model based on the findings of Liang and Xue [70] to study how knowledge affected computer users' behavior by making 161 regular computer users fill up an online questionnaire. Davinson and Sillence [71] experimented with how education affected users through a teaching exercise to calculate risk levels. 'Anti-Phishing Phil,' the training program that he created taught users how to identify phishing threats. Dodge *et al.* [72] studied the education program on user information assurance. Feledi *et al.* [73] examined the sharing of information security knowledge through Web-Prote'ge', a web portal. The studies showed that Ontologies could model the domain of information security. Parsons *et al.* [74] evaluated the validity and reliability testing using the results from 500 Australian employees to determine how awareness of policy related to procedures. They found that only if the knowledge and attitude of users go hand in hand, training will be fruitful. Safa *et al.* [75] showed that a skeptic attitude keeps one away from phish. They identified some crucial factors of security breaches, namely, being unaware, carelessness, laziness, malice, and conflicting attitude. Shillair *et al.* [76] showed that being diligent, with involvement and being aware, can enhance online safety behaviors. Tsohou *et al.* [77] analyzed how incomplete information can affect a user's behavior. They suggested how knowledge-sharing ideas can help.

10.3.4   Phishing Recovery and Avoidance

Arachchilage and Love [78] suggested Technology Threat Avoidance Theory (TTAT), a game design framework, to motivate users to abstain from phish. It also proved useful in avoiding viruses and other malware. Baek *et al.* [79] studied why online users do not adopt protective behaviors. Bansal and Zahedi [80] examined dual breaches—hacking and illegal distribution and investigated different responses viz., excuse, refutation, and no answer. The authors showed how the nature of the breach affected the process of restoration. Bose and Leung [81] suggested that those who started using anti-phishing software showed a positive return in market value compared with those who did not. Their study showed that investors rewarded companies that adopt countermeasures. Carpenter *et al.* [82] addressed the importance of avoiding unnecessary identity exposure behaviors. The authors also identified other types of psychological attacks and measures to prevent them.

Alsharnouby *et al.* [83] used eye-tracking to study, which signals attracted users' attention in determining the authenticity of any webpage. They showed how users could identify only half of the illegitimate sites. They found that longer the user gazed at a website, the more was the possibility of identifying an illicit website. Huang *et al.* [84] found that theft of passwords can be avoided by not using passwords at all. To answer the potential security question, the author proposed an efficient authentication service based on the instant messaging service, which eradicates the necessity of credentials to authenticate the user, thus removing phishing itself considerably. Vossaert *et al.* [85] suggested user-centric identity management, using trusted modules that combined several privacy features in identity management systems. Lei *et al.* [86] proposed a virtual password concept through functions to safeguard credentials with the help of manual computing. This approach could be implemented in Cash-vending machines across the Internet and even in devices as well. Mayhorn [98] investigated alert messages or warnings which may affect a user's security behavior.

10.3.5   Visual Methods

Rao and Ali [87] used a Computer-vision-based technique called SURF detector to extract discriminatory key features for websites. De Kimpe *et al.* [88] identified that user behaviors like copying digital content, inadvertent disclosure of personal details, use of the social network, and online shopping played a significant role in becoming phishing targets. Dalgic *et al.* [89] used machine learning algorithms like SVM and Random Forest models to detect phishing pages through color and edge-based visual information. Adebowale *et al.* [90] have proposed a method to identify the phishing websites by integrating the features of images, frames, and text using supervised learning schemes. Rao and Pais [91] used heuristics and similarity-based features to identify phishing sites. Some of the visual methods used for identifying phishing websites are:

1. Logo matching [92],
2. Page layout similarity [93],
3. Keypoint matching [87],
4. Holistic page image matching by Contrast Context Histograms [94],
5. The visual signature of the webpage using MPEG-7 like features [95], CSS features [96],
6. Spatial layout similarity [97].

Even though visual similarity-based studies score well in identifying phishing websites, they demand high computational power compared to text-based methods.

10.4 Conclusion

The authors have presented a review on Phishing. The review analyses the various approaches to detect and prevent phishing with special emphasis to visual methods.

Acknowledgments

The authors would like to thank the Management of SASTRA Deemed University and the Department of Science and Technology – Fund for Improvement of Science and Technology Infrastructure in Universities and higher educational institutions, Government of India SR/FST/MSI-107/2015.

References

1. Ross, A., Online bank fraud rises as phishing criminals redouble efforts, 1–2, 2012. http://www.cio.co.uk/news/security/online-bank-fraud-rises-as-phishing-criminals-redouble-efforts/
2. Xiang, G., Hong, J., Rose, C.P., Cranor, L., CANTINA+: A feature-rich machine learning framework for detecting phishing web sites. *ACM Trans. Inf. Syst. Sec.*, 14, 2, 1–28, 2011.
3. Abdelhamid, N., Ayesh, A., Thabtah, F., Phishing detection-based associative classification data mining. *Expert Syst. Appl.*, 41, 13, 5948–5959, 2014.
4. Ramanathan, V. and Wechsler, H., Phishing detection and impersonated entity discovery using Conditional Random Field and Latent Dirichlet Allocation. *Comput. Secur.*, 34, 123–139, 2013.
5. Barraclough, P.A., Hossain, M.A., Tahir, M.A., Sexton, G., Aslam, N., Intelligent phishing detection and protection scheme for online transactions. *Expert Syst. Appl.*, 40, 11, 4697–4706, 2013.
6. Huang, G.-B., Zhu, Q.-Y., Mao, K.Z., Siew, C.-K., Saratchandran, P., Sundararajan, N., "Can threshold networks be trained directly?," in IEEE Transactions on Circuits and Systems II: Express Briefs, 53, 3, 187–191, 2006.

7. Zhang, Y., Hong, J.I., Cranor, L.F., Cantina: A contentbased approach to detecting phishing web sites. *16th International World Wide Web Conference*, WWW2007, pp. 639–648, 2007.

8. Mavrommatis, P. and Provos, N., All your iFRAMEs point to us. *Symposium a quarterly journal in modern foreign literatures*. 1–15, 2008.

9. Afroz, S. and Greenstadt, R.j, PhishZoo: Detecting phishing websites by looking at them. *Proceedings—5th IEEE International Conference on Semantic Computing*, ICSC 2011, pp. 368–375, 2011.

10. Le, A., Markopoulou, A., Faloutsos, M., PhishDef: URL names say it all. *Proceedings—IEEE INFOCOM.*, pp. 191–195, 2011.

11. Shahriar, H. and Zulkernine, M., Trustworthiness testing of phishing websites: A behavior model-based approach. *Future Gener. Comput. Syst.*, 28, 8, 1258–1271, 2012.

12. Juan, C. and Chuanxiong, G., Online detection and prevention of phishing attacks (invited paper). *First International Conference on Communications and Networking in China*, ChinaCom '06, 2007.

13. Martin, A., Anutthamaa, Na. Ba., Sathyavathy, M., Francois, Marie Manjari Saint, Venkatesan, Dr. Prasanna, V., A framework for predicting phishing websites using neural networks. *IJCSI*, 8, 2, 330–336, 2011.

14. Aburrous, M., Hossain, M.A., Dahal, K., Thabtah, F., Intelligent phishing detection system for e-banking using fuzzy data mining. *Expert Syst. Appl.*, 37, 12, 7913–7921, 2010.

15. Sheng, S., Wardman, B., Warner, G., Cranor, L.F., Hong, J., Zhang, C., An empirical analysis of phishing blacklists. *6th Conference on Email and Anti-Spam*, CEAS 2009, 2009.

16. Thabtah, F., Eljinini, M.A.H., Zamzeer, M., Hadi, M., Naïve Bayesian Based on Chi Square to Categorize Arabic Data, Communications of the IBIMA. 10, 158–163, 2009.

17. Wenyin, L., Huang, G., Xiaoyue, L., Min, Z., Deng, X., Detection of phishing webpages based on visual similarity. *14th International World Wide Web Conference*, WWW2005, pp. 1060–1061, 2005.

18. Dhamija, R., Tygar, J.D., The battle against phishing: Dynamic security skins. *ACM Int. Conf. Proc. Ser.*, 93, 77–88, 2005.

19. Abdelhamid, N., Multi-label rules for phishing classification. *Appl. Comput. Inf.*, 11, 1, 29–46, 2015.

20. Hamid, I.R.A. and Abawajy, J.H., An approach for profiling phishing activities. *Comput. Secur.*, 45, 27–41, 2014.

21. Ahmadinejad, S.H. and Fong, P.W.L., Unintended disclosure of information: Inference attacks by third-party extensions to Social Network Systems. *Comput. Secur.*, 44, 75–91, 2014.

22. Alam, S., Horspool, R.N., Traore, I., Sogukpinar, I., A framework for metamorphic malware analysis and real-time detection. *Comput. Secur.*, 48, 212–233, 2015.

23. Alazab, M., Profiling and classifying the behavior of malicious codes. *J. Sys. Software*, 100, 91–102, 2015.

24. Chang, J.S. and Chang, W.H., Analysis of fraudulent behavior strategies in online auctions for detecting latent fraudsters. *Electr. Commerce Res. Appl.*, 13, 2, 79–97, 2014.

25. Chatzipoulidis, A., Michalopoulos, D., Mavridis, I., Information infrastructure risk prediction through platform vulnerability analysis. *J. Sys. Software*, 106, 28–41, 2015.

26. Chena, R. and Sharma, S.K., Understanding Member Use of Social Networking Sites from a Risk Perspective. *Procedia Technol.*, 9, 331–339, 2013.

27. Zhang, Y., Age, gender, and Internet attitudes among employees in the business world. *Comput. Hum. Behav.*, 21, 1, 1–10, 2005.

28. Liao, C., Liu, C.C., Chen, K., Examining the impact of privacy, trust and risk perceptions beyond monetary transactions: An integrated model. *Electr. Commerce Res. Appl.*, 10, 6, 702–715, 2011.

29. Crossler, R.E., Johnston, A.C., Lowry, P.B., Hu, Q., Warkentin, M., Baskerville, R., Future directions for behavioral information security research. *Comput. Secur.*, 32, 90–101, 2013.

30. Greenleaf, G. and Park, W.Il, South Korea's innovations in data privacy principles: Asian comparisons. *Comput. Law Sec. Rev.*, 30, 5, 492–505, 2014.

31. Liébana-Cabanillas, F., Nogueras, R., Herrera, L.J., Guillén, A., Analysing user trust in electronic banking using data mining methods. *Expert Syst. Appl.*, 40, 14, 5439–5447, 2013.

32. Herzberg, A., Why Johnny can't surf (safely)? Attacks and defenses for web users. *Comput. Secur.*, 28, 1-2, 63–71, 2009.

33. Lee, Jung, H.L., Won, G., Lim, J.I., A study of the security of Internet banking and financial private information in South Korea. *Math. Comput. Modell.*, 58, 1-2, 117–131, 2013.

34. Schultz, E., Security views. *Comput. Secur.*, 24, 5, 349–358, 2005.

35. Schultz, E., Security views. *Comput. Secur.*, 24, 5, 349–358, 2007.

36. Mohammad, R.M., Thabtah, F., McCluskey, L., Tutorial and critical analysis of phishing websites methods. *Comput. Sci. Rev.*, 17, 1–24, 2015.

37. Parsons, K., McCormac, A., Pattinson, M., Butavicius, M., Jerram, C., The design of phishing studies: Challenges for researchers. *Comput. Secur.*, 52, 194–206, 2015.

38. Rughiniş, C. and Rughiniş, R., Nothing ventured, nothing gained. Profiles of online activity, cyber-crime exposure, and security measures of end-users in European Union. *Comput. Secur.*, 43, 111–125, 2014.

39. Zhang, D., Yan, Z., Jiang, H., Kim, T., A domain-feature enhanced classification model for the detection of Chinese phishing e-Business websites. *Inf. Manage.*, 51, 7, 845–853, 2014.

40. Yan, Q., Han, J., Li, Y., Zhou, J., Deng, R.H., Leakage-resilient password entry: Challenges, design, and evaluation. *Comput. Secur.*, 48, 196–211, 2015.

41. Chen, X., Bose, I., Leung, A.C.M., Guo, C., Assessing the severity of phishing attacks: A hybrid data mining approach. *Decis. Support Syst.*, 50, 4, 662–672, 2011.

42. Nishanth, K.J., Ravi, V., Ankaiah, N., Bose, I., Soft computing based imputation and hybrid data and text mining: The case of predicting the severity of phishing alerts. *Expert Syst. Appl.*, 39, 12, 10583–10589, 2012.

43. Ankaiah, N. and Ravi, V., A Novel Soft Computing Hybrid for Data Imputation. *7th international conference on data mining (DMIN)*, p. 057, 2011.

44. Gowtham, R. and Krishnamurthi, I., A comprehensive and efficacious architecture for detecting phishing webpages. *Comput. Secur.*, 40, 23–37, 2014.

45. Han, W., Cao, Y., Bertino, E., Yong, J., Using automated individual white-list to protect web digital identities. *Expert Syst. Appl.*, 39, 15, 11861–11869, 2012.

46. He, M., Horng, S.J., Fan, P., Khan, M.K., Run, R.S., Lai, J.L., Chen, R.J., Sutanto, A., An efficient phishing webpage detector. *Expert Syst. Appl.*, 38, 10, 12018–12027, 2011.

47. Kazemian, H.B. and Ahmed, S., Comparisons of machine learning techniques for detecting malicious webpages. *Expert Syst. Appl.*, 42, 3, 1166–1177, 2015.

48. Ramesh, G., Krishnamurthi, I., Kumar, K., Sampath, S., An efficacious method for detecting phishing webpages through target domain identification. *Decis. Support Syst.*, 61, 1, 12–22, 2014.

49. Lakshmi, V., Santhana, Vijaya, M.S., Efficient prediction of phishing websites using supervised learning algorithms. *Procedia Eng.*, 30, 2011, 798–805, 2012.

50. Wenyin, L., Fang, N., Quan, X., Qiu, B., Liu, G., Discovering phishing target based on semantic link network. *Future Gener. Comput. Syst.*, 26, 3, 381–388, 2010.

51. Li, Y., Xiao, R., Feng, J., Zhao, L., A semi-supervised learning approach for detection of phishing webpages. *Optik*, 124, 23, 6027–6033, 2013.

52. Rahman, R.A. and Anwar, I.S.K., Effectiveness of fraud prevention and detection techniques in malaysian islamic banks, *Procedia. Soc. Behav. Sci.*, 145, 97–102, 2014.

53. Almasizadeh, J. and Abdollahi, A.M., Mean privacy: A metric for security of computer systems. *Comp. Commun.*, 52, 47–59, 2014.

54. Bose, I. and Leung, A.C.M., Assessing anti-phishing preparedness: A study of online banks in Hong Kong. *Decis. Support Syst.*, 45, 4, 897–912, 2008.

55. Carminati, M., Caron, R., Maggi, F., Epifani, I., Zanero, S., BankSealer: A decision support system for online banking fraud analysis and investigation. *Comput. Secur.*, 53, 175–186, 2015.

56. Chen, C.M., Huang, J.J., Ou, Y.H., Efficient suspicious URL filtering based on reputation. *J. Inf. Sec. Appl.*, 20, 26–36, 2015.

57. Das, M.L. and Samdaria, N., On the security of SSL/TLS-enabled applications. *App. Comput. Inf.*, 10, 1-2, 68–81, 2014.

58. Dosis, S., Homem, I., Popov, O., Semantic representation and integration of digital evidence. *Procedia Comput. Sci.*, 22, 1266–1275, 2013.

59. Virvilis, N., Mylonas, A., Tsalis, N., Gritzalis, D., Security Busters: Web browser security vs. rogue sites. *Comput. Secur.*, 52, 90–105, 2015.

60. Khalid, U. and Ghafoor, Abdul and Irum, Misbah and Shibli, Muhammad A., Cloud based secure and privacy enhanced authentication & authorization protocol. *Procedia Comput. Sci.*, 22, 680–688, 2013.

61. Lai, F., Li, D., Hsieh, C.T., Fighting identity theft: The coping perspective. *Decis. Support Syst.*, 52, 2, 353–363, 2012.

62. Gouda, M.G., Liu, A.X., Leung, L.M., Alam, M.A., SPP: An anti-phishing single password protocol. *Comput. Networks*, 51, 13, 3715–3726, 2007.

63. Ojo, N.J. and Ige, N.J., Methods for using intrusion logs to establish criminal evidence against intruders. *Procedia Comput. Sci.*, 21, 465–470, 2013.

64. Vos, A., Marinagi, C., Trivellas, P., Eberhagen, N., Skourlas, C., Giannakopoulos, G., Risk Reduction Strategies in Online Shopping: E-trust Perspective. *Procedia Soc. Behav. Sci.*, 147, 418–423, 2014.

65. Layton, R. and Watters, P.A., A methodology for estimating the tangible cost of data breaches. *J. Inf. Sec. Appl.*, 19, 6, 321–330, 2014.

66. Luo, X., Zhang, W., Burd, S., Seazzu, A., Investigating phishing victimization with the Heuristic-Systematic model: A theoretical framework and an exploration. *Comput. Secur.*, 38, 28–38, 2013.

67. Contena, B., Loscalzo, Y., Taddei, S., Surfing on Social Network Sites: A comprehensive instrument to evaluate online self-disclosure and related attitudes. *Comput. Hum. Behav.*, 49, 30–37, 2015.

68. Vishwanath, A., Herath, T., Chen, R., Wang, J., Rao, H.R., Why do people get phished? Testing individual differences in phishing vulnerability within an integrated, information processing model. *Decis. Support Syst.*, 51, 3, 576–586, 2011.

69. Arachchilage, N.A.G. and Love, S., Security awareness of computer users: A phishing threat avoidance perspective. *Comput. Hum. Behav.*, 38, 304–312, 2014.

70. Liang, H. and Xue, Y., Understanding security behaviors in personal computer usage: A threat avoidance perspective. *J. Assoc. Inf. Syst.*, 11, 7, 394–413, 2010.

71. Davinson, N. and Sillence, E., It won't happen to me: Promoting secure behaviour among internet users. *Comput. Hum. Behav.*, 26, 6, 1739–1747, 2010.

72. Dodge, R.C., Carver, C., Ferguson, A.J., Phishing for user security awareness. *Comput. Secur.*, 26, 1, 73–80, 2007.

73. Feledi, D., Fenz, S., Lechner, L., Toward web-based information security knowledge sharing. *Inf. Sec. Tech. Rep.*, 17, 4, 199–209, 2013.

74. Parsons, K., McCormac, A., Butavicius, M., Pattinson, M., Jerram, C., Determining employee awareness using the Human Aspects of Information Security Questionnaire (HAIS-Q). *Comput. Secur.*, 42, 165–176, 2014.

75. Safa, N.S., Sookhak, M., Von Solms, R., Furnell, S., Ghani, N.A., Herawan, T., Information security conscious care behaviour formation in organizations. *Comput. Secur.*, 53, 65–78, 2015.

76. Shillair, R., Cotten, S.R., Tsai, H.Y.S., Alhabash, S., Larose, R., Rifon, N.J., Online safety begins with you and me: Convincing Internet users to protect themselves. *Comput. Hum. Behav.*, 48, 199–207, 2015.

77. Tsohou, A., Karyda, M., Kokolakis, S., Analyzing the role of cognitive and cultural biases in the internalization of information security policies: Recommendations for information security awareness programs. *Comput. Secur.*, 52, 128–141, 2015.

78. Arachchilage, N.A.G. and Love, S., A game design framework for avoiding phishing attacks. *Comput. Hum. Behav.*, 29, 3, 706–714, 2013.

79. Baek, Y.M., Kim, E.M., Bae, Y., My privacy is okay, but theirs is endangered: Why comparative optimism matters in online privacy concerns. *Comput. Hum. Behav.*, 31, 1, 48–56, 2014.

80. Bansal, G. and Zahedi, F.M., Trust violation and repair: The information privacy perspective. *Decis. Support Syst.*, 71, 62–77, 2015.

81. Bose, I. and Leung, A.C.M., The impact of adoption of identity theft countermeasures on firm value. *Decis. Support Syst.*, 55, 3, 753–763, 2013.

82. Carpenter, S., Zhu, F., Kolimi, S., Reducing online identity disclosure using warnings. *Appl. Ergon.*, 45, 5, 1337–1342, 2014.

83. Alsharnouby, M., Alaca, F., Chiasson, S., Why phishing still works: User strategies for combating phishing attacks. *Int. J. Hum. Comp. Stud.*, 82, 69–82, 2015.

84. Huang, C.Y., Ma, S.P., Chen, K.T., Using one-time passwords to prevent password phishing attacks. *J. Network Comput. Appl.*, 34, 4, 1292–1301, 2011.

85. Vossaert, J., Lapon, J., De Decker, B., Naessens, V., User-centric identity management using trusted modules. *Math. Comput. Modell.*, 57, 7-8, 1592–1605, 2013.

86. Lei, M., Xiao, Y., Vrbsky, S.V., Li, C.C., Virtual password using random linear functions for on-line services, ATM machines, and pervasive computing. *Comput. Commun.*, 31, 18, 4367–4375, 2008.

87. Rao, R.S. and Ali, S.T., A computer vision technique to detect phishing attacks. *Proceedings—2015 5th International Conference on Communication Systems and Network Technologies*, CSNT 2015, pp. 596–601, 2015.

88. De Kimpe, L., Walrave, M., Hardyns, W., Pauwels, L., Ponnet, K., You've got mail! Explaining individual differences in becoming a phishing target. *Telematics Inf.*, 35, 5, 1277–1287, 2018.

89. Dalgic, F.C., Bozkir, A.S., Aydos, M., Phish-IRIS: A New Approach for Vision Based Brand Prediction of Phishing Web Pages *via* Compact Visual Descriptors. *ISMSIT 2018—2nd International Symposium on Multidisciplinary Studies and Innovative Technologies, Proceedings*, pp. 1–8, 2018.

90. Adebowale, M.A., Lwin, K.T., Sánchez, E., Hossain, M.A., Intelligent web-phishing detection and protection scheme using integrated features of Images, frames and text. *Expert Syst. Appl.*, 115, December 2017, 300–313, 2019.

91. Rao, R.S. and Pais, A.R., Jail-Phish: An improved search engine based phishing detection system. *Comput. Secur.*, 83, 246–267, 2019.

92. Chiew, K.L., Chang, E.H., Sze, S.N., Tiong, W.K., Utilisation of website logo for phishing detection. *Comput. Secur.*, 54, 16–26, 2015.

93. Bozkir, A.S. and Sezer, E.A., Use of HOG descriptors in phishing detection, 4th International Symposium on Digital Forensics and Security. *ISDFS 2016—Proceeding*, pp. 148–153, 2016.

94. Chen, K.T., Chen, J.Y., Huang, C.R., Chen, C.S., Fighting phishing with discriminative keypoint features. *IEEE Internet Comput.*, 13, 3, 56–63, 2009.

95. Maurer, M.-E. and Herzner, D., Using visual website similarity for phishing detection and reporting. pp. 1625, 2012.

96. Mao, J., Li, P., Wei, T., Liang, Z., BaitAlarm: Detecting phishing sites using similarity in fundamental visual features. *Proceedings—5th International Conference on Intelligent Networking and Collaborative Systems*, INCoS 2013, pp. 790–795, 2013.

97. Zhang, W., Lu, H., Xu, B., Yang, H., Web phishing detection based on page spatial layout similarity. *Informatica (Slovenia).*, 37, 3, 231–244, 2013.

98. Mayhorn, C.B. and Wogalter, M.S., Laughery, K.R., Special issue on warnings: Advances in delivery, application, and methods, Applied Ergonomics. 45, 5, 1267–1269, 2014.

Index

Abnormality, 184
Aerial dataset, 5
Antiphishing, 221
Artificial intelligence, 119, 146
Attribute data, 4
Australia, 126–127
Avocado,
  dip, 151–160

Benchmark, 183, 193, 195–196
Bilateral filtering, 9
Bivariate frequency histogram, 154,
  158–159
Blindness, 183–184
Blood vessel, 192
Bridge, 126, 142, 166, 167, 175, 176,
  178
Browser, 218, 225
Built-up area, 12–14, 19, 21, 23

Chain codes, 91, 92, 93
Character recognition, 201
Characteristic, 183
Classification, 1–3, 6–9, 12, 13, 16–21,
  25–28, 31–36, 218, 221
Clinical, 183, 185, 188–191, 195–196
Clustering, 14, 19
Color,
  analysis, 151–152, 154
  distribution, 154–157
  evolution, 155–156
  invariance, 154, 159–160
  plots, 156–157
  space, 152–156, 159

Computed PSNR value, 77, 78
Computed PT, 78, 79
Computed SNR value, 77, 78
Computer vision, 151–152, 159–161
Convolutional neural network,
  203–2012
Coverage, 1–3, 5–7, 21, 23, 30, 33, 34

Damage, 119, 121, 122, 126, 142,
  143, 147, 163, 164
Data acquisition, 72
Datamining, 221–223
Decision tree, 26, 35
Defects, 162, 163, 164, 166, 168, 170,
  172, 177, 178
Diabetes, 183–196
Diabetic retinopathy, 183–186, 194
Diagnose, 183, 185, 196
Disaster, 164, 165, 168
Disaster in Pakistan, 120, 122, 123
Dynamic security skins, 220

Edge detection, 72
Edge enhancement, 9
E-mail, 222, 223, 225
Enhancement, 186, 190, 194, 195,
  197

Feature extraction, 73
Felzenszwalb's method, 22
Floods, 119–146
Food,
  industry, 151
  science, 159–162

231

Fourier descriptors, 102, 103
Foursquare data, 1, 3, 5, 6, 8, 11, 20–22, 31–33, 35

Gaussian noise, 9, 11
GIS, 4
GLCM matrix, 16

Handwritten character recognition, 202
Hu invariant moments, 100

Image, 152, 154–156, 160
    acquisition, 152–153
    analysis, 151–152
Image processing, 119, 132, 141, 142, 143, 147, 153–154, 162, 163, 164, 166, 168, 170, 172, 177, 178

Kappa coefficient, 30
K-means, 9

Land-cover, 1–8, 10, 12, 18, 25, 28, 32–36
Landmarks, 182, 185–186, 195
Land-use, 1–8, 10, 11, 20, 21, 23–25, 28, 31–35
Lesions, 183–197
Lightness a* b* ($L^*a^*b^*$), 152, 154–156, 160

Machine learning, 218, 220–224, 227
MATLAB codes, 106–118
Microwave treatment, 151, 162
Moments, 96, 97, 98, 99, 100

Naïve Bayesian, 25, 26
Noise, 132, 133, 142, 146, 166, 167, 174, 177

Openstreetmap data, 4

Pakistan, 120, 122, 123
Password, 218, 225, 227

Pest detection model, 73
Pest identification, 73
Pests, 71
Phishing,
    avoidance, 226
    blacklist-based approaches, 219
    CANTINA-based approaches, 220
    content-based approaches, 218
    detection, 223
    heuristics-based approaches, 219
    image-based approaches, 220
    prevention, 224
    recovery, 226
    visual methods, 227
    whitelist-based approaches, 220
Phishtank, 219, 223, 224
Point data, 4
Polygonal approximation, 93, 94, 95
Pre-processing, 7, 11
Processing of CFB, 76
Processing of GW, 76
Processing of LGB, 75
Processing of RRFB, 75
Processing of RW, 74

Quadtree, 103, 104, 105, 106
Quality control, 152, 154–155
Quick shift method, 22

Random forest, 9, 13, 16–19, 25
Red green blue (RGB), 152–155
Referenced data, 4
Retina, 183–197
Roads, 126, 143, 144, 147, 166, 167, 175, 176, 178

Satellite images, 1, 5–11, 13, 21, 24, 25, 28, 33
Screening, 185 –191, 197
SED methods, 70
Segmentation, 14, 36
SG, 70
Spatially referenced data, 4
SVM, 25, 26

TF-IDF, 218, 220, 224
Threshold, 11, 20, 22, 23, 32
Training and education, 226

UAV, 72
URL, 218, 219
USB camera, 153, 159–160

VGI, 2, 5, 11, 32, 33
Visualization, 1–4, 8, 23, 24, 25, 31, 34

YUY2 color space, 153

Zernike moments, 101